# STUDIES IN ANTIQUITY AND CHRISTIANITY

*The Roots of Egyptian Christianity*
Birger A. Pearson and James E. Goehring, editors

*Gnosticism, Judaism, and Egyptian Christianity*
Birger A. Pearson

*Ascetic Behavior in Greco-Roman Antiquity: A Sourcebook*
Vincent L. Wimbush, editor

*Elijah in Upper Egypt: "The Apocalypse of Elijah"
and Early Egyptian Christianity*
David Frankfurter

*The Letters of St. Antony: Monasticism and the Making of a Saint*
Samuel Rubenson

*Women and Goddess Traditions: In Antiquity and Today*
Karen L. King, editor

*Ascetics, Society, and the Desert:
Studies in Early Egyptian Monasticism*
James E. Goehring

*The Formation of Q: Trajectories in Ancient Wisdom Collections*
John S. Kloppenborg

*Reading the Hebrew Bible for a New Millennium:*
Volume 1: *Theological and Hermeneutical Studies*
Volume 2: *Exegetical and Theological Studies*
Wonil Kim, Deborah Ellens, Michael Floyd,
and Marvin A. Sweeney, editors

*Images of the Feminine in Gnosticism*
Karen L. King, editor

*Mimesis and Intertextuality in Antiquity and Christianity*
Dennis R. MacDonald, editor

# STUDIES IN ANTIQUITY AND CHRISTIANITY

The Institute for Antiquity and Christianity
Claremont Graduate University
Claremont, California

STUDIES IN ANTIQUITY & CHRISTIANITY

# Mimesis and Intertextuality in Antiquity and Christianity

*Edited by*
*Dennis R. MacDonald*

TRINITY PRESS
INTERNATIONAL
HARRISBURG, PA

Trinity Press International, P.O. Box 1321, Harrisburg, PA 17105
Trinity Press International is a division of the Morehouse Group.

Cover art: Ulysses and Calypso, red-figured vase, fifth century B.C.E. Museo Archeologico Nazionale, Naples, Italy. Erich Lessing/Art Resource, NY.

Cover design: Jake Haas

**Library of Congress Cataloging-in-Publication Data**
Mimesis and intertextuality in antiquity and Christianity / edited by Dennis R. MacDonald.
      p.  cm. – (Studies in antiquity & Christianity)
   Chiefly papers read at a conference in June 1998 at the Institute for Antiquity and Christianity at Claremont Graduate University.
   Includes bibliographical references.
   ISBN 1-56338-335-7 (alk. paper)
   1. Christian literature, Early – History and criticism – Congresses.  2. Christian literature, Early – Classical influences – Congresses.  3. Imitation in literature – Congresses.  4. Intertextuality – Congresses.  I. MacDonald, Dennis Ronald, 1946-
   II. Studies in antiquity and Christianity.

BR67 M47  2001
270.1 – dc21

                                                                        00-062867

Printed in the United States of America

01    02    03    04    05    06             10    9    8    7    6    5    4    3    2    1

# Contents

# Contributors

FRANÇOIS BOVON, Harvard University, The Divinity School

THOMAS LOUIS BRODIE, Dominican House of Study, Dublin, Ireland

ELLEN FINKELPEARL, Scripps College

RONALD F. HOCK, University of Southern California

DENNIS R. MACDONALD, Claremont School of Theology and Claremont Graduate University

GEORGE W. E. NICKELSBURG, The University of Iowa

JUDITH PERKINS, Saint Joseph College

GREGORY J. RILEY, Claremont School of Theology and Claremont Graduate University

# Abbreviations

| | |
|---|---|
| AB | Anchor Bible |
| *AncSoc* | *Ancient Society* |
| *APh* | *Acta Philippi* |
| BETL | Bibliotheca ephemeridum theologicarum Lovaniensium |
| *BNGJ* | *Byzantinisch-neugriechische Jahrbücher* |
| BZAW | Beihefte zur Zeitschrift für die alttestamentliche Wissenschaft |
| *CBQ* | *Catholic Biblical Quarterly* |
| CBQMS | Catholic Biblical Quarterly Monograph Series |
| *CdÉ* | *Chronique d'Égypte* |
| CRINT | Compendia rerum iudaicarum ad Novum Testamentum |
| CSCO | Corpus scriptorum christianorum orientalium |
| DJD | Discoveries in the Judean Desert |
| *EA* | *Epigraphica Anatolia* |
| *ÉdP* | *Étude de papyrologie* |
| *HSCP* | *Harvard Studies in Classical Philology* |
| *HTKNT* | *Herders theologischer Kommentar zum Neuen Testament* |
| *HTR* | *Harvard Theological Review* |
| *IBS* | *Irish Biblical Studies* |
| *JHS* | *Journal of Hellenic Studies* |
| *JSNT* | *Journal for the Study of the New Testament* |
| JSNTSup | JSNT Supplement Series |
| OBO | Orbis biblicus et orientalis |
| *PIBA* | *Proceedings of the Irish Biblical Association* |
| *RE* | Pauly-Wissowa. *Real-Encyclopädie der classischen Altertumswissenschaft* |
| *REA* | *Revue des études anciennes* |
| *RE Sup* | *RE Supplement* |
| *RevQ* | *Revue de Qumran* |
| *RhM* | *Rheinisches Museum* |
| SBL | Society of Biblical Literature |

| | |
|---|---|
| SBLTT | SBL Texts and Translations |
| *StudPal* | *Studien zur Palaeographie und Papyruskunde* |
| *ThR* | *Theologische Rundschau* |
| TU | Texte und Untersuchungen zur Geschichte der altchristlichen Literatur |
| *ZAW* | *Zeitschrift für die alttestamentliche Wissenschaft* |
| *ZNW* | *Zeitschrift für die neutestamentliche Wissenschaft* |
| *ZPE* | *Zeitschrift für Papyrologie und Epigraphik* |
| *ZWTh* | *Zeitschrift für wissenschaftliche Theologie* |

# Acknowledgments

This volume contains most of the papers read at a conference held in June 1998, at the Institute for Antiquity and Christianity, at Claremont Graduate University. Professors James M. Robinson and Karen Jo Torjesen invited me to convene senior scholars from Europe and North America on a topic of my choice. For more than a decade I had been interested in various forms of literary imitation in early Christianity and had benefited greatly from the work of others, several of whom agreed to participate in the conference and publish original contributions in this volume. Dr. Jon Ma Assgeirson, then the Associate Director, saw to innumerable details at the conference and provided encouragement to see these contributions to publication. All contributors accepted editorial advice graciously and provided improved versions in a timely fashion. Professor Philip Sellew read the manuscript and offered his encouragement, erudition, and support. Henry Carrigan of Trinity Press International advocated the manuscript to the Editorial Board. As editor of the volume, I will take responsibility for the editing but I could not have done so without the impressive and faithful assistance of Dolly Bush, a student in New Testament at Claremont Graduate University who spent many hours compiling the bibliography, disciplining the abbreviations and footnotes, reformatting files, typing, and any number of other tasks. The result is a unique collection devoted to various aspects of one of the most neglected topics in the study of Christian origins: literary imitation and intertexuality in light of ancient rhetorical practice.

Finally, contributors to this volume have been enriched by the insights of our students to whom we too seldom give sufficient credit. I know that my own work in this field emerges in large part from discussions in and outside the classroom that are impossible fully to acknowledge. It therefore would seem fitting to dedicate this volume to our students, who have helped us better to understand and appreciate the complexity of literary imitation and intertextuality in antiquity and Christianity.

# Introduction

*Dennis R. MacDonald*

On June 4–6, 1998, the Institute for Antiquity and Christianity of Claremont Graduate University hosted a conference on Mimesis and Intertextuality in Early Christianity, the first conference ever devoted specifically to this topic. This is not to say that the topic had been ignored; on the contrary, scholars long before had studied and debated various aspects of early Christian intertextuality, such as the Synoptic Problem, the use of sources in the Gospels and Acts, and the relationships among the Gospels of John and Thomas and the Synoptics. Furthermore, scholars had already acknowledged theoretical discussions of intertextuality ranging from quotations and obvious allusions to faint echoes and even non-genetic comparisons. Few scholars of early Christian literature, however, had enriched their observations with studies of mimesis, the process of training students to write through imitation of recognized models. It was to correct this deficiency that the Institute sponsored this conference in June of 1998.

My own interest in mimesis began in 1984 with a discovery of extensive imitation of Homeric and Euripidean poetry in the apocryphal *Acts of Andrew*. The authors of this text were no slaves to their models; in fact, they competed with them to show the superiority of Christianity to Greek mythology and religion. Nearly every character in the *Acts* represents a Greek god or hero, and Andrew's preaching consistently overcomes their ethical shortcomings, corrects their physical defects, and raises fallen heroes to life. Educated Greeks called such contrasting imitations *zeloi*; Romans called them *aemulationes*. A *zelos* or *aemulatio* was a strategic improvement on the model. For example, Andrew's preaching in his *Acts* prompts a Zeus-like proconsul to stop chasing women, an Ares-like soldier to abandon his weapons, and a Dionysus-like character to forsake wealth and become manly. Andrew exorcises a Heracles-like demoniac, cures a Hephaestus-like cripple, and raises to life a Hector-like corpse. Andrew himself embodies virtues like those of Achilles, Odysseus, and especially Socrates. Virtually every character in the *Acts* finds an analog in Greek mythology or philosophy. I published my mimetic reading of the *Acts* in 1994 as *Christianizing Homer*.[1] While working on this book I became convinced that several other early Christian texts likewise imitated Homeric epic, including the Book of Tobit, Luke-Acts, and especially the Gospel of Mark.

Such discoveries of imitations of classical Greek literature account for another unique aspect of the conference. Scholars previously have observed the influence of Jewish texts on the production of early Christian narratives, but seldom have they argued the same for the closest equivalent to the Bible in the Greco-Roman world: the Homeric epics. Several contributions to the conference advance our understanding of Homeric influence on Christian as well as Jewish narratives.

One question repeatedly emerges in treatments of mimesis: What criteria ought one use to identify the presence of a literary model? In some cases authors loudly announce their reliance, like Vergil's use of Homer in the *Aeneid*, but just as often authors occulted or disguised their reliance.

Over the years I have developed six criteria for detecting mimesis in ancient texts, criteria that work even when authors disguise their reliance on models. The first two criteria pertain to the popularity of the proposed model. The criterion *accessibility* refers to the physical distribution of the model and its likely availability to the author of the imitation. Criterion two, *analogy*, seeks for examples of imitations of the same story by other authors. If no analogy exists, the case for dependence weakens; if one finds several analogies, the case strengthens. Criteria three through five examine similarities between two texts that might indicate mimesis. The third criterion, *density*, assesses the volume of parallels between two texts. The fourth criterion, *order*, looks for similar sequences for the parallels. The more often two texts share content in the same order, the stronger the case for dependence. The fifth criterion is *distinctive traits*. Occasionally two texts contain unusual characteristics that set them apart, and often one can explain the peculiarity in the model as the distinctive contribution of its author, whereas the peculiarity in the hypertext issues from imitation. Ancient authors frequently included unusual details to alert readers to the presence of their models; one might call them intertextual flags. The sixth and final criterion

---

1. *Christianizing Homer: The "Odyssey," Plato, and the "Acts of Andrew"* (New York: Oxford University Press, 1994).

is *interpretability*, which may include emulation. This involves an assessment of why the author may have targeted the model for imitation, such as the replacement of its values and perspectives with different ones, as is the case with the *Acts of Andrew*.

At the conference I illustrated these criteria by comparing the death and burial of Jesus with the death and burial of Hector at the end of the *Iliad*. I decided not to present the full version of the conference paper in this volume because it and related essays have been published.[2] It will be useful, however, to summarize that paper to demonstrate the application of the criteria for detecting literary imitations and the promise of mimesis for illuminating even the best known stories of ancient Christianity.

According to the *Iliad*, Zeus and Apollo repeatedly had rescued Hector from harm, and the hero hoped they would come to his aid once again against Achilles. To steel himself for battle, Hector refused the honey-mixed wine offered him by his mother, Hecuba, to dull his senses to pain. When he saw his opponent in the armor of Hephaestus, Hector fled. In one last act of benefaction, Apollo gave him strength to outrun Achilles, but only until Zeus raised his dreaded scales. Then "Phoebus Apollo abandoned him."[3] Athena disguised herself as Hector's brother Deïphobos, promising to fight at his side. Achilles and Hector traded taunts and threw their spears in vain. Hector then turned to Deïphobos for another, but his brother had vanished. It was then that Hector knew his gods had abandoned him: "Well now! Truly have the gods called me to my death....So I imagine long since this was the pleasure of Zeus, and the son of Zeus, the god who strikes from afar."[4] Achilles then slew him mercilessly, gloated over the corpse of "the one the Trojans glorified like a god," and dragged his corpse behind his chariot in a notorious act of savagery. The Trojans watched these events in horror from the walls of the city, and three women led the lament: Hecuba, Andromache, and Helen. They knew that the death of their hero symbolized the destruction of Troy; the city would be destroyed "from top to bottom."[5]

Achilles continued desecrating Hector's corpse, but the gods kept it from decay, birds, and dogs. Priam, Hector's father, set out at night

---

2. *The Homeric Epics and the Gospel of Mark* (New Haven: Yale University Press, 2000).
3. *Iliad* 22.213.
4. *Iliad* 22.297 and 301–2.
5. *Iliad* 22.408 and 24.728–29.

across the plain bringing with him a lavish ransom for the body of his son. Hermes donned his sandals that allowed him to walk over the waters from Olympus to the Troad and then accompanied Priam to the Greek bivouac. There Achilles granted the body to the king and had it anointed and shrouded. Priam drove it back to the city, where the women raised their laments and buried the hero under a barrow of huge stones. Now that its champion lay dead, the fall of Troy was inevitable and near at hand.

Even before comparing the death and burial of Hector with Mark's account of the death and burial of Jesus, one can apply the first two criteria for establishing the plausibility that Mark could have used the end of the *Iliad* as his model. The parallels surely satisfy criterion one, *accessibility*. The *Iliad* was the most readily available book in Greek antiquity and retained its elite position well into the Roman Imperial Period. Furthermore, if Mark imitated the death and burial of Hector, he had good company, including Aeschylus, Euripides, Sophocles, the tyrant Dionysius I, Astydamas, Ennius, Vergil, Statius, and an anonymous Hellenistic poet.[6] A school text paraphrases the death of Hector, proof that teachers targeted it for mimesis.[7] Josephus was sufficiently conversant with *Iliad* 22 to imitate an obscure section of it.[8] Dionysius of Halicarnassus caviled the historian Hegesias of Magnesia, who lamely imitated "those lines of Homer in which Achilles is made to outrage Hector after his death."[9] Dionysius surely would have objected as well to the imitation of the dragging of Hector's corpse in the *Acts of Andrew and Matthias*.[10] Porphyry concocted an allegory of the conflict between Achilles and Hector as the conflict between Christ and the Devil.[11] The death of Hector and the ransom of his body were the most common

---

6. R. A. Coles, "A New Fragment of a Post-Classical Tragedy from Oxyrhynchus," *Bulletin of the Institute of Classical Studies* 15 (1968) 110–18.

7. P. J. Sijpesteijn, "Scholia minora zu Homer Ilias 22.184–256," *Mnemosyne* 40 (1987) 158–61.

8. Compare Homer's description of the two springs outside Troy in *Iliad* 22.145–56 with Josephus's description of two springs in *Jewish War* 2.186–89. The Jewish historian borrows a phrase from Homer in describing Isaac as Abraham's son when he was "on the threshold of old age" (*Antiquities* 1.222). This phrase appears twice in the *Iliad* (22.60 and 24.487) and once in the *Odyssey* (15.348). If he had in mind a single text, it probably was *Iliad* 22.60.

9. *On Literary Composition*, 18.

10. *Acts of Andrew and Matthias*, 25–28; see *Christianizing Homer*, 53–55.

11. Gerhard Binder, "Eine Polemik des Porphyrios gegen die allegorische Auslegung des Alten Testaments durch die Christen," *ZPE* 3 (1968) 81–95.

Homeric episodes for representation on Greek vases. Mark's putative imitation of the death and burial of Hector in his account of the death and burial of Jesus obviously had *analogs* (criterion 2).

The parallels between *Iliad* 22 and 24 and the death and burial of Jesus in Mark are extensive, sequential, unusual, and almost certainly the result of mimesis. Indeed, the parallels are every bit as persuasive as the imitations I just listed. Like the epic, the Gospel of Mark ends with the death and burial of its hero, which sets the stage for the destruction of an entire city. Just as Trojan warriors fled into Troy, leaving Hector to face his end alone, Jesus' disciples fled and abandoned him.[12] In the accounts of Jesus' trials one finds no parallel to the *Iliad;* the parallels resume with the crucifixion scene. Like Hector, who refused the honey-mixed wine offered to ease his suffering, Jesus refused the myrrh-mixed wine offered by the soldiers. The taunts of the bystanders at the cross conform to the conventions of Homeric taunts, such as the use of titles, bluster, provocation, and irony. The outcome of the taunt later ricochets against the taunter. When Deïphobos was nowhere to be found, Hector recognized his gods had abandoned him. When darkness engulfed the world at noon, Jesus recognized his God had abandoned him. The cry of dereliction, a clumsy transliteration of the Aramaic *"Eloi, Eloi, lema sabachthani,"* prompted the bystanders to think he was calling for Elijah, much as Hector had called for Deïphobos. Neither Deïphobos nor Elijah responded to the call. According to Homer, when Hector died, his soul flew away, audibly bewailing its fate. According to Mark, Jesus breathed his last after uttering "a loud cry."

When the Trojans saw Hector die, they took it as a portent that their city would fall "from top to bottom." When Jesus died, the veil of the temple was rent "from top to bottom," portending the fall of Jerusalem and the destruction of the Temple. Achilles gloated over Hector, mocking the corpse of the one the Trojans used to pray to "as to a god." Jesus' executioner, the Roman centurion, gloated over Jesus with enormous irony: "Surely this man was a son of God!" Mark states that three women watched the crucifixion "from afar," like Andromache, Hecuba, and Helen, who observed the outrages against Hector from the walls of Troy.

These parallels between the deaths of Hector and Jesus are *dense, sequential,* and *distinctive* (criteria 3, 4, and 5), but no more so than the parallels between the burials of Hector and Jesus. The right column re-

---

12. *Iliad* 22.1 and Mark 14:50–52.

produces Mark 15:42–16:2 verbatim, and virtually every motif appears in the paraphrase of *Iliad* 24 on the left, usually in the same order.

| *Iliad* 24 | Mark 15:42–16.2 |
|---|---|
| Priam, king of Troy, set out at night | When it was late, and since it was the day of Preparation, that is, the day before the sabbath, Joseph of Arimathea, a distinguished member of the council, who was also himself waiting |
| to rescue the body of his son, Hector, from his murderer, Achilles. The journey was full of danger.[13] He entered Achilles' abode, "came close to Achilles,"[14] and asked for the body of Hector.[15] | expectantly for the kingdom of God, <br><br> dared to go to Pilate and asked for the body of Jesus. |
| Achilles was amazed that Priam dared to enter his very home. Achilles sent two soldiers to get the ransom, and "called forth" maidservants to "wash and anoint him."[16] | Then Pilate was amazed that he might already be dead; and summoning the centurion, he asked him whether he had been dead for some time. [A woman earlier had anointed Jesus.] When he learned from the centurion that he was dead, he granted the body to Joseph. |
| Hector's body had been saved from desecration. "So when the handmaids had washed the body and anointed it with oil and had wrapped it in a fair cloak and a tunic, then Achilles himself lifted it and placed it on a bier." [Hector's bones would be placed in an ossuary, buried in the ground, and covered with stones.] [Priam left with the body while it was yet night, and brought it to Troy for a fitting burial.] Cassandra was the first to see Priam coming with the bier in the wagon. Three women led in the lament: Andromache, Hecuba, and Helen. | [Jesus' rapid death and burial saved the corpse from desecration.] Then Joseph bought a linen cloth, and taking down the body, wrapped it in the linen cloth and placed it in a tomb that had been hewn out of the rock. He then rolled a stone against the door of the tomb. <br><br> Mary Magdalene and Mary the mother of Joses saw where the body was laid. |
| After elaborate preparations, they burned Hector's body at dawn. | When the sabbath was over, Mary Magdalene, and Mary the mother of James, and Salome brought spices, so that they might go and anoint him. And very early on the first day of the week, when the sun had risen, they went to the tomb. |

---

13. E.g., *Iliad* 24.152, 181, 281–321, and 357–467.
14. *Iliad* 24.477–78.
15. *Iliad* 24.486–506.
16. *Iliad* 24.582.

Mark's use of *Iliad* 22 and 24 also is *interpretable* (criterion 6) insofar as Jesus' heroism and victory over death contrast with Hector's naïve optimism and permanent death. The Trojan hero thought until the end that he might prevail and called on Deïphobos to help. Jesus, however, knew he would die in Jerusalem and went there bravely; he did not cry to Elijah for help, as those at the cross surmised. The Trojans had glorified Hector like a god, but now he was dead, his body rotting in a tomb and his soul flitting about in Hades. After three days, Jesus' tomb was empty; as the Son of God he rose from the dead. God accomplished for Jesus what Priam could not accomplish for Hector; Achilles rightly told the king, "you will gain nothing by grieving for your son, nor will you raise him up."[17] The *Iliad* ends as a tragedy; Mark ends as a comedy.

My summary of the argument here does not suffice to establish the veracity of my claim about Mark and the *Iliad*; for this the reader should consult my book. But the abbreviated treatment here may suffice to illustrate the application of the criteria for detecting mimesis in early Christian narratives.

In lieu of my paper on Mark and the *Iliad* I have substituted a similar study of the influence of the first four books of the *Odyssey* on the Book of Tobit. In some respects, these parallels are even more astonishing insofar as Tobit was not composed in Greek but in Aramaic. Despite its language of composition and Jewish content, Tobit's characterizations, plot elements, changes in venue, and motifs so consistently parallel Homer's epic that one can scarcely doubt direct literary dependence.

George W. E. Nickelsburg agrees with my claim that the author of Tobit used the beginning of the *Odyssey,* but he shows that this dependence was not exclusive, for the author also used the legend of Ahikar, the story of Job, and especially the patriarchal narratives of Genesis. Nickelsburg also suggests that ancient authors may not have been conscious of their imitations and, even when they were conscious of them, may not have consulted texts but may have drawn from their memories. This proposal of multiple literary models lying behind Tobit is consistent with ancient mimetic practice, which often was consciously eclectic. Authors frequently disguised literary dependence by employing as many as five models.

Ronald F. Hock collects and interprets evidence for the use of Homeric epic in Greco-Roman education. He shows that the epics were a

---

17. *Iliad* 24.550–51.

youngster's companion from the time one shuffled off to school for the
first time until one graduated from advanced rhetorical studies. Homeric names served as models for learning to read; Homeric tales were
topoi for classroom compositions; and Homeric speeches were emulated
in declamations. The breadth and depth of Homeric knowledge is astonishing to modern readers and suggests that ancients were equipped
to detect allusions to the epics that are invisible to all but the most
perceptive contemporary critics.

Ellen Finkelpearl shows how classicists distinguish allusion from
topoi, employ intertextual terminology (e.g., allusion, reference, imitation, and borrowing), interpret the prosification of poetry, and describe
the enormous variety of ancient mimetic practices. She investigates several texts in Apuleius that illustrate the flexibility and complexity of
ancient mimesis and the difficulty in isolating the sources of allusions.
By demonstrating the way that Apuleius incorporates secular or value-
neutral phrases into philosophical and religious contexts, she implicitly
provides a model for the interpretation of early Christian appropriation
and transvaluation of pre-Christian texts.

Gregory J. Riley argues that ancient Christian imitation of Greek classics finds an analog in the imitation of Greek cultural ideals, especially
ideals related to the cult of heroes. Developing insights from his book
*One Jesus, Many Christs,* Riley shows how early Christians modeled their
lives — and sometimes their martyrdoms — after the Greek idealiza-
tion of heroes who won eternal renown through suffering and violent
deaths.

Thomas Louis Brodie, a pioneer in the application of literary imitation to the study of the New Testament, claims that the author
of Luke-Acts had an intimate familiarity with several letters of the
apostle Paul and reworked some of this material into his narratives. He
compares two accounts of the Last Supper, 1 Cor 11:16–34 and Luke
22:14–30, and argues that they share remarkable similarities. The differences between them are most interpretable if one views Luke as directly
indebted to 1 Corinthians 11. If correct, this observation opens up the
possibility for other rewritings of the epistles in Luke's works.

Intertextuality for Judith Perkins includes ideological tensions between exemplars of a common genre. She argues that the Greek romances and the so-called Acts of Christian Martyrs share generic
traits, including an interest in suffering — such as deprivations, imprisonments, tortures — but with radically different valuations. "In the

romance Greek urban elite used the image of the tortured and constrained body to build social cohesion and solidify their social identity.
In the Acts, Christians co-opted the same representation as a focus of
resistance to the dominant social power and as an opening of a new
site for social enunciation." Voices of this new religious movement came
from two unlikely sites: the prison and the arena. It was from here that
Christian authors frequently articulated their interpretation of suffering
as divine blessing. "The state broke the bodies of dissidents to proclaim
and graphically symbolize its enduring unity and power. The martyrs,
however, usurped this bodily inscribed language of power and recycled
and redirected it to bolster Christian corporate existence."

François Bovon demonstrates how freely the author of the apocryphal
*Acts of Philip* employed biblical traditions: "There is an ongoing process
of revelation and manifestation of divine love through the centuries,"
and this process can be observed in biblical texts, apostolic memories,
and apocryphal traditions. The great moments of the biblical story out-
weigh the biblical text per se; the words of Jesus carry freight whether
transmitted through the New Testament, apocryphal traditions, or even
in the composition of the *Acts of Philip* itself.

The participants universally considered this conference a success and
hoped for a similar conference on this topic in the future. The application of mimetic theory on ancient texts — especially on early Christian
texts — is in its infancy. We offer the following essays in the hope of
stimulating more research on mimesis and intertextuality in antiquity
and Christianity.

# 1

## Tobit and the *Odyssey*

### Dennis R. MacDonald

The Book of Tobit tells this tale. An oppressive Assyrian regime con-
fiscated the property of a faithful exile named Tobit. Later, Tobit
surreptitiously buried the corpse of a murdered Jew and slept outside
his home because of ritual uncleanness from having touched the corpse.
As he slept, sparrow droppings fell into his eyes, blinding him. To make
ends meet, his wife Anna took up weaving. Tobit then sent Tobiah,
his only son, to Ecbatana and Rages to claim a treasure he had de-
posited there with a friend during more prosperous times. The angel
Raphael, disguised as a young Jew named Azariah, offered to accompany the lad on his journey, and along the way, they captured a fish
in the Tigris, whose heart, liver, and gall contained magical properties.
When they arrived in Ecbatana, at the home of wealthy Raguel and
Edna his wife, Tobiah and the angel found Sarah, their daughter, tor-
mented by a demon that repeatedly slew her would-be husbands on the
nuptial bed. Tobiah dispelled the demon by burning the fish's heart and
liver, and married Sarah. For fourteen days the family feasted to cel-
ebrate the union, while Raphael traveled to Rages for Tobit's treasure.
After Raphael returned, he escorted Tobiah and Sarah back to Nineveh,
to the jubilation of Tobit and Anna. When Tobiah applied the fish's gall
to his father's eyes, Tobit recovered his sight. Finally, Raphael revealed
his angelic identity and disappeared, evoking fearful praise from Tobit
and Tobiah.

In 1911 the classicist Carl Fries published an article that identified a
striking number of parallels between the Book of Tobit and the so-called
*Telemachia* of Homer's *Odyssey*, that is, Books 1–4 and 15.[1] Like Tobit, the
*Telemachia* narrates the devastation of a father's estate (Odysseus's by the
suitors), the weaving of a disconsolate mother (Penelope), the journey of
an only son (Telemachus) in the company of a disguised, supernatural

---

1. "Das Buch Tobit und die Telemachie," *ZWTh* 53 (1911) 54–87. Interpreters of Tobit
have virtually ignored this article, as I would have, had not Norman R. Petersen and
George W. E. Nickelsburg brought it to my attention.

guide (Athena), a distant wedding feast, the return of the son with great wealth, the parents' joy at the son's arrival, and the restoration of the hero's fortune. As we shall see, the stories also share an impressive number of minor details.

These agreements, according to Fries, issued from an ancient oriental myth. To explain how the Greek bard and the Jewish novelist, though separated by several centuries and much of the Mediterranean, knew the same tale, Fries argued as follows. Even though the Book of Tobit as we have it could not have been written earlier than the fourth century B.C.E., several centuries after the writing of the *Odyssey,* its "basic elements" go back to "the earliest historical time."[2] At "a very early date," argued Fries, before the *Odyssey,* a Jewish author reworked these "old oriental motifs" into a novel about the journey of Tobiah, a source lying behind our Book of Tobit. The author of the *Telemachia* could have used this Tobiah novel "more or less directly."[3] Later, another author recast this novel into the Book of Tobit as we now know it, adding the framing narrative about Tobit's blindness and eventual healing.[4]

The *Odyssey,* too, had a complex history of composition, according to Fries. The final redactor incorporated two earlier poems about Telemachus into his epic about Odysseus. One still detects the poems behind Books 3 and 4.[5] The two *Telemachias* share a remarkable number of agreements, evidence that they both derive from a common myth that also informed the Tobiah novel underlying the Book of Tobit, where it appears in its most pristine form.[6] The poet of the *Odyssey* awkwardly

---

2. Fries, "Buch Tobit," 71. Tobit's burial of the dead calls to mind the "Antigone motif" developed by Sophocles but whose origins were oriental and ancient; Sarah's dangerous marriage bed modifies the Mesopotamian myth of Ishtar who slew her would-be lovers (*Gilgamesh Epic,* Table VI; according to Fries, the Ishtar myth also informed ancient characterizations of Atalanta, Circe, Helen, and Penelope [73–74]); and the depiction of Tobit echoes legends concerning Ahikar that in turn may have come from an earlier mythological character (71–76).

3. Ibid., 72.

4. Ibid., 75–76 and 83–87.

5. In the first, Athena takes the form of Mentor and accompanies Telemachus to Pylos, where the youth originally married Polycaste, Nestor's daughter. Athena/Mentor then goes off to collect an old debt from the Cauconians (*Odyssey* 3.365–67). The goddess then would have returned to Pylos and escorted the youth back to Ithaca.

Fries also argued that an even earlier *Telemachia* lay behind *Odyssey* 4, which told a similar tale. Peisistratus, Nestor's son, played a role like that of Athena/Mentor by accompanying Telemachus from Pylos to Sparta, where Odysseus's son acquired a wife. A residuum of romance exists in the double wedding of the children of Menelaus and Helen and the giving of wedding gifts to Telemachus (ibid., 80–81).

6. Ibid., 81–82.

combined these two poems into an introduction for the more dominant story of Odysseus.

One might diagram Fries's complex argument as follows:

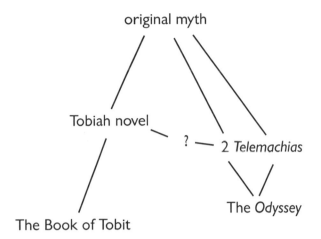

Biblical scholars will recognize from Fries's treatment of Tobit his rather freewheeling use of source criticism; classicists will see in his treatment of the *Odyssey* his commitment to the so-called analytical school of Homeric scholarship. Even nonspecialists might be suspicious of the complexity of this explanation. In light of recent research, Fries's isolation of sources now seems naive. Tobit is the work of a single author who possessed no written source concerning Tobiah.[7] Similarly, analytical treatments of the *Odyssey* are less attractive today than either "unitarian" interpretations or oral-formulaic theories of epic composition.[8] Most Homeric scholars now view the *Telemachia* not as a separate poem (or poems) but as an integral part of the composition of the epic.[9]

7. E.g., Irene Nowell, "The Book of Tobit: Narrative Technique and Theology" Ph.D. diss., Catholic University of America, 1983).

8. For brief discussions of Homeric scholarship in the twentieth century see Bernard Knox in Robert Fagles, *The Iliad* (New York: Viking, 1990) 5–22, and Alfred Heubeck, ed., *A Commentary on Homer's Odyssey*, vol. 1, Introduction and Books I–VIII, with Stephanie West and John Bryan Hainsworth, 3–23 (New York: Oxford University Press, 1988).

9. The following quotation is representative of the consensus on the relationship of the *Telemachia* to the rest of the epic.

> [T]he inclusion of the Telemachy in the epic is a master-stroke on the part of the poet, since it allows him to start events in different places at the same time, and so to create from the beginning two strands of narrative which run parallel until he brings them together at the conclusion. The gods — and the poet — have carefully

One might argue, though apparently no one has, that Tobit and the *Odyssey* nevertheless recast the same ancient myth. Against such a claim are the enormous temporal, cultural, and geographical distances between the two works. The fourth-century date for Tobit favored by Fries probably is too early. A more likely date is the early second century B.C.E.[10] Furthermore, Fries assumed that Tobit had been written in Greek, but Aramaic and Hebrew fragments have emerged among the Dead Sea Scrolls and, when compared with the Greek versions, suggest a Semitic original. Even so, one cannot rule out prima facie a common folkloric ancestry. Folktales often show remarkable stability over millennia and transferability from one culture and region to another.

Were the parallels between the two works limited to those treated by Fries and summarized thus far, one might indeed attribute the similarities to a shared folktale, but the density of the parallels, their common and unusual sequence, and the capacity of details in the *Odyssey* to explain peculiarities in Tobit suggest a literary connection. The author of the Aramaic (or Hebrew) Tobit apparently consulted a Greek copy of the epic during composition. Other Jewish authors of the period imitated Homer, but they wrote in Greek and in verse.[11] If correct, Tobit's use of the epic witnesses to an unusual and fascinating liaison between Semitic-speaking Judaism and classical Greek poetry.

The author of Tobit clearly used other models for his work in addition to Homer's *Telemachia*. Analogies to the Bible abound, especially to

---

arranged that at almost the same moment as the father on a distant island embarks on the craft he has built himself, the son leaves this home to find news of his father in the world outside. We thus have here two opposite courses of action which are destined to come together and to culminate in common endeavor and achievement; in other words, they are two aspects of the same process: that of bringing Odysseus home.

This device was surely the poet's own invention, and he must have been delighted by it, all the more perhaps because he could have found no example of such virtuosity in construction either in the *Iliad* or the earlier oral epics. (Heubeck, *Commentary*, 17)

See also Karl Reinhardt, "Homer und die Telemachie," in *Von Werken und Formen. Vorträge und Aufsätze* (Godesberg: Küpper, 1948) 37–51, and Ralph Hexter, *A Guide to the Odyssey: A Commentary on the English Translation of Robert Fitzgerald* (New York: Vintage Books, 1993) 8–9.

10. See the discussion by Carey A. Moore, *Tobit: A New Translation with Introduction and Commentary*, AB 40A (New York: Doubleday, 1996) 40–42.

11. E.g., Theodotus *On the Jews* and Philo Epicus *On Jerusalem* (Eusebius *Praeparatio evangelica* 9.17–20, 22–24, and 35–38). An obscure medieval note states that a certain "Sosates, the Jewish Homer, flourished in Alexandria" sometime between 142 and 51 B.C.E. (Shaye J. D. Cohen, "Sosates the Jewish Homer," *HTR* 74 [1981] 391–96).

Job and Genesis 24 and 29.[12] The author borrowed from the legend of Ahikar;[13] Asmodeus's curse on Sarah's marriage bed instantiates a motif common in folktales around the world.[14] George W. E. Nickelsburg's contribution to this volume will demonstrate sustained similarities between Tobit and Genesis 27–35. Even so, no anterior tradition or text more thoroughly informs the book than Homer's *Odyssey*. In other words, Tobit's imitation of his models was eclectic, a clever melding of patriarchal and Homeric elements.

Much of the discussion here presents parallels between the two works in columns and repeats some of the evidence cited by Fries. They need repeating insofar as few commentators have referred to this article that merits, after eighty years, a thorough discussion. Furthermore, Fries failed to recognize many of the parallels presented here.

---

12. The plight of Tobit at the beginning of the novel and his final vindication resemble the frame story of Job (Fries, "Buch Tobit," 84). Compare Tob 1:3–3:6 with Job 1:1–3:26 and Tob 13:1–4:15 with Job 42:10–17. See especially Devorah Dimant, "Use and Interpretation of Mikra in the Apocrypha and Pseudepigrapha," in Martin Jan Mulder and Harry Sysling, eds., *Mikra: Text, Translation, Reading and Interpretation of the Hebrew Bible in Ancient Judaism and Early Christianity*, CRINT 2.1 (Philadelphia: Fortress Press, 1988) 417–19.

Genesis 24 tells of Abraham's sending of his servant (Eliezer?) to get a wife for Isaac from his homeland in the East. The similarities with Tobit include the insistence on getting a wife from a family of relatives (Gen 24:3–4 and 37–38 and Tob 1:9, 4:12–13, and 6:18), the promise of Abraham that God would "send his angel before" the servant (Gen 24:8 and Tob 3:16–17), the exemplary hospitality of the hosts (Gen 24:15–33 and Tob 7:1–11), the refusal to eat until the errand was disclosed (Gen 24:33 and Tob 7:11), the agreement on a wedding between the young people (Gen 24:50 and Tob 7:11–13), the resumption of eating (Gen 24:54 and Tob 7:14), the request of the host that the girl delay her departure (Gen 24:55 and Tob 8:20), the insistence to be going (Gen 24:56 and Tob 10:7–8), the blessing at the departure (Gen 24:60 and Tob 10:11–12), the sighting of the return party from a distance (Gen 24:63 and Tob 11:5–6), and the introduction of the girl to her new family (Gen 24:64–67 and Tob 11:17). See Moore, *Tobit*, 8–9.

The use of earlier Jewish texts has preoccupied much scholarship on Tobit. See especially Alexander A. DiLella, "The Deuteronomic Background of the Farewell Discourse in Tobit 14:3–11," *CBQ* 4 (1979) 380–89, Paul Deselaers, *Das Buch Tobit. Studien zu seiner Entstehung, Komposition und Theologie*, OBO 43 (Göttingen: Vandenhoeck & Ruprecht, 1982) 293–304, and Merten Rabenau, *Studien zum Buch Tobit*, BZAW 220 (Berlin: Walter de Gruyter, 1994) 94–115.

13. Jonas C. Greenfield, "Ahikar in the Book of Tobit," in Maurice Carrez, et al., eds., *De la Torah au Messie. Études d'exégèse et d'herméneutique bibliques offertes à Henri Cazelles* (Paris: Desclée, 1981) 329–36.

14. Frank Zimmermann, *The Book of Tobit: An English Translation with Introduction and Commentary*, Jewish Apocryphal Literature (New York: Harper, 1958), and T. Francis Glasson, "The Main Source of Tobit," *ZAW* 71 (1959) 275–77. For a critique of folkloric assessments see William Soll, "Misfortune and Exile in Tobit: The Juncture of a Fairy Tale Source and Deuteronomic Theology," *CBQ* 51 (1989) 209–12, and especially "Tobit and Folklore Studies with Emphasis on Propp's Methodology," in David Lull, ed., *SBL 1988 Seminar Papers* (Atlanta: Scholars Press, 1988) 39–41.

The translations of the *Odyssey* used in this study for the most part conform to the Loeb edition (Murray-Dimock). The translations of Tobit generally follow the New Revised Standard Version, which renders the Greek of Codex Sinaiticus (the Hanhart edition).[15] When Aramaic or Hebrew fragments exist, I reproduce the translations of Joseph A. Fitzmyer and underline unquestionably attested readings to distinguish them from the Greek Tobit.[16] Alterations of these translations, of course, conform to the best critical editions. Often passages from the *Odyssey* and Tobit appear in parallel columns to assist comparison. The lexical similarities between the epic and the Greek Tobit (of which there are many) for the most part are coincidental, insofar as Greek was not Tobit's original language of composition, but occasionally overlapping vocabulary shows how the translator of Greek Tobit used expressions similar to Homer's own Greek.

## TWO PROBLEMS AND ONE DIVINE SOLUTION

The *Odyssey* and the Book of Tobit similarly commence with two seemingly intractable problems, one at the hero's home and the other far away.[17] During his twenty-year absence, Odysseus's home had become infested with 108 suitors vying for the hand of Penelope, who delayed her wedding by weaving a shroud for her father-in-law during the day and unraveling it at night.[18] Indeed, Penelope was endowed "above other women" with "knowledge of beautiful handiwork."[19] In the meantime, the constant feasting of the suitors threatened Odysseus's estate with ruin, and Telemachus, the son of Penelope and Odysseus, was helpless against their superior numbers and strength.

Far from Ithaca a second tragedy persisted: the goddess Calypso had trapped Odysseus on her island as her love pet, preventing his return. His sufferings were all the more tragic in view of his righteousness; he

---

15. *Tobit*, Septuaginta: Vetus Testamentum graecum auctoritate Academiae Scientiarum Gottingensis editum 8.5 (Göttingen: Vandenhoeck & Ruprecht, 1983) 59–185.

16. In Magen Brochi, et al., eds., *Qumran Cave IV, XIV: Parabiblical Texts, Part 2,* DJD 19 (Oxford: Clarendon Press, 1995) 1–76.

17. See the treatment of George W. E. Nickelsburg, "Stories of Biblical and Early Post-Biblical Times," in Michael E. Stone, ed., *Jewish Writings of the Second Temple Period: Apocrypha, Pseudepigrapha, Qumran Sectarian Writings, Philo, Josephus,* CIRNT 2 (Philadelphia: Fortress Press, 1984) 42–44.

18. *Odyssey* 2.103–5.

19. *Odyssey* 2.116–17.

was "beyond all mortals in wisdom, and beyond all has paid sacrifice to the immortal gods."[20] So dearly did he pine for home that he longed to die.[21]

The role of Odysseus falls to Tobit in the Jewish novel.[22] Like Odysseus, Tobit was scrupulous with sacrifices and suffered greatly from the confiscation of his possessions.[23] In despair of his poverty and blindness, he, like Odysseus, prayed for death.[24] To make ends meet, his wife Anna took up "women's work," namely, weaving.[25] Here, and again frequently later, Anna plays the role of Penelope.[26]

As in the *Odyssey,* so also in Tobit: a second problem exists far from home, in distant Ecbatana. The demon Asmodeus loved Sarah, the

---

20. *Odyssey* 1.65–67; cf. 60–61.

21. *Odyssey* 1.59; cf. 5.82–84 and 151–58. Compare also Tobit's burial of the dead with Odysseus's burial of Elpenor in 12.1–15.

22. The opening sentences of both works (as well as their eventual titles) indicate the books will concern an individual, Odysseus or Tobit, though the narrative soon switches the attention to their sons, Telemachus and Tobiah.

23. Tob 1:4 and especially 6–7a:

I would hurry off to Jerusalem with the first fruits of the crops and the firstlings of the flock, the tithes of the cattle, and the first shearings of the sheep. I would give these to the priests, the sons of Aaron, at the altar; likewise the tenth of the grain, wine, olive oil, pomegranates, figs, and the rest of the fruits to the sons of Levi who ministered at Jerusalem.

Even in exile he maintained his righteousness, caring for the hungry and poor and burying the bodies of the faithful slain by Assyrians (2:7–10).

24. Tob 3:1, 6 (cf. 4:2):

Then with much grief and anguish of heart I wept, and with groaning began to pray: "...So now deal with me as you will; command my spirit to be taken from me, so that I may be released from the face of the earth and become dust. For it is better for me to die than to live, because I have had to listen to undeserved insults, and great is the sorrow within me. Command, O Lord, that I be released from this distress; release me to go to the eternal home, and do not, O Lord, turn your face away from me. For it is better for me to die than to see so much distress in my life and to listen to insults."

25. Tob 2:11–12.

26. The name Anna means "grace," an apt designation also for Penelope. One day Anna cut a length of cloth from her loom and sent it to her clients, but besides her wages they gave her a young goat. Convinced that Anna had stolen the goat, Tobit commanded her to return it; she, however, insisted that her patrons had given it to her as an honest gift (Tob 2:13–14). Ancient readers generally praised Penelope for her patience and chastity; one of the few blemishes on her character was the suspicion of theft prompted by Homer's statement that she tricked lavish gifts from the suitors (*Odyssey* 18.270–83). This is the very charge Tobit leveled at Anna for the goat.

daughter of Raguel and Edna, and slew seven bridegrooms on her wedding couch.[27] Bereft of a husband and honor, Sarah, too, like Odysseus and Tobit, prayed to die.[28]

According to Homer, Zeus decided to intervene and rectify the twin disasters. He sent Athena, disguised as Mentes and later as Mentor, to Odysseus's son Telemachus to travel with him to Pylos and Sparta; he sent Hermes to Ogygia, Calypso's island, to free Odysseus.[29] So also in Tobit: God decided to intervene to correct both situations by sending Raphael in disguise.

> [T]he prayers of both of them [Tobit and Sarah] were heard in the glorious presence of God. So Raphael was sent to heal both of them:[30] Tobit, to cure the white scales from his eyes, so that he might see the light of heaven with his eyes; and Sarah, daughter of Raguel, to give her in marriage to Tobiah son of Tobit, and to set her free from the wicked demon Asmodeus.[31]

Tobiah will leave home with Raphael disguised as a mortal to retrieve his father's fortune;[32] Telemachus will leave home with Athena disguised as a mortal to learn his father's fate. In other words, the journey of each lad served the interests of his father.[33] In the epic, the father is far from home on his *nostos* from Troy; in Tobit the father remains at home, like Abraham who sent his servant to find a bride for Isaac in Genesis 24, and like blind Isaac who stayed home as Jacob went to find his bride in Genesis 27. Both the epic and the novel assure the reader almost from the outset that the Divine Will will win in the end, though the characters themselves remain oblivious to it. This disparity between the knowledge of the reader and the ignorance of the characters allows for dramatic irony in both works.[34]

---

27. Both Calypso and Sarah are dangerous brides. The nymph was all too familiar with the Olympian double standard of allowing gods to couple with mortal women, but disallowing goddesses the same pleasure with mortal men. Artemis slew Orion, the lover of Eos, and Zeus slew Iason, the lover of Demeter (*Odyssey* 5.118–28). Asmodeus similarly slew Sarah's seven suitors.

28. *Odyssey* 3.11–15.

29. *Odyssey* 1.82–89.

30. The name Raphael aptly means "God heals."

31. Tob 3:16–17 (4QpapTob[b] a, frag. 7. Ls. 1–2).

32. Cf. Gen 24:8.

33. Fries, "Buch Tobit," 55.

34. On irony in Tobit, see Nowell, "Book of Tobit," 192–200.

## PREPARATIONS FOR THE JOURNEY

To prepare for his death, Tobit summoned Tobiah to his side. The author's characterization of Tobiah shares much with Homer's Telemachus; both are beloved only sons who suffer undeserved troubles, and several of Tobit's instructions to Tobiah in 4:3–19 are apt of Telemachus.[35] Tobit ends this discourse by informing Tobiah about ten talents he had left with Gabael in Media that he must retrieve.[36]

Tobiah promised to do as instructed but complained that he did "not know the roads to Media, or how to get there."[37] Tobit told him to find a guide.[38] The subsequent negotiations and arrangements with the angel Raphael echo Telemachus's preparations for his trip with Athena. Both lads go and find the disguised heavenly strangers standing alone before them.[39]

Both boys (and Tobit) asked the strangers whence they came and from what families. The columns that follow are the first of many that allow easier comparison of the two works.[40] Underlining identifies those words attested from the Dead Sea Scroll Aramaic and Hebrew fragments.

---

35. Athena (disguised as Mentes and Mentor), Nestor, and Menelaus all serve Telemachus as father surrogates (e.g. *Odyssey* 1.308). Athena/Mentor and Tobit both give instructions concerning proper funeral rites for their fathers (Tob 4:3 and *Odyssey* 1.291–92; cf. 2.221–23). Tobit tells Tobiah to treat his mother with respect "because she faced many dangers for you while you were in her womb" (Tob 4:4) = 4QTob^e, frag. 2, L. 2: "*and* (she) *bore you in* [her] *womb.*" Telemachus shows filial respect by refusing to abandon "the mother that bore me" (*Odyssey* 2.130–31). Tobiah was to demonstrate generosity to the poor (Tob 4:5–11), a characteristic also of Telemachus (*Odyssey* 1.118–43, 3.34–53, 337–55, 464–80, 4.26–67, 587–624, and 15.68–142). Tobit instructed his son to marry a Jewish girl (Tob 4:12–13a); Menelaus and Helen talked with Telemachus about his future bride (*Odyssey* 15.24–26 and 125–27).

36. Before leaving for Troy, Odysseus likewise entrusted his estate to his friend Mentes for safekeeping (*Odyssey* 2.225–27). Odysseus was absent from Ithaca for twenty years, precisely the same duration that Tobit's money was with Gabael (Tob 5:3).

37. Tob 5:2.

38. Tob 5:3.

39. Compare the following:

| *Odyssey* 1.119–20 | Tob 5:4 |
|---|---|
| [Telemachus] went straight to the outer door; for in his heart he counted it shame that a stranger should stand alone at the gates. [Athena was in disguise.] | [Tobiah] went out and found the angel Raphael standing in front of him; but he did not perceive that he was an angel of God. |

40. For the most part they will appear in their Homeric order.

**Odyssey 1.170 and 174–76**

Telemachus spoke to flashing-eyed Athene, ...
"Who are you among men,
and from where (πόθεν)? Where (πόθι) is your
city and where your parents? ...

And tell me this also truly,
that I may know it well, whether this is your
first visit here, or whether you are indeed
a friend of my father's house (πατρώιος)."

**Tob 5:5 and 11–12**
**(4QTob^b ar. frag. 3. L. 2)**
[H]e [Tobiah] said to him,
"Where do you come from (πόθεν),
young man? ... "
Tobit said to him, "Brother,
of what lineage (πατριᾶς) are you
and from what tribe?"
"Tell me, brother. ..."
I want to know the truth, brother,

whose son you are and what your
name is."

Notice that Telemachus and Tobit both want guarantees of noble pater-
nity ("tell me this also truly, that I may know it well"; "Tell me, ... I
want to know the truth").

The goddess and the angel both lied concerning their identities ("I
am") and ancestries ("the son of ...") and claimed to be in the area
on business. Jewish angels seldom lie;[41] Homer's deities, like Athena,
often do.

**Odyssey 1.180–84**
Then the goddess, flashing-eyed Athene,
answered him, "Therefore I will tell you all.
I declare that I am Mentes, the son of wise
Anchialus ... on my way to Temese for copper;
and I bear with me shining iron."

**Tob 5:13 (4QTob^b ar, frag. 3, L. 3)**
He replied,

"I am Azariah, the son of the great
Hananiah, one of your relatives."
["I have come here to work." (5:5)]

Both strangers, though lying, give satisfactory reassurances; both were
longstanding friends of the fathers and had shared experiences with
them.

**Odyssey 1.187–88 and 209–11**
[Athena:] "Friends of one another do we
declare ourselves to be, just as our fathers were,
friends from old."
" ... [F]or many were the times we consorted
with one another before he embarked for
the land of Troy, whither others, too,
the bravest of the Argives, went in their
hollow ships."

**Tob 5:14**
[Tobit:] "It turns out that you are a
kinsman, and of good and noble
lineage.
For I knew Hananiah and Nathan,
the two sons of Shameliah the great,
and they used to go with me to
Jerusalem and worshiped with me
there, and were not led astray."

Both strangers also predicted divine resolutions soon for the fathers.[42]

---

41. Attending angels are common in Jewish texts; e.g., Gen 24:7, 40, and 48:15–16,
and Ps 91:11.

42. Compare the following:

The heavenly messengers both promised to travel with the young men on their dangerous missions. Someone ordered each lad to prepare supplies.

*Odyssey* 2.285–89
[Athena, now disguised as Mentor:]
"But for yourself, the journey on which
your heart is set shall not be long delayed,
so true a friend of your father's house am I,
who will equip for you a swift ship, and
myself go with you. But go now to the
house and join the company of the suitors;
make ready stores, and stow them all in
vessels." (Cf. 2.337–60)

Tob 5:16–17
[Raphael:]

"I will go with him; so do not fear. . . ."

[Tobit:] "Son, prepare things for the
journey and set out with your brother."

Just as Tobiah and his angelic guide were about to leave, "his mother [Anna] wept."[43] Telemachus knew that his mother Penelope would never let him sail for Pylos,[44] so he left without notifying her, "that she may not mar her fair flesh with weeping."[45] He did tell his nurse, Eurycleia, who, like Anna, wept. Anna and Eurycleia both began their laments with two questions objecting to the journeys.

*Odyssey* 2.361–64
So he spoke, and the staunch nurse, Eurycleia,
uttered a shrill cry, and lamenting spoke to him
winged words: "Ah, dear child, how has
this thought come into your mind?
Whither do you intend to go over the wide earth,
you who are an only son and well-beloved?"

Tob 5:18
But his mother began to weep,
and said to Tobit,
"Why is it that you have sent my
child away?
Is he not the staff of our hands as he
goes in and out before us?"

In both works someone (Telemachus or Tobit) comforts the woman by claiming divine protection for the journey.

*Odyssey* 2.371–72
Then wise Telemachus answered her,
"Take heart, nurse, . . .

for not without divine sanction is this plan."

Tob 5:21–22 (4QTob^b ar, frag. 4, Ls. 3–4)
[H]e said to her,
Do not fear and do not become
anxious about him, my sister.
For a good angel will accompany him;
his journey will be successful."

With these words, both Eurycleia and Anna were comforted.[46]

*Odyssey* 1.203–4
[Athena:]
"Not much longer shall he be absent
from his own native land."

Tob 5:10
[Raphael:] "Take courage;
the time is near for God to heal you;
take courage."

43. Tob 5:18.
44. *Odyssey* 2.356–60 and 371–76.
45. *Odyssey* 2.376; cf. 749.
46. Cf. *Odyssey* 4.758 and Tob 6:1.

## THE JOURNEY AND THE WELCOME

Tobiah, his dog, and Raphael left on their journey, and at the Tigris a "fish leaped up from the water to swallow the foot of the youth."[47] They brought the fish to land and removed its gall, heart, and liver, each of which possessed magical properties.[48] As they approached Ecbatana, Raphael told Tobiah to take Sarah to wife, and not to worry about her dangerous bridal chamber, for the odor produced by burning the liver and heart of the fish would forever dispel the demon.[49] They entered Ecbatana and went immediately to the home of Raguel, who noted privately to his wife Edna how much Tobiah resembled his father Tobit. When those present learned of Tobit's blindness, they wept.

This reception at Ecbatana resembles Telemachus's reception in *Odyssey* 4.[50] He and his new traveling companion, Peisistratus,[51] entered Sparta. In the columns that follow, the traveling pairs arrive at their destination, go to the splendid homes of Menelaus or Raguel,[52] and find the hosts at home.

| *Odyssey* 4.1–4 Tob 7:1 | (=4QpapTob<sup>a</sup> ar, frag. 14ii, L. 6) |
|---|---|
| And they came to the hollow land of Lacedaemon | And when they entered into Ecbatana.... |
| with its many ravines, | So he [Raphael/Azariah] |
| and drove to the palace of glorious Menelaus. | took him to Raguel's house (εἰς τὸν οἶκον) |
| Him they found giving a marriage feast (τόν δ᾽ εὗρον δαινύντα γάμον) | and they found Raguel sitting (εὗρον αὐτὸν καθήμενον) |
| to his many kinsfolk for his flawless son and daughter within his house. | before the gate of his dwelling. |

---

47. Tob 6:3 (4QTob<sup>b</sup> ar, frag. 4i, Ls. 6–7).

48. Tob 6:4–9. This episode shares much with *Odyssey* 10.275–309, where Hermes, disguised as a young man, gives Odysseus the magical root *moly* for neutralizing the effects of Circe's spells that transformed humans into swine.

49. Compare Tob 6:10–18, the exchange between Raphael/Azariah and Tobiah just prior to entering the house of Raguel, with *Odyssey* 3.14–28, the exchange between Athena/Mentor and Telemachus just prior to their joining the feast of Nestor. In both, a heavenly guide emboldens a timid youth concerning what to do in a new situation (*Odyssey* 3.14: "[N]o longer need you feel shame"; Tob 6:18 [4QTob<sup>b</sup> ar, frag. 4iii, L. 17]: "do not fear").

50. It also resembles Telemachus's reception at Pylos in Book 3. Although the author of Tobit seems to follow the events in Book 4 more closely, parallels also exist with Book 3.

51. Peisistratus plays a role similar to that of Athena/Mentor in Book 3.

52. Raguel means "friend of God"; Menelaus likewise is dear to Zeus, having married his daughter Helen (e.g., *Odyssey* 4.561–69).

Homer continues: "His daughter [Hermione] he was sending to the son of Achilles... and now the gods were bringing the marriage to pass."[53] There will be a marriage also, of course, in Ecbatana.

Telemachus and Peisistratus "halted at the gate of the palace."[54] Menelaus showed hospitality by having squires "lead the men into the divine palace."[55] The two lads enjoyed a sumptuous feast during which Menelaus expressed his fondness for Odysseus.[56] After dinner, Helen joined the men and immediately noticed the similarities between Telemachus and his father. In Tobit, Edna, whose name significantly means "pleasure," plays a role similar to that of Helen. Compare this passage with the speech of Raguel to Edna.

*Odyssey* 4.137 and 141–44

[Helen] questioned her husband on each matter... "For never yet, I declare, saw I one so like another... as this man is like the son of great-hearted Odysseus, Telemachus." [Menelaus responded that he noticed the likeness as well (4.146–50; cf. 3.123–25).]

Tob 7:2 (4QpapTob[a] ar, frag. 14ii, Ls. 7–8 and 4QTob[b] ar, frag. 4iii, Ls. 4–5)
He [Raguel] said to his wife Edna,

"How this youth resembles Tobi, the son of my uncle!" (Cf. 9:6)

Peisistratus told Menelaus and Helen that the lad was indeed Odysseus's son; Tobiah told Raguel and Edna that he was Tobit's son.[57] Both hosts expressed their joy at the identities of their guests,[58] and those present wept over the sufferings of the boys' fathers.[59]

---

53. *Odyssey* 4.5 and 7.
54. *Odyssey* 4.20; cf. Tob 7:1 (4QpapTob[a] ar, frag. 14ii, L. 6): "before the gate of his dwelling."
55. *Odyssey* 4.43; cf. Tob 7:1 (4QpapTob[a] ar, frag. 14ii, L. 7): "And he brought them into his house."
56. *Odyssey* 4.100–12; cf. Tob 7:7–9.
57. Tob 7:3, 4QTob[b] ar, frag. 4iii, Ls. 5–6.

*Odyssey* 3.68, 71, 75–76, and 81
[T]he horseman, Nestor of Gerenia, spoke first: ...
"Strangers, who are you? Whence (πόθεν) do you sail over the watery waves?"
Then wise Telemachus took courage, and made answer, ...
"We have come from Ithaca (ἡμεῖς ἐξ Ἰθάκης)."

Tob 7:3 (4QTob[b] ar, frag. 4iii, Ls. 5–6)
Edna asked them and said to them,
"Where are you from (πόθεν),
my brothers?"
They said to her,

"We are from the Naphtalites
(ἐκ τῶν υἱῶν Νεφθαλεὶμ ἡμεῖς),
[who] are captives in Nineveh."

Both boys then speak of their fathers (*Odyssey* 3.83–101 and Tob 7:5). The exchange between the strangers and the hosts in Tob 7:4–6 according to the two existing Aramaic texts also bears strong resemblances with the Hebrew of Gen 29:4–6.
58. *Odyssey* 4.169–72 and Tob 7:5–6.
59. *Odyssey* 4.183–86 and Tob 7:7–8.

*Odyssey* 4.183–86
[Menelaus ended a speech lamenting the sufferings of righteous Odysseus.]
So he spoke, and in them all aroused the desire of lament.
Argive Helen wept (κλαῖε), the daughter of Zeus.
Telemachus wept (κλαῖε), and Menelaus, son of Atreus, nor could the son of Nestor keep his eyes tearless.

Tob 7:7–8 (4QTob<sup>b</sup> ar, frag. 4iii, Ls. 9–10)
[Raguel ended a lament for "a righteous man."]
He fell upon the neck of Tobiah the son of his kinsman, and wept (ἔκλαυσεν).

His wife Edna also wept (ἔκλαυσεν) for him, and their daughter Sarah likewise wept (ἔκλαυσεν).

## THE WEDDING

Tob 7:9–8:18 narrates the first night together for Tobiah and Sarah, which was uneventful thanks to the apotropaic stench of the burning fish's liver and heart that sent Asmodeus to "the remotest parts of Egypt."[60] This section of Tobit recasts the folktale of the Dangerous Bride,[61] though several details have parallels also in the epic. The setting for Telemachus's visit in Sparta was a double wedding just before Menelaus and Helen sent their only daughter, Hermione, away with her new husband Neoptolemus, the son of Achilles.[62] Both Hermione and Sarah were the only daughters and beautiful,[63] and their parents sent both with wealth to the homes of their husbands.[64] Helen gave Telemachus a gift for his future bride.[65] The author of the Jewish novel apparently transformed the wedding celebration at Sparta into a wedding for Tobiah and Sarah under the influence of Genesis 24 (Isaac and Rebekah) and 29 (Jacob and Rachel) and the folktale of the Dangerous Bride.[66]

Two feasts dominate the activities at the homes of both Menelaus and Raguel. The first feast in both settings takes place immediately on the arrival of the two strangers.

*Odyssey* 4.48–49, 51, 55, 57–60, 65–68, 294–95, and 302–3
[T]hey went into the polished baths and bathed (λούσαντο). And when the maids had bathed (λοῦσαν) them and anointed them with oil . . . they sat down on chairs. . . . And the revered housekeeper brought and set before them bread.

Tob 7:9–10 and 14 and 8:1 (4QTob<sup>b</sup> ar, frag. 4iii, Ls. 11–12)
He [Raguel] slaughtered a ram of the flock, and received them very warmly. When they had bathed (ἐλούσαντο) and washed themselves and had reclined

---

60. Tob 8:3. Compare with *Odyssey* 1.22–26, where Poseidon was with the Ethiopians.
61. On the Bride of the Monster folktale, see Zimmermann, *Tobit,* 5–12.
62. *Odyssey* 4.1–19.
63. *Odyssey* 4.5–14 and Tob 3:15 and 6:12.
64. *Odyssey* 4.8–9 and Tob 10:10.
65. *Odyssey* 4.125–20.
66. For the influence of the folktale, see Zimmermann, *Tobit,* 5–12.

...And a carver lifted up and set before them platters of all sorts of meats, and set by them golden goblets.[67] Then fair-haired Menelaus greeted the two and said: "Take the food and be glad...." So saying he took in his hands roast meat and set it before them, the same fat ox chine which they had set before himself as a mark of honor. So they put forth their hands at the good cheer lying ready before them. But when they had put from them the desire for food and drink... [After a big meal and long conversation, Telemachus was ready for bed:] "But come, send us to bed, that lulled now by sweet sleep we may rest and take our joy.[70] ...So they slept there in the porch of the palace, the hero Telemachus and the glorious son of Nestor.

to eat and to drink... Raguel...said to the lad, "Eat, drink, and be merry tonight...."[68]

Then they began to eat and drink....[69]

When they had finished eating and drinking,

they wanted to retire,

so they took the young man and brought him into the bedroom.

Even though the narration of feasts can be formulaic, these two feasts are particularly parallel: both begin after baths, the hosts encourage the seated guests to enjoy themselves and the meals include roasted flesh and wine. After eating and drinking, the guests desire to sleep.

The second feast at Sparta takes place just before Telemachus departs; the second in Tobit is the wedding feast itself. The two feasts again echo each other insofar as both hosts command their wives to cook; the men take responsibility for the meat.

*Odyssey* 15.92–94 and 97–98
Menelaus...at once bade his wife with her maid servants to make ready a meal in the halls from the abundant store that was within [everything but the livestock].... [Eteoneus] Menelaus bade kindle a fire and roast some of the flesh;

and he heard, and obeyed (cf. 15.134–43).

Tob 8:19 (4QTob[b] ar, frag. 5, L. 3)
After this he [Raguel] asked his wife to bake many loaves of bread;

and he went to the herd and brought two steers and four rams and ordered them to be slaughtered. So they began to make preparations.[71]

---

67. Cf. *Odyssey* 3.62–63 and 430–74.

68. In Gen 24:33 and Tob 7:11 a guest negotiating for the hand of a maiden refuses to eat until he can disclose the purpose of his visit.

69. In Tob 7:14, as in Gen 24:54, the meal resumes after a deal is struck for the bride (Sarah and Rebekah).

70. Compare also the preparations of the beds and the maidservants with lamps in *Odyssey* 4.296–305 and Tob 7:15–16 and 8:1 and 13. Compare also *Odyssey* 4.304–5 and Tob 8:9a, on couples falling asleep together.

71. See also Gen 18:6–8.

## THE REQUEST TO LINGER AND THE ACQUISITION OF THE TREASURE

Ecstatic about Sarah's non-lethal wedding night, Raguel and Edna asked Tobiah to stay for two weeks, and offered later to send him off a wealthy man.[72] Menelaus made a similar offer to Telemachus.

| Odyssey 4.587–91 | Tob 8:20–21 (4QTob<sup>b</sup> ar, frag. 5, L. 6) |
|---|---|
| But come now, tarry (ἐπίμεινον) in my halls until the eleventh or the twelfth day is come. | You shall not leave here for fourteen days, but shall stay (μενεῖς) here eating and drinking with me; and you shall cheer up my daughter.... |
| Then will I send you forth with honor and give you splendid gifts, three horses and a well-polished chariot; and besides I will give you a beautiful cup.[73] | Take at once half of what I own and carry (it) <u>with you to the house of</u> your <u>fa</u>ther; the other half will be yours when my wife and I die. |

At this point in Tobit, Raphael/Azariah took four servants and two camels to retrieve the money from Gabael.[74] This theme of a heavenly messenger in disguise also appears in the *Odyssey*, not in Book 4 but in Book 3, where Athena/Mentor left Telemachus alone in Pylos while she went to collect a debt from the Cauconians.[75] Tobiah sent Raphael/Azariah off at once, so that his own absence from home would be as brief as possible; his father was waiting for him.[76] Telemachus, too, was eager to travel home so as not to keep his comrades waiting.[77]

### ANGUISHED MOTHERS BACK HOME

Penelope learned from the suitors that Telemachus had gone on his dangerous journey and that the suitors were plotting to slay him on his return. "[H]er knees were loosened where she sat, and her heart melted. For long she was speechless, and both her eyes were filled with tears, and the flow of her voice was checked."[78] She understandably feared for

---

72. Tob 8:19–21. In Gen 24:55–56 one also reads of a request for the bride to stay several days and an insistence by the visitor to depart.

73. Menelaus gives Telemachus his costliest possession: "a well-wrought mixing bowl" (*Odyssey* 4.615–17).

74. Tob 9:1–6; cf. *Odyssey* 3.475–80. After Raphael arrived, Gabael loaded the money on camels (Tob 9:5). Menelaus put his gifts for Telemachus on a horse-drawn wagon (*Odyssey* 15.51 and 131–32).

75. *Odyssey* 3.365–70. Fries notes the similarities also with Odysseus's journey to get his famed bow in *Odyssey* 21.15–41 ("Buch Tobit," 65–66).

76. Tob 9:3–4.

77. *Odyssey* 4.593–99 and especially 15.64–91; cf. Gen 24:56.

78. *Odyssey* 4.703–5; see also 4.715–20.

his life and insisted that she never would have let him go had she known
of his plans.[79] To comfort her, Athena sent a phantom of Iphthime, Penelope's sister, in a dream, assuring her that her son would return safely.[80]
In Tobit, Anna similarly complains to Tobit: " 'My child has perished
and is no longer among the living.' And she began to weep and mourn
for her son, saying, 'Woe to me, my child, the light of my eyes, that I let
you make the journey.' "[81] Like Iphthime in Homer, Tobit consoles the
disconsolate mother by appealing to the reliability of the boy's guide.

*Odyssey* 4.824–28
Then the dim phantom answered her and said:
"Take heart and be not in your mind too
greatly afraid;

since such a guide goes with him as other men
too have prayed to stand by their side."

Tob 10:6
But Tobit kept saying to her,
"Be quiet and stop worrying, my dear;
he is all right.
Probably something unexpected has
happened there.
The one who went with him is trust-
worthy and is one of our own kin.
Do not grieve for him, my dear;
he soon will be here."[82]

Anna remained distressed and "would rush out every day and watch
the road her son had taken and would eat nothing."[83]

### FAREWELLS

Homer continues narrating events back in Ithaca for the remainder of
Book 4 (625–847); Book 5 turns the reader's attention to the plight of
Odysseus on Calypso's island. Books 5–12 narrate his *nostos*, or 'return',
and Books 13–14 tell of his disguise as a beggar and his reception by
Eumaeus, his swineherd. Not until the beginning of Book 15 does the
narrator return to Telemachus's sojourn in Sparta. The narrator of Tobit
returns to Tobiah's situation in Ecbatana at 10:7, after the completion of

79. *Odyssey* 4.710, 817–23, and 727–34.
80. *Odyssey* 4.795–87.
81. Tob 10:4. Penelope calls Telemachus "sweet light (of my eyes)" in *Odyssey* 17.41.
82. See also *Odyssey* 4.804–7.
83. Tob 10:4. I prefer the reading ἐγεύσατο to ἐπείθετο. In this case, Anna's condition
calls to mind Penelope's in *Odyssey* 4.787–90: "But she, the wise Penelope, lay there in
her upper chamber, touching no food, tasting neither meat nor drink, pondering whether
her flawless son would escape death, or be slain by the insolent suitors." Compare also
Anna's watching for Tobiah's return (10:7) with the suitors' watching for Telemachus's
return (*Odyssey* 4.842–47). Both passages follow almost immediately the comforting of
the mothers. According to Tob 10:7, Edna wept all night, without sleeping a wink. At
the beginning of *Odyssey* 15, "sweet sleep did not hold Telemachus, but all through the
immortal night anxious thoughts for his father kept him wakeful" (15.7–8).

the fortnight's wedding celebration and Tobiah's request to be sent home. This request again parallels the epic. The following columns narrate the requests of Telemachus and Tobiah to return home, the commands of their hosts to stay longer, and the insistence of the lads to be sent off.

| *Odyssey* 15.62–67, 75–76, 86, and 88 | Tob 10:7–9 (4QTob$^e$, frag. 4, Ls. 1–7) |
|---|---|
| [At the end of many days:]<br>Then Telemachus…came up to Menelaus, and addressed him, saying:<br><br><br>'[S]end me back (μ' ἀπόπεμπε) now at last to my own fatherland (ἐς πατρίδα γαῖαν), for now my heart is eager to return home."<br>Then Menelaus…answered him,<br>"…But stay (μέν'), till I bring handsome gifts and put them on your chariot."…<br>Then wise Telemachus answered him,<br>"…[R]ather would I go at once to my home."[84] | And when <u>the fourteen days of</u> the wedding <u>were over for them,</u>…<u>Tobiah came</u> to him <u>and said to him,</u><br>"<u>Send me off; I know already that</u> my father does not believe, and <u>also my mother does not believe that she will see me</u> again. <u>Now I beg you, my father, that you send me off</u> (ἐξαποστείλῃς με) <u>so that I may go to my father</u> (πρὸς τὸν πατέρα μου). <u>I have already told you how I have left them behind."</u><br><u>Raguel then said to Tobiah,</u><br>"<u>My son, stay</u> (μεῖνον) <u>with me, and I shall send messengers to Tobi</u>…"<br>But he said,<br>"No! I beg you to send me back to my father."[85] |

Both hosts reluctantly agreed to send the boys home; Menelaus sent Telemachus home with his priceless mixing bowl and a double-handled cup. Helen gave him one of her most elegant "richly embroidered robes" for his future wife.[86] Raguel sent Tobiah home with "half of his property: male and female slaves, oxen and sheep, donkeys and camels, clothing, money, and household goods."[87] Furthermore, Menelaus and Helen as well as Raguel and Edna sent the boys off with benedictions. Men first.

| *Odyssey* 15.110–12 and 128–29 | Tob 10:11 |
|---|---|
| Menelaus spoke to him and said:<br><br>"Telemachus, may Zeus…in truth bring to pass for you your return just as your heart desires."…<br>[Helen:] "I wish that with joy you may reach your well-built house and your native land." | Then he [Raguel] saw them safely off; he embraced Tobiah and said,<br>"Farewell, my child; have a safe journey."[88]…<br>[Edna:] "My child and dear brother, the Lord of heaven bring you back safely.…May we all prosper together all the days of our lives." |

---

84. Telemachus also wanted to avoid Nestor, who would have delayed his return through excessive hospitality (*Odyssey* 15.209–14).

85. Cf. Gen 24:55–56.

86. *Odyssey* 15.101–29.

87. Tob 10:10; cf. *Odyssey* 4.8–9 and the gifts Menelaus gave Hermione when he sent her off to the home of Neoptolemus ("horses and chariots"), and 15.84–85 (and gifts of "a fine bronze tripod or cauldron, or a pair of mules, or a golden cup") and 206–7.

88. Cf. *Odyssey* 15.151–53.

At last, both boys departed for home and arrived safely. Telemachus eluded the ambush of the suitors because of the warning of Athena; Tobiah had vanquished Asmodeus because of the magic of Raphael.

## WELCOMES AT HOME

On his way home, Telemachus gained yet another traveling companion, Theoclymenus, but just as they arrived at Ithaca, the two youths parted ways. Theoclymenus went to the home of Peiraeus, and Telemachus himself to the hut of the swineherd Eumaeus.[89] Similarly in Tobit, just as the travel party approached Nineveh, Sarah stayed with the servants while Tobiah and Raphael/Azariah went to the home of Tobit and Anna.[90] Eumaeus (who plays the role of Telemachus's father in Odysseus's absence: "as a loving father...") and Tobit discover the presence of the returned youths and welcome them with hugs.

| *Odyssey* 16.12, 14–18, 20–23, and 41 | Tob 11:10–11, 13–14, and 15 (4QTob$^e$, frag. 5, Ls. 1–2 and 5–6) |
|---|---|
| In amazement up sprang the swineherd.... And he went to meet (ἦλθεν) his lord, [who "stood in the doorway (προθύροισι)" (12)], and kissed his head and both his beautiful eyes and his two hands, and a big tear fell from him. And as a loving father greets his own son, who comes in the tenth year from a distant land, ...even so did the noble swineherd then clasp in his arms godlike Telemachus, and kiss him all over as one escaped from death; and sobbing he addressed him with winged words: "You are come, Telemachus, sweet light (γλυκερὸν φάος)...." Telemachus [and Eumaeus] went in.... and passed over the stone threshold. | Then Tobit got up and came stumbling out to <u>meet</u> (ἐξῆλθεν) <u>his son as far as</u> the courtyard door (θύραν). Tobiah went to him with the <u>gall of the fish in his hand</u>, <u>and he scattered</u> (some of it) on his eyes,... [Thus Tobit was healed.] <u>And he saw</u> his son and fell on his neck,[91] and he wept, and said to him, "I see you, my <u>son,</u> the light of my eyes (τὸ φῶς τῶν ὀφθαλμῶν μου)!" So Tobit went in rejoicing. |

Later, Homer narrates the rendezvous of Telemachus and Penelope, a passage that parallels Anna's reception of Tobiah. Both women go to meet their sons, embrace them with tears, and link the boys' returns to their own deaths. Penelope thought she would die without seeing her son; Anna can die in peace now that she has seen her son.

---

89. *Odyssey* 15.439–57.
90. Tob 11:4.
91. A Greek variant, followed by the Syriac, adds Tobit's kissing of Tobiah.

| *Odyssey* 17.36 and 38–42 | Tob 11:9 |
|---|---|
| Then out from her chamber came wise | Anna ran up to see her son |
| Penelope . . . and bursting into tears | |
| she flung her arms about her dear son | and fell on the neck of her son, |
| and kissed his head and both his beautiful eyes; | |
| and with sobs she spoke to him winged words: | saying,[92] |
| "You have come Telemachus, | "Now that I have seen you, my child, |
| sweet light (γλυκερὸν φάος); | |
| I thought I should never see you again." | I am ready to die." And she wept. |

One might attribute much that these scenes share with each other to the stock elements of literary welcomes: weeping, hugging, conversing, and entering the home. More distinctive is the metaphor "light" used for each lad. This address is altogether appropriate for Tobiah, who, because of his father's blindness, was indeed the "light of his eyes." It is worth noting, however, that nowhere else in the Bible is someone called the "light" of someone else's "eyes." The parallel passage in the *Odyssey*, however, refers to Telemachus as Penelope's "sweet light."

## DISCLOSING IDENTITIES

When the wedding celebration for Tobiah and Sarah ended, Tobit remembered his obligation to pay Azariah his wages for guiding his son safely to and from Media.[93] Azariah refused to take anything and revealed that he was the angel Raphael. In the epic there is no symmetrical revelation by Athena/Mentor. Instead, Raphael's revelation parallels Odysseus's revelation to Telemachus in Book 16.

To protect him from detection by the suitors, Athena had disguised the hero as a beggar. Telemachus did not recognize the beggar to be his father until Odysseus, now sure of his son's fidelity, revealed himself. In both columns one reads of a decision to reveal the stranger's identity, a disclosure in the first-person singular (εἰμί) with the appropriate predicate, and a fearful response. Such a pattern is common in recognition scenes, so it need not indicate direct literary imitation, but the passages do appear in the same order both in the epic and the novel.

---

92. Variants in Latin add *cum lacrimis* or *lacrimans*.

93. Compare *Odyssey* 15.506–7: "I [Telemachus] will set before you, as wages for your journey, a good feast of meat and sweet wine."

**Odyssey 16.167–68, 178–79, and 188–89**

[Athena:] "Odysseus . . . now tell
your son your secret
and do not hide it."
[Athena transformed Odysseus's appearance.]
[Telemachus] marveled, and, shaken,
turned his eyes aside for fear it was a god.
[Odysseus:] "I am (εἰμι) your father, for whose
sake with groaning you suffer many a woe."

**Tob 12:11 and 15–16**

[Raphael:] "I will now declare
the whole truth to you
and will conceal nothing from you. . . .

I am (ἐγώ εἰμι) Raphael, one of the seven
angels who stand ready and enter before
the glory of the Lord." The two of them
were shaken; they fell face down, for
they were afraid.

Odysseus and Raphael both reassure the men and calm their fears. The angel then ascends, just as Athena had in Book 1.[94] Later, Tobiah will find Sarah and introduce her to his parents;[95] Telemachus will find Theoclymenus and introduce him to his mother.[96]

Other parallels between the two works are possible as well. For example, one could compare Odysseus's sea monsters with the fish that attacks Tobias, the epic's dangerous women (Circe and Calypso) with Sarah, and Hermes' instructions to Odysseus for using the magical herb *moly* to avoid Circe's fatal spells with the angel's instructions to Tobias for using the magical organs of the fish to avoid Asmodeus's fatal jealousy. If the author of Tobit knew the *Telemachia*, he certainly could have known the *Nostos* as well.[97]

This completes the isolation of parallels between the two works. For the most part, the characters in Tobit conform to specific counterparts in the epic.

---

94. Cf. the following.

**Odyssey 1.319–23**

[Athena] departed, flying upward like a bird;
and in her heart she put strength and courage,
and made him think of his father. . . .
And in his mind he marked what had
happened and marveled, for he suspected
that she was a god. (cf. 3.371–84)

**Tob 12:20–22 (4QTobᵉ, frag. 6, L s. 1–3)**

And he [Raphael] ascended.
Then they stood up,
and they saw him no more.
But they were blessing and praising God,
and acknowledging him because of his
great deeds and the amazing fact that an
angel of God had appeared to them.

95. Tob 11:16–18; cf. Gen 24:64–67, the introduction of Rebekah to Isaac's family.

96. *Odyssey* 17.52–84.

97. I am grateful to Amy-Jill Levine for pushing me to include these parallels in my consideration.

Odysseus = Tobit[98]
Penelope = Anna
Telemachus = Tobiah
Zeus = God
Athena = Raphael
Menelaus = Raguel
Helen = Edna
Hermione = Sarah
dogs = dog

There are, however, a few exceptions to these equations. In the *Telemachia* the servant Eurycleia serves as a second mother to Telemachus. In Book 1 Telemachus keeps his departure a secret from Penelope, but when Eurycleia learns that he is leaving, she weeps as though she were his mother and has to be comforted. In Tobit the role of Eurycleia is taken over by Anna herself and Tobit comforts her.[99] Later in the epic, Penelope herself learns of Telemachus's journey and weeps. Her sister Iphthime comes to her in a dream to comfort her. In Tobit, this role of the comforter again is played by Tobit himself.[100] Homer makes much of the swineherd Eumaeus, who functions in the epic as a second father to Telemachus, in place of absent Odysseus. In Tobit, this role is played by Tobit himself insofar as he never left home.[101] Finally, Raphael's revelation of his true identity to Tobit and Tobiah corresponds to the revelation of Odysseus to Telemachus.[102] Apart from these exceptions, the characterizations between the two works are notably persistent.

Furthermore, the parallels between Tobit and the *Telemachia* almost invariably appear in the same order. Not a single major division of the narrative in Tobit appears out of its Homeric sequence, despite huge omissions of content. The following columns display the common narrative elements between the two books. Elements out of sequence with the other book appear within square brackets ([ . . . ]).

---

98. The identification of Tobit with Odysseus also might explain the unusual first person narration of Tobit's situation in 1:3–3:6. Odysseus speaks of his adventures in the first person in *Odyssey* 9–12, but perhaps it is wiser to attribute the first person speech to imitation of the tale of Ahikar.

99. Tob 5:18–22.

100. Tob 5:18–22.

101. Tob 11:10–11.

102. Tob 12:11–16.

| *Odyssey* | **Tobit** |
|---|---|
| *Two Problems and One Divine Solution* | |
| Odysseus's home is devastated by suitors. | Tobit's home is devastated by Assyrians. |
| The hero himself, faithful in sacrifices, is held by Calypso and wants to die (1.59). | Tobit, faithful in sacrifices, is blind and wants to die (3:6; cf. 4:2). |
| Penelope weaves. | Anna weaves. |
| [Gods slay lovers of goddesses, like Calypso.] | Asmodeus slays Sarah's suitors (3:11–15). |
| Zeus decides to intervene and sends Athena to Telemachus (1.95–104). | God decides to intervene and sends Raphael to Tobiah (3:16–17). |
| *Preparations for the Journey* | |
| Athena appears to Telemachus as Mentes and later as Mentor (1.119–20 and 2.267–68). | Raphael appears to Tobiah as Azariah (5:4). |
| Telemachus asks Athena/Mentes where he is from (1.170–76). | Tobiah and Tobit ask Raphael/Azariah where he is from (5:5 and 11–12). |
| The stranger lies about her identity, "I am Mentes," in the area on business (1.180–84). | The stranger lies about his identity, "I am Azariah," in the area for work (5:13 and 5). |
| The stranger is a family friend (1.187–88). | The stranger is a family friend (5:14). |
| The stranger predicts a quick resolution (1.200–205). | [The stranger predicts a quick resolution (5:10).] |
| The stranger promises to travel with the lad on a dangerous journey (2.285–89). | The stranger promises to travel with the lad on a dangerous journey (5:16–17). |
| Eurycleia weeps at the lad's departure (2.361–64). | Anna weeps at the lad's departure (5:18). |
| Telemachus comforts Eurycleia (2.371). | Tobit comforts Anna (5:21–22). |
| *The Journey and the Welcome* | |
| The lad and the goddess leave on their journey (2.413–34; cf. 3.477–97). | The lad and the angel leave on their journey (6:2–3). |
| They arrive in Sparta and find Menelaus giving a wedding feast (4.1–4). | They arrive in Ecbatana and find Raguel sitting at his gate (7:2). |
| Helen and Menelaus recognize resemblances between son and father (4.146–50). | Raguel recognizes resemblances between son and father (7:2). |
| At the mention of the father's sufferings those present weep (4.183–86). | At the mention of the father's sufferings those present weep (7:7–8). |
| *The Wedding* | |
| Menelaus is celebrating a double wedding for his daughter and son (4.1–19). | [Later, Raguel will be celebrating a wedding for his daughter (8:19–10:7).] |
| Before the feast, the strangers bathe (4.48–49). | Before the feast, they bathe (7:9). |
| They sit and eat meat (4.55 and 57–60). | They sit and eat meat (7:9). |
| When they finished eating, they retired (4.294–303). | When they finished eating, they retired (7:14 and 8:1). |
| [A second feast takes place when Telemachus is about to depart (15.92–98).] | A second feast takes place as the wedding celebration (8:19). |

| *Odyssey* | Tobit |
|---|---|

### The Request to Linger and the Acquisition of the Treasure

| | |
|---|---|
| Menelaus asks Telemachus to stay for eleven or twelve days and offers him wealth (4.587–91). | Raguel asks Tobiah to stay for fourteen days and offers him wealth (8:20–21). |
| [Athena/Mentor had gone off to collect a debt from the Cauconians (3.366–70).] | Raphael/Azariah leaves to get the money from Gabael (9:1–6). |
| Telemachus is eager to return home (4.593–99 and 15.64–91). | Tobiah is eager to return home (9:3–4). |

### Anguished Mothers back Home

| | |
|---|---|
| The narrator switches back to Ithaca (4.621). | The narrator switches back to Nineveh (10:1). |
| Penelope weeps for her son, fearing for his life (4.703–20). | Anna weeps for her son, fearing for his life (10:4). |
| Iphthime comforts Penelope, assuring her that the guide is trustworthy (4.824–28). | Tobit comforts Anna, assuring her that the guide is trustworthy (10:6). |

### Farewells

| | |
|---|---|
| The narrator again switches to Sparta (15.1). | The narrator again switches to Ecbatana (10:7). |
| Telemachus asks to be sent home (15.62–66). | Tobiah asks to be sent home (10:7). |
| Menelaus asks him to stay (15.67–85). | Raguel asks him to stay (10:8). |
| Telemachus insists (15.86–91). | Tobiah insists (10:9). |
| Menelaus gives the boy lavish gifts (15.101–29). | Raguel gives the boy lavish gifts (10:10). |
| Menelaus and Helen send him off with a benediction (15.110–12 and 128–29). | Raguel and Edna send him off with a benediction (10:11). |
| Telemachus arrives home safely. | Tobiah arrives home safely. |

### Welcomes at Home

| | |
|---|---|
| Telemachus leaves Theoclymenus with a friend and goes to the hut of Eumaeus (15.439–57). | Tobiah leaves Sarah with the servants and goes with Raphael to his home (11:1–4). |
| Telemachus is welcomed by his dogs (16.4–10). | Tobiah returns home with his dog (11:4). |
| Eumaeus goes to meet the lad, weeps, hugs, and calls him "sweet light" (16.12–23). | Tobit goes to meet the lad, weeps, hugs, and calls him, "light of my eyes" (11:10–11). |
| Penelope goes to meet the lad, weeps, and hugs, saying she thought she would never see him again (17.36–42). | [Anna goes to meet the lad, weeps, and hugs, saying, "I have seen you . . . , I am ready to die" (11:9).][103] |

### Disclosing Identities

| | |
|---|---|
| Odysseus says he will keep nothing hidden (16.167–68). | Raphael says he will keep nothing hidden (12:11). |
| Odysseus declares, "I am your father" (16.188). | Raphael declares, "I am Raphael" (12:15). |
| [Telemachus had feared when he saw his father transfigured (16.178–79).] | Tobit and Tobiah feared at the declaration of the angel's identity (12:16). |

103. When Telemachus returned home, the first person to welcome him was Eumaeus, and then Eurycleia and Penelope. In Tobit one might expect the order to be the reception

The density and order of these stories surely point to some relationship between them, and three kinds of connections are possible. First, one might argue that Fries basically was correct in suspecting a common background in oral folktales. Second, one might propose that the author of Tobit consciously imitated the *Telemachia* as he or she remembered it, but did not consult a copy of the epic. Third, one might deduce that these parallels provide sufficient evidence for direct literary imitation. To determine which of these models is most appropriate, it is useful to note Tobit's retention of distinctive Homeric features. Because Tobit retains details of the *Telemachia* not characteristic of such folktales generally, one should conclude that the parallels result from conscious *mimesis* of the epic, whether from memory or manuscript.

Dogs play distinctive but merely cosmetic roles in both stories. Tobiah's dog appears in Tobit only twice. It first appears as Tobiah and Azariah left Nineveh, "and the dog went along, and together they traveled."[104] It appears for a second and final time when they returned, "And the dog went along behind them."[105]

Dogs were Telemachus's special signature. According to *Odyssey* 2.11 and 17.62, two dogs followed Telemachus about. When he finally returned home and came to the hut of Eumaeus,

> the loud-barking dogs fawned [about him], and did not bark as he drew near. And noble Odysseus noticed the fawning of the dogs, and the sound of footsteps fell upon his ears; and at once he spoke to Eumaeus winged words: "Eumaeus, surely some comrade of yours will be coming, or at least someone you know, for the dogs do not bark, but fawn about him, and I hear the sound of footsteps."[106]

Typically, Greek artists portrayed Odysseus's son walking with a spear in one hand, accompanied by two dogs. Domestic dogs are rare in Jewish texts that usually treat hounds as savage nuisances. The association of both boys with friendly hounds surely derives from a genetic relationship between the two works.[107]

---

by Tobit and then Anna, but their welcomes are in reverse order because of Tobit's blindness. Sighted Anna is the first to see her son coming in the distance; she welcomes him. Tobit's welcome will wait until after he regains his sight.

104. Tob 6:2 (4QTob^b ar, frag. 4i, L. 5).

105. Tob 11:4.

106. *Odyssey* 16.4–10.

107. Odysseus's dog Argos also plays a significant role in the epic insofar as he, before any human, recognizes Odysseus's identity, and, after doing so, dies (*Odyssey* 17. 291–327).

This assessment gains conviction if one prefers an alternative reading of Tob 11:6 (no Qumran Aramaic or Hebrew version survives). According to the variant, "[T]he dog ran ahead of them," not behind them, so when Anna looked down the road, "she saw the dog running ahead, and she ran and said to his father, 'Look, your son is coming, and the man who went with him!' "[108] This additional reference to the dog might have dropped out of the other versions because Anna's statement to Tobit mentions the coming not of the dog but only of Tobiah and Azariah. If one favors this variant, both Anna and Odysseus first learn of the returns of their sons because of dogs: Odysseus "noticed the fawning of the dogs" without barking and deduced, "surely some comrade... will be coming";[109] when Anna saw the dog running, she assumed her son was not far behind and told Tobit, "your son is coming."[110]

Likewise distinctive of the tales in Tobit and the *Odyssey* is the switching of venues at precisely the same juncture. Homer leaves Telemachus in Sparta in suspended animation from 4.621 until the end of Book 14. This narrator shifts attention from Sparta back to Ithaca in a "remarkable and subtle transition" to focus on the continuing ruination of Odysseus's home. Book 4 ends with a contingent of the suitors setting an ambush at sea, "lying in wait for Telemachus." They and the reader must wait for Telemachus for ten Books, after Odysseus's peregrinations from the island of Calypso to Ithaca. Not until the beginning of Book 15 does Athena appear to Telemachus advising him to return home. This artful switching of venues clearly is the work of the epic poet and "reveals the complex narrative structure of the *Odyssey*."[111] The Book of Tobit switches venues between Ecbatana and Nineveh at precisely the same point in the story: after the request of the host for the youth to stay with him several days despite his eagerness to be sent on his way.[112] At this point, the narrative returns to Nineveh and the anguish of the par-

---

108. The variant survives in Hanhart's recension *d* (represented by two fourteenth-century Greek manuscripts) and in Syriac. In Gen 24:63 Isaac saw camels coming from a distance bearing the servant and Rebekah, a context similar to that in Tobit. If, as is likely, Tobit imitated Genesis 24 as well as the *Odyssey*, he may have mated Telemachus's dogs with Jacob's camels to produce Tobiah's dog.

109. *Odyssey* 16.8.

110. Tob 11:6. Zimmermann argues in favor of this variant but thinks the dog originally served a role in subduing Asmodeus (*Tobit*, 10, 78–79, and 104–5).

111. Hexter, *Guide*, 189.

112. Cf. *Odyssey* 4.587–620 and Tob 8:20–9:6.

ents, especially of Anna, at the absence of their only son.[113] The Book of Tobit resumes its parallels with the epic with the next appearance of Telemachus at the beginning of Book 15. As in the epic, the narrator once again focuses on the youth away from home and the negotiations with his host for his return.[114] This shifting of the narratives between the two settings at the same two points in the development of their plots is a sign of literary, not oral, dependence.

Finally, the dependence of Tobit on the *Telemachia* elegantly explains a notorious problem in Tob 7:7. Edna asked Tobiah and Azariah if they knew their relative Tobit, and they answered: " 'We do know him.' 'Is he well ?' They said to her, 'He is well.' And Tobiah said, 'He is my father.' Then Raguel jumped up, kissed him, and broke into tears. He also spoke as follows, 'Blessings upon you, my son; you are the son of a righteous man.' "[115] Raguel's knowledge of Tobit had proved to him that he was "righteous," and now he has learned that his friend was in good health. Entirely without preparation, the narrator then supplies Raguel with information he did not receive from Tobiah and Azariah. Despite their statement that Tobit was well, Raguel laments his blindness: "O most miserable of calamities that such a righteous and philanthropic man has become blind."[116] Unfortunately, no Aramaic or Hebrew text survives for this crucial passage, but the Greek version translated here surely preserves the substance of the original; the subsequent lamentations of Raguel, Edna, and Sarah require it. This inconcinnity between the announcement of Tobit's health and Raguel's weeping over his blindness obviously bothered the hand responsible for the other major Greek recension, which adds: "When he [Raguel] heard that Tobit had lost his sight...." At this point in the *Odyssey* there is no such incongruity. When Menelaus learned that his guest was the son of Odysseus, he wept, and for good reason: he knew better than Telemachus himself of Odysseus's sufferings.[117] The author of Tobit, in following the flow of *Odyssey* 4, apparently failed to recognize the problem he or she was creating by attributing to Raguel Menelaus's knowledge of the father's tragedy. Such an error points to clumsy literary imitation.

---

113. Tob 10:1–7a.
114. Cf. *Odyssey* 15.1–129 and Tobit 10:7b-11.
115. Tob 7:4–7a.
116. Tob 7:7b.
117. *Odyssey* 4.155–86.

By comparing this passage with Gen 29:4–6, the meeting of Jacob and some Aramaeans, one might better understand why the author of Tobit lost his concentration. The young patriarch, like Tobiah, traveled to the East, to his father's homeland, searching for a bride from his extended family. The exchange between Jacob and the Aramaeans closely parallels the exchange between Edna, Tobiah, and Raphael; the response of Laban parallels that of Raguel.

**Gen 29.4–6 and 13–14**

Jacob said to them,
"My brothers, where do you come from?"
They said, "We are from Haran."

He said to them,
"Do you know Laban son of Nahor?"
They said, "We do know him."
He said to them,
"Is it well with him?"
They said, "He is well,
and here is his daughter Rachel,
coming with the sheep."
[Rachel meets Jacob and goes to tell her father.]
When Laban heard the news about his sister's son Jacob, he ran to meet him; he embraced him and kissed him, and brought him to his house.

Jacob told Laban all these things, and Laban said to him,
"Surely you are my bone and flesh!"

**Tob 7:3–7 (4QpapTob³ ar, frag. 14ii, Ls. 8–11 and 4QTobᵇ ar, frag. 4iii, Ls. 5–10)**

Edna asked them and said to them,
"Where are you from, my brothers?"
They said to her, "We are of the Naphtalites, who are captives in Nineveh."
She said to them,
"Do you know Tobi our kinsman?"
They said to her, "We do know him."

"Is he well?"
They said to her, "He is well."
And Tobiah said, "He is my father."

Then Raguel
jumped up,
kissed him, and broke into tears.
[Cf. 7:1: "and he brought them into his house."]

He also spoke to him as follows,
"Blessings upon you, my son; you are the son of a righteous man."[118]

Later in Genesis and Tobit, the young visitor negotiates the hand of the fair maiden, encounters difficulties in achieving his matrimonial goal, and in the end takes her home. The Aramaic of Tobit looks like a direct imitation of Genesis 29.[119]

It would appear that the author of Tobit used both *Odyssey* 4 and Genesis 29 in the composition of Tobiah's welcome at Ecbatana. This is what seems to have happened. The author consulted the epic for composing 7:2.

118. Similarities to Aramaic Targums suggest the author may have used a Targum instead of the Hebrew text. In any case similarities with the Targums show Tobit's Aramaic to be a close rendition of Gen 29:4–7 and 13–14.

119. Moore, *Tobit*, 218.

| *Odyssey* 4.137 and 141–44 | Tob 7:2 (4QpapTob^a ar, frag. 14ii, Ls. 7–8 and 4QTob^b ar, frag. 4iii, Ls. 4–5) |
|---|---|
| [Helen] questioned her husband on each matter ... "For never yet, I declare, saw I one so like another... as this man is like the son of great-hearted Odysseus, Telemachus." | He [Raguel] said to his wife Edna, "How this youth resembles Tobi, the son of my uncle!" |

Then the author turned to Genesis 29 for composing 7:3–7a and returned to the epic for composing 7:7a-8.

| *Odyssey* 4.183–86 | Tob 7:7–8 (4QTob^b ar, frag. 4iii, Ls. 9–10) |
|---|---|
| [Menelaus ended a speech lamenting the sufferings of righteous Odysseus.] So he spoke, and in them all aroused the desire of lament. Argive Helen wept (κλαῖε), the daughter of Zeus. Telemachus wept (κλαῖε), and Menelaus, son of Atreus, nor could the son of Nestor keep his eyes tearless. | [Raguel ended a lament for "a righteous man."] He fell upon the neck of Tobiah the son of his kinsman, and wept (ἔκλαυσεν). His wife Edna also wept (ἔκλαυσεν) for him, and their daughter Sarah likewise wept (ἔκλαυσεν). |

In this reversion to the epic, the author failed to notice he had omitted a crucial bit of information: the notification to Raguel of Tobit's blindness.

The author of Tobit was no slave to his sources; he emulated them. He transformed Homer's story so thoroughly with Jewish concerns that one would hardly expect a Greek model. Tobit scrupulously observed Jewish law; the three wisdom speeches issue from topoi of Jewish wisdom literature;[120] much of the narrative and some of the discourses parallel Job;[121] and the frequent prayers manifest typical Jewish piety. In the next essay George W. E. Nickelsburg will show that the author borrowed extensively also from Genesis 27–35. The author of Tobit seems to have spray-painted Phidias's Zeus with Jewish colors.[122] The result is a narrative that dramatically transforms its model in religious and cultural significance.

The dependence of Tobit on Homer advocated here is not limited to the *Telemachia*. Parallels exist not only to Books 1–4, but also Books 15, 16, and perhaps 17. Parallels to the *Nostos* also are possible. In other words, it would appear that our author had access to six or seven Books

---

120. Tob 4:3–12, 12:6–10, and 14:3–11.

121. Tob 3:2–6 and 11–15, 8:5–8 and 15–17, 11:14–15, and 13:1–18.

122. For an assessment of Tobit's multiple sources and compositional license see Lothar Ruppert, "Das Buch Tobias. Ein Modellfall nachgestaltender Erzählung," in Josef Schreiner, ed., *Wort, Lied und Gottesspruch. Festschrift J. Ziegler*, vol 1: *Beiträge zur Septuaginta*, Forschung zur Bibel 1 (Würzburg: Echter Verlag, 1972) 109–19, and George W. E. Nickelsburg, "The Search for Tobit's Mixed Ancestry: A Historical and Hermeneutical Odyssey," *RevQ* 17 (1996) 339–49.

of the twenty-four that constitute the *Odyssey*. The dependence is all the more remarkable in an Aramaic narrative so xenophobic of non-Jewish society.[123]

Why did this Jewish author imitate a Greek epic? Surely one cannot answer this question definitively, but one might suggest that the author recognized parallels between the journey of Telemachus with Athena/ Mentor and the journeys of Abraham's servant (Genesis 24) and of Jacob (Genesis 29) to Aram, Abraham's patria, for the purpose of acquiring a wife from the same tribe. According to Gen 24:7, God would send an angel with the servant to assist in the winning of an appropriate wife for Isaac. There can be little doubt that Genesis 24 and 29 informed the story of Tobit, Tobiah, and Sarah. By borrowing both from Genesis and from Homer, the author generated his dominating characterizations and plot in order to promote the importance of God's providence and of Jewish endogamy.

---

123. Though see Tob 14:6–7.

# 2

## Tobit, Genesis, and the *Odyssey:*
## A Complex Web of Intertextuality

### George W. E. Nickelsburg

Of all the Apocrypha and Pseudepigrapha, the Book of Tobit probably offers the most to a discussion of intertextuality. This complex
tale of life in the eastern Diaspora during the Assyrian period, composed pseudonymously during the Hellenistic period, epitomizes the
challenges, ambiguities, and frustrations of intertextual analysis. One
need only browse the history of its interpretation to see how the story
has been associated with almost every literary genre of antiquity and
has had its roots traced to a broad range of cross-cultural texts and traditions.[1] Is it a folk tale, a romance, or a wisdom novel? It comprises the
genres of narrative, testament, prayer, song of praise, parenesis, a journey in the company of an interpreting angel, and an apocalypse.[2] In the
Israelite tradition, it has been tied to Genesis, 2 Kings, Job and 1 Enoch.
Outside that tradition, it has parallels in the Story of Ahikar, the Tale
of the Grateful Dead and other folk tales, and the *Telemachia* in Homer's
*Odyssey.* The sorting out of these many possibilities is a complicated
scholarly juggling act, to say the least.

A few years ago, I began writing an article for the Milik Festschrift,
hoping to develop some of the suggestions I had made in a piece called
"Tobit and Enoch: Distant Cousins with a Recognizable Resemblance."[3]
The more I worked at the problem, the more I recognized that any connections between these two texts — and I still think there are some —
had to be placed in the context of Tobit's clear connections with other

---

1. See, e.g., Robert Henry Pfeiffer, *History of New Testament Times, with an Introduction
to the Apocrypha* (New York: Harper, 1949) 266–71; Zimmerman, *Tobit,* 5–15; Robert Doran,
"Narrative Literature," in *Early Judaism and its Modern Interpreters,* ed. Robert A. Kraft and
George W. E. Nickelsburg (Philadelphia: Fortress Press, 1986) 297–98; and Moore, *Tobit,*
15–21.

2. George W. E. Nickelsburg, "Tobit and Enoch: Distant Cousins with a Recognizable Resemblance," in David J. Lull, ed., *SBL 1988 Seminar Papers.* (Atlanta: Scholars Press,
1988) 54–68.

3. See Nickelsburg, "Mixed Ancestry," 340–4; idem., "Tobit and Enoch."

41

literature. And that was where I finally left it, with some methodological observations and questions, to which I shall return later. About the
time the offprints of my article arrived, I also received from Dennis
MacDonald, a draft entitled "Tobit and the *Telemachia.*" It was a substantial, intelligent development of an idea presented by the classicist
Carl Fries in a 1911 article that has been all but ignored by subsequent
scholarship.[4] I found MacDonald's treatment compelling, both in most
of its details and in its overall sweep, so I decided to use it in a course
on Religious Syncretism in Antiquity. However, as I prepared for the
class, I happened to be tuned to my Genesis frequency. At the end of
his chapter MacDonald referred to parallels between Tobit and the Genesis stories of Jacob, Laban, and Abraham's sending for a bride for Isaac.
The closer I looked at the Genesis text, the more Tobiah's journey across
Mesopotamia began to look less like Telemachus's search for his father
and more like Jacob's journey in search of a bride. The situation became more complex when I read the rewriting of that biblical story in
the *Book of Jubilees.* So I had arrived back at the intertextual complexity I
had observed in the article in the Milik Festschrift.

    This is the problem I shall lay out in this paper. MacDonald's article
is reproduced in this volume under the title, "Tobit and the *Odyssey.*" To
set the stage for my own exposition, I shall sketch the lines and some
of the details of his argument, then I shall present the parallels between
Tobit and the Jacob story, as it is presented in Genesis and then as it
is rewritten in *Jubilees.* In conclusion, I shall offer some methodological
observations and suggestions. In my presentation I keep in mind Mac-
Donald's benchmarks for determining intertextual connection: density
of parallels, narrative order, similarities in wording, and the ability of
one text to explain problems or obscurities in another text.


### TOBIT AND THE ODYSSEY

MacDonald begins his paper by reviewing and critiquing Fries's article.
Fries argued that the Jewish folk tale behind the Book of Tobit and
two versions of the *Telemachia* used by the author of the *Odyssey* had

---

    4. Fries, "Buch Tobit," 54–87. Norman R. Petersen first called my attention to this
article and later cited it in "Tobit," in Bernhard W. Anderson, ed., *The Books of the Bible.*
(2 vols.; New York: Charles Scribner's Sons, 1989) 2.36. Otherwise, until MacDonald's
paper, I have found it cited only in Pfeiffer, *History,* 271; and Moore, *Tobit,* 16, n. 38.

drawn on a common myth. MacDonald's thesis is that the author of Tobit knew and used the *Odyssey* itself. The bases of his comparison are the Greek texts of the *Odyssey* and Tobit and the Qumran fragments of the Aramaic text and Hebrew translation of Tobit. He finds many lexical similarities between the Greek of Tobit and that of the *Odyssey*, but concludes that these are probably coincidental and that the author of the Aramaic Tobit knew the Greek epic.

MacDonald follows the story line of the two texts and concludes that the elements in Tobit's plot line follow, almost without exception in sequence, corresponding elements in the *Odyssey*, often with the same wording. The two stories have a corresponding cast of characters:

| | | |
|---|---|---|
| Father | Odysseus | Tobit |
| Wife | Penelope | Anna |
| Son | Telemachus | Tobiah |
| Deity | Zeus | God of Israel |
| Divine Helper | Athena | Raphael |
| Second Father | Menelaus | Raguel |
| Wife | Helen | Edna |
| Daughter | Hermione | Sarah |
| Pet | Dog | Dog |

The major parallel elements in the plots of the two stories are as follows.

### Two Problems and One Divine Solution

The stories begin with a complication. Two men, Odysseus and Tobit, faithful to their God, are in trouble. Their homes have been devastated; the one is absent from his family, in the arms of Calypso, the other is home, but blind. Their wives weave. There is a second problem. In Tobit a jealous demon-lover of Sarah, a relative of the Tobits, has killed seven husbands in a row on her wedding nights. The parallel in the *Odyssey*, which MacDonald brackets, is that gods slay lovers of goddesses like Calypso. The respective deity decides to intervene.

### Preparations for the Journey

The sons of the respective fathers prepare for a journey — Telemachus to seek his father, Tobiah to recoup his father's fortune and to find a bride (though he does not yet know it). Before they begin, a divine being appears to each of them, pretending to be a known human being, and agrees to serve as a guide on the journey. The scenes end with Eurycleia, Telemachus's nurse, weeping and Telemachus comforting her, and Anna, Tobiah's mother, weeping and Tobit comforting her.

### The Journey and the Welcome

Telemachus and Athena leave, arrive in Sparta, and find Helen and Menelaus preparing for a family wedding. Helen and Menelaus recognize Telemachus's resemblance to his father, and at the mention of his sufferings, all weep. Tobiah and Raphael leave and arrive in Ecbatana. Raguel recognizes Tobiah's resemblance to his father, and at the mention of his sufferings, all weep.

### The Wedding

In each story there is a wedding. Menelaus is celebrating the double wedding of his son and daughter. Raguel will be celebrating the wedding of his daughter Sarah to Tobiah. After bathing there is a feast, and then everyone retires. There will be a second feast.

### The Request to Linger and the Acquisition of Treasure

Menelaus and Raguel ask Telemachus and Tobiah respectively to stay on and offer them wealth. Raphael leaves to get Tobit's money; Athena has gone off to collect a debt. Each of the young men is eager to return home.

### Anguished Mothers back Home

In both stories, the narrator switches scenes to the young men's homes, where the mother weeps for her absent son and is comforted with the knowledge that he has a trustworthy guide.

### Farewells

Another switch in venue takes us back to the young men in strikingly similar scenes of farewell. The youth asks to be sent home, but his host asks him to stay; the youth insists; the host then gives lavish gifts, and he and his wife send the youth off with a benediction.

### Arrivals and Welcomes at Home

The young men arrive at their homes safely. Telemachus leaves his companion with a friend and goes to the hut of Eumaeus; Tobiah leaves

Sarah with their servants and goes with Raphael to his home. Telemachus is welcomed by his dogs and Tobiah arrives with his dog. Eumaeus goes to meet Telemachus and weeps and hugs him; Tobit goes to meet Tobiah and weeps and hugs him. The respective mothers do the same.

### Disclosing Identities

Odysseus says he will hide nothing from Telemachus, and states, "I am your father." Raphael says he will hide nothing and states, "I am Raphael." There is an element of fear in each scene.

### Conclusions

In summarizing this close comparison of these two texts, MacDonald notes the following striking facts. The density and order of the parallels indicate a relationship between the two stories, and a few details in the *Odyssey* explain obscure elements in Tobit. Especially noteworthy is the presence of Tobiah's dog. Dogs simply are not household pets in Jewish stories. Certain switches in venue occur at precisely the same point in both stories. A dependence on the *Odyssey* explains a notorious problem in Tobit. When Tobiah and Raphael arrive at Raguel's house, the latter asks about Tobit's health, is assured he is well, and responds accordingly. But a moment later, he indicates that he knows about the father's suffering. This odd incongruity is explained by the corresponding scene in the *Odyssey*, where Odysseus's sufferings are well known to Menelaus. MacDonald attributes this slip of the pen to the fact that the author of Tobit moved from his model in the *Odyssey* to a similar point in the story of Jacob and Laban in Genesis, and he goes on to indicate the parallels between Tobit and Genesis 29 and the *Odyssey* respectively. He concludes that "the author of Tobit seems to have spray-painted Phidias's Zeus with Jewish colors." The author of Tobit "recognized parallels between the journey of Telemachus with Athena/Mentor and the journeys of Abraham's servant (Genesis 24) and Jacob (Genesis 29)" and borrowed from both Genesis and Homer.

I agree with MacDonald that the density, order, and wording of the parallels between the two texts and the explanatory value of a few of the details in the *Odyssey* indicate a substantial, literary relationship between them. There are, however, a few points where the comparison wavers a bit and where the Jacob story, to which he briefly refers, solves these problems to a greater degree than he himself indicates. At the same time, this creates some other intertextual complications and problems.

The major problem in MacDonald's comparison between Tobit and the *Odyssey* is the purpose of the two journeys and the elements relating to the two weddings. In Tobit, Tobiah goes on a journey to recover his father's money. Before he leaves, his father instructs him to marry a woman from his own tribe, and thanks to God's providence, he finds that bride in the course of the journey. In the *Odyssey* Telemachus goes off to find his father. On the road, he happens onto a wedding at the house of Menelaus and Helen. It is not his own wedding. There are a few other loose ends, which MacDonald duly notes. The one I mention here comes at the end of the departure scene. In Tobit, after Tobiah leaves, his mother weeps and his father comforts her. In the *Odyssey*, before Telemachus leaves, his nurse weeps and Telemachus comforts her. These differences are paralleled by similar elements in Genesis and its later Jewish exposition. These, in turn, help explain elements in the story of Tobit for which the *Odyssey* cannot account.

## A COMPARISON OF THE JOURNEYS OF TOBIAH AND JACOB

Both Tobit 2–12 and Genesis 27–35 recount the story of a man who goes on a journey in search of a bride and returns home safely. The parallels are many and encompass more than the journey itself.

### Circumstances at Home

Tobit, the father of Tobiah, is blind. Isaac, the father of Jacob, is blind. Anna, the wife of Tobit, brings home a young goat that she has been given as a bonus for her work. Tobit accuses her of stealing the animal and deceiving him in her explanation. Rebekah, the wife of Isaac, in fact, deceives her husband by having Jacob bring in two young goats whose meat Jacob will feed his father under the pretense that he is Esau.

### "Deathbed" Instructions: Take a Bride from Your Own Family

Expecting that he will die, Tobit instructs Tobiah not to marry a foreign woman but to take a bride from his own family. Isaac does not know when he is going to die. He instructs Jacob not to marry Canaanite women but to travel to Mesopotamia to marry one of the daughters of Laban, his mother's brother.

The Journey

Both sons set out on a journey, Tobiah to another city in Mesopotamia, Jacob also to a city in Mesopotamia. Each story recounts the first night on the road. Tobit, in the company of an angel, obtains the magical apparatus that will grant him success both in Ecbatana and on his return to Nineveh. Jacob stops at Bethel and has a dream in which angels appear and God speaks, promising to accompany him, protect him and return him safely. (As MacDonald has noted, the motif of angelic accompaniment occurs in Genesis 24, the story of Abraham's servant's trip to Mesopotamia in search for a bride for Isaac. Additionally, Raphael plays the role of marriage broker ascribed to Abraham's servant.)

The Arrival

As Tobiah and Raphael approach Ecbatana, the angel tells Tobiah about Sarah and assures him that she is beautiful. Tobiah falls in love at first non-sight. After Jacob meets Rachel, we will be told that Rachel is beautiful and that Jacob loves her. Tobiah and Raphael arrive at Raguel's house. Jacob comes to the well and meets Rachel. She brings him to the house of Laban.

The Recognition

Raguel recognizes Tobiah and discovers that he is the son of his kinsman Tobit. Jacob identifies himself to Rachel as her father's kinsman, and after she brings him home, Laban acknowledges, "Surely you are my flesh and bone."

The Wedding

Raguel agrees that Tobiah will marry his daughter, and a wedding feast ensues. Laban agrees that Jacob will marry Rachel after seven years of service. When the tie is completed, there is a wedding feast.

An Unusual Wedding Night

Tobiah and Sarah go into the wedding chamber. Tobiah exorcises the rival demonic bridegroom who wishes to possess Sarah, and Tobiah and Sarah consummate their marriage. Jacob consummates his marriage with a rival bride.

Debate about the Return Home

In both instances, the bridegroom expresses his intention to return home — Tobiah after fourteen days of feasting, Jacob after fourteen years with Laban. The father-in-law objects in each case, but the bridegroom insists.

The Return

In both cases, the bridegroom returns home a rich man, Tobiah with Raguel's blessing, Jacob in spite of Laban's threat. Tobiah comes home to Tobit with his bride. Jacob comes back to Isaac, although Rachel has died meanwhile. Both stories conclude with the death and burial of the father.

Summary

These parallels indicate substantial similarity in the purposes of the two journeys and in some of their details. In these respects, Tobiah's journey is better paralleled by the Jacob story than by the *Telemachia*. I agree with Dennis MacDonald that the author of Tobit is well aware of the Genesis story, but I have argued that the Genesis story has influenced Tobit in more ways than MacDonald indicates. But the comparison has further complications.

## THE STORY OF TOBIAH AND
## THE ACCOUNT OF JACOB'S STORY IN JUBILEES

In discussing the possible relationship between Tobit and the Book of Genesis, we should consider not just the biblical text itself, but also how Genesis was interpreted in the Hellenistic period. Specifically, the *Book of Jubilees* provides some striking parallels to Tobit not found in the *Odyssey* or in the biblical text of Genesis.[5]

The Grief of the Mother

When Tobiah leaves home, his mother weeps over his departure and Tobit comforts her. To this scene MacDonald compares the interaction between Telemachus and his nurse. However, *Jubilees* 27 provides a closer parallel, one not found in Genesis.

---

5. See John C. Endres, *Biblical Interpretation in the Book of Jubilees*, CBQMS 18 (Washington: Catholic Biblical Association of America, 1987) 95–97.

After Jacob had set out to go to Mesopotamia, Rebecca grieved in her spirit for her son and kept *weeping.* Isaac said to Rebecca, "My sister, do not weep for Jacob my son because *he goes* safely (lit. *in peace*) and *will return* safely (lit. *in peace*). The most high God will guard him from every evil and *will be with him* because he will not abandon him throughout his entire lifetime. For I know well that *his ways will prosper* wherever he goes until *he returns* safely (lit. *in peace*) to us and *we see* that he is safe (lit. *in peace*). *Do not be afraid* for him, my *sister,* because he is *just in his way.* . . . So Isaac was consoling Rebecca regarding her son Jacob (13–18).[6]

Here is the comparable scene involving Anna and Tobit:

And his mother *wept.* . . . And he (Tobit) said to her, "*Do not be afraid.* Our child *goes* safely (lit. *in peace*) *and will come* (back) safely (lit. *in peace*) to us,[7] and your eyes *will see* (him) on the day when he comes to you safely (lit. *in peace*). Have no care, *do not fear* concerning them, sister. A good angel *will go with him,* and *his way will prosper,* and he will return safely. And she stopped weeping (Tob 5:18–21).

Not only are the two scenes played out between the parents, but the similar wording indicates a connection.

### The Return

There is a second point of comparison between Tobit and *Jubilees* not found in Genesis. When Tobiah returns home, there is a wonderful reunion scene between the son and his parents. First, Anna embraces her son and expresses her readiness to die now that she has seen him; then Tobiah comes to his father and heals his blindness and the two embrace. In *Jub* 31:3–9 Jacob sends word that he is arriving. Isaac asks that Jacob come to him, "so that I may see him before I die." Jacob arrives. His mother embraces him. Jacob comes to his father. The two embrace, and Isaac regains his sight.

### The Prayers of Rebekah and Raguel

One other curious parallel between Tobit and *Jubilees* may or may not account for anything. It is in the wording of Rebekah's prayer before Jacob's departure and of Raguel's prayer after his daughter and son-in-

---

6. Translation with a few adjustments is that of James C. VanderKam, *The Book of Jubilees,* CSCO 511 (Louvain: Peeters, 1989) 173. Italics indicate similar details.

7. The Greek in this passages employs the participle ὑγιαίνων. *The* Aramaic *bslm* of 4QTobitb ar (4Q197) 4 1:2 (Fitzmyer, "Tobit," in Brochi, et al., eds., *Qumran Cave IV, XIV,* 44) corresponds exactly to the Ethiopic *basalâm* of Jub 27:14, 16).

law have survived the ordeal of the demon. Rebekah prays to "the *God who created the heavens* and the earth":

> May God *be blessed*
> and may his name be blessed *forever and ever* —
> who gave me Jacob a *pure and holy* offspring,
> for he belongs to you.

Raguel prays to the *God* of *heaven,*

> *Blessed* are you with every *pure and holy* blessing,
> and may your holy ones and all your creatures . . . bless you *for all ages.*

We might also note that in Tobit, Tobiah claims that he is not taking Sarah out of *porneia,* and Jacob assures his mother that he has not engaged in *fornication.*

### The Relationship between Tobit and Jubilees

Our comparison with *Jubilees* indicates that the story of Tobit is closer to the *Jubilees* account of the story of Jacob than it is to the Genesis version. What might be the relationship between Tobit and the *Jubilees* version of the story of Jacob? That there could be a relationship is at least supported by the fact that manuscripts of both texts have been found at Qumran. But how might they be related? There are some problems.

Tobit is normally dated before *Jubilees.*[8] So a dependence of Tobit on Jubilees seems unlikely. But the problem is more complex. Among the Qumran manuscripts are the fragments of four copies of a text designated as "Reworked Pentateuch" (4Q 363–367).[9] Among these fragments is a piece that appears to preserve the grieving scene between Isaac and Rebecca.[10] So, even if we date Tobit to the third century, its author could have known the interpretation attested in Jubilees — an interpretation that included a grieving scene between Rebekah and Isaac and, possibly, one that depicted a reunion between Jacob and his parents and the restoration of Isaac's eyesight. Perhaps this is the case. It would explain

---

8. On the date of Tobit, see Nickelsburg, "Stories,"45; on the date of Jubilees, see idem, "The Bible Rewritten and Expanded," in Michael E. Stone, ed., *Jewish Writings of the Second Temple Period: Apocrypha, Pseudepigrapha, Qumran Sectarian Writings, Philo, Josephus,* CRINT 2.2 (Assen: Van Gorcum, 1984) 101–3.

9. For these texts, see Emmanuel Tov and Sidnie White, "Reworked Pentateuch," in Harold Attridge, et al., eds., *Qumran Cave 4, VIII: Parabiblical Texts. Part II,* DJD 13 (Oxford: Clarendon Press, 1994) 187–351.

10. See 4Q364 3 2:1–6 (ibid., 206–7). Here, too one finds "in peace" (Heb. *běšlwm*).

why Tobit's grieving scene is closer to Jubilees than it is to the *Odyssey*. But there is another possible scenario.

The grieving scene in Tobit is natural. Anna remonstrates with her husband because he has sent Tobiah off to fetch his money, which she considers less important than the presence of their son. In *Jubilees*, it is Rebekah who suggests that Jacob leave to find a wife, and then she grieves when he has left. Moreover, in Tobit the blindness of Tobit and the restoration of his sight are of the essence of the story,[11] whereas the restoration of Isaac's sight in Jubilees is gratuitous and completely unexpected. This may suggest that the author of Tobit shaped his story on the basis of material from the *Odyssey* and from Genesis. The author of *Jubilees* or his tradition knew the story of Tobit, recognized in that story some dependence on the Jacob story, and incorporated some elements from Tobit into his recasting of the Jacob story. The two alternatives can be diagrammed as follows:

Odyssey                     Genesis            Genesis              Odyssey
   |        Interpretation     |                  \        Tobit        /
Tobit                       Jubilees            Jubilees or its source

## THE COMPLEX WEB OF INTERTEXTUALITY

However we explain the relationships among Tobit, the *Odyssey*, Genesis, and *Jubilees*, it is clear that we are dealing with a complex set of relationships. That the author of Tobit knew and used the *Odyssey* has been demonstrated by MacDonald. At the same time, the author of Tobit was able to "switch gears" and make an identification between Telemachus and Jacob, and he could then construe the journey of Tobiah, in its purpose, if not in all of its details, more in terms of the Jacob story than that of Telemachus. Beyond that the author may have worked with a traditional interpretation of the Genesis story rather than with the biblical text per se. Alternatively, the process has gone full circle, and the author of *Jubilees* or his source has worked Tobit's reuse of Genesis into his own recasting of the story. Pending closer study, I leave open the alternatives.

---

11. See the analysis of the plot in Nickelsburg, "Stories," 42–3.

## SOME METHODOLOGICAL CONSIDERATIONS
## IN THE DISCUSSION OF INTERTEXTUALITY

At this point, I return to some considerations that I raised in my article in the Milik Festschrift.[12] In short, how do we imagine the process of intertextual composition, with its many hooks and fingers, fitting into the great intercultural tradition? How do we imagine the author of Tobit at his *Schreibtisch* ? To what extent was the poetic process conscious and to what extent was it unconscious? From his text we know that he knew Genesis, Kings, Job, Ahikar, the *Odyssey* and perhaps some other texts or traditions.[13] He knew the genres of narrative, testament, two-ways, parenesis, prayer, and apocalypse, to name the obvious ones.[14] In what form did he know these things? MacDonald's benchmarks are helpful at this point: density, order, verbatim parallels, and explanatory value. They make a compelling case for this author's conscious dependence on the text of the *Odyssey* and the text of Genesis or a traditional exposition of it. The author explicitly refers to the story of Ahikar and to some elements in the history of the Assyrian Captivity of Israel. But what of the other texts and traditions to which he alludes and the genres that he employs? At this point, I am less certain. The question has implications for the broader question of intertextuality. How, in any given case, do we imagine the process of intertextual poetics?

As we try to understand complex texts from antiquity, to what extent do we impose on a creative writer — to use a modern term — a manner of composition that reflects more the style of writing that we scholars employ? We sit down with our notes, our sources, and our outlines and start to cast our articles and books. We are aware of the need to document, and at least we try conscientiously to footnote our sources. Of course, this is something of an oversimplification, but it is more on than off the mark. I suggest that often we analyze ancient texts or construe our analyses of these texts as if their authors wrote in somewhat the same fashion. We assume that our outlines of their texts correspond to something of which they must have been conscious. Our identification of their sources and allusions — even if we have had to search them out through concordance and computer — must have been up front in their minds. Wording that can be traced to Isaiah must have been in-

---

12. Nickelsburg, "Search," 347–9.
13. Ibid., 340–3.
14. See Nickelsburg, "Tobit and Enoch."

tended as an allusion to Isaiah, and perhaps even to its context. I do not deny that this was the case sometimes; there is enough evidence of explicit citation — not just quotation — to indicate that these authors knew their Scriptures. But in other cases, they may well have employed biblical language and rhetoric without intending allusion or reference — the equivalent of a preacher speaking King James English.

If the conscious, deliberate way that we scholars do our work sometimes affects the way we imagine the poetics of the texts we interpret, perhaps we need to attend more to the poetic processes at work among non-scholarly writers. Here is a modern example. The American playwright David Rabe wrote a play in the 1980's entitled *Hurlyburly*. When I first heard the title of this play, I thought, "Oh, Macbeth, Act I." My footnoting mind was at work. This is what Rabe writes about the title in the published Afterword:

> I had a long list of titles, none of which seemed quite appropriate. Then one day while the play was in rehearsal I was looking at a piece of prose I had been working on in which the word "hurlyburly" occurred, and I thought, "That could be it. . . . " One morning I awoke to find myself thinking that I should look in *Macbeth* and I would find justification for the title there. I opened my favorite copy . . . and there it was in the first four lines. "When the hurlyburly's done, When the battle's lost and won." Certainly I had read *Macbeth* before, and certainly I knew that the word was "Shakespearean," but until that moment I had no conscious knowledge that the word was in *Macbeth* and in the first four lines.[15]

This interesting commentary, by an author on his own writing, should perhaps discourage facile judgments about the process of intertextuality. A few other of Rabe's comments on the genesis of this play are perhaps also pertinent.

When David Rabe writes a play, he sits at the keyboard and enters the dialogue. There are no names attached, just conversation. He describes how the plot of *Hurlyburly* and its resolution developed not from an *a priori* scenario but through the actual writing of the dialogue, and he goes on to describe the rehearsal of the play. "Questions were addressed to me and I had no answers. I had no knowledge as to what a character was up to or intended, or what a scene was meant to convey." The meaning of the play emerged in the rehearsal, as the actors and actresses brought the text to life.[16]

---

15. David Rabe, *Hurlyburly: A Play* (New York: Grove Press, 1985) 170.
16. Ibid., 162–3.

I conclude from this modern example that the poetics of texts consti-
tutes a mysterious process that involves a remarkable dialectic between
the conscious and the unconscious. We may well find material that
is really there — apropos our present discussion — intertextual relationships that are firm and verifiable. But we need to imagine the
atmosphere and the process by which they got to be there and not jump
too quickly to notions of intertextuality that emphasize the text as written, whether consulted or consciously remembered. We need controls.
Explicit citation is one. MacDonald's benchmarks of density, order, distinctive traits, and interpretability, taken together, are another. They
are a valuable tool for identifying conscious intertextuality and help-
ing us to sort this out from other forms of literary and non-literary
interdependence and interrelationship.

## APPENDIX
## INTERTEXTUALITY IN TOBIT, GENESIS, AND JUBILEES

| Tobit | Genesis 27–35 | Jubliees | Genesis 24 |
|---|---|---|---|
| 2:7–10 Tobit becomes blind | 27:1 Isaac is blind | | |
| 2:11–14 Anna given a goat. Tobit blames her for deception | 27:5–29 Rebekah concocts deception regarding goat | | |
| 4:2 Tobit makes preparations with his son before his death | 27:2 Isaac makes preparations with son before his death | | |
| 4:12–13 Tobit instructs his son not to marry a foreign woman, but to follow example of Abraham, Isaac, Jacob | 28:1 Isaac instructs his son not to marry a Canaanite woman, but one of own family | | 3 Abraham instructs servant not to marry a son to Canaanite woman |
| 5:17 May God bring you there safely and return you safely | 28:15 I will bring you back | | |
| May God's angel accompany you | 28:12 Sees vision of angels | | 7 God will send his angel before you |

| Tobit | Genesis 27–35 | Jubliees | Genesis 24 |
|---|---|---|---|
| 5:18–22<br>Anna weeps.<br>Tobit assures her. He<br>goes in peace, will<br>return in peace.<br>Your eyes will see<br>him. When he<br>returns in peace.<br>Fear not: angel will<br>accompany him; his<br>ways will prosper;<br>he will return in<br>peace. She is silent | | 27:13–18<br>Rebekah weeps.<br>Isaac assures her,<br>he goes in peace, in<br>peace he will<br>return, God will be<br>with him; his ways<br>will prosper . . .<br>until he returns in<br>peace . . . and we<br>see him in peace.<br>Fear not, he is on<br>upright path. Isaac<br>comforted her | |
| 6:2–6 Spends night,<br>get magical<br>apparatus | 28:10–17 Spends<br>night, promised<br>success | | |
| 6:10–7:1 Arrival in<br>Mesopotamia | 29:1 Arrival in<br>Mesopotamia | | |
| 6:12 Sarah is<br>very beautiful | 29:17 Rachel is<br>very beautiful | | |
| 6:18 Tobiah loves<br>Sarah very much | 29:18 Jacob loved<br>Rachel | | |
| 7:1 Arrival at<br>Raguel's house | 29:13 Arrival at<br>Laban's house | | |
| 7:2–7 Recognition<br>scene: son of<br>kinsman | 29:14 Recognition:<br>you are my bone<br>and flesh | | |
| 7:9–13 Marriage<br>arrangements | 29:16–20 Marriage<br>arrangements | | |
| 7:14 Wedding meal | 29:22 Wedding feast | | |
| 7:15–8:14 Wedding<br>night | 29:23–25 Wedding<br>night | | |
| 10:7–9<br>Discussion between<br>Tobiah and Raguel<br>over return home | 30:25–30<br>Discussion between<br>Jacob and Laban<br>over return home | | |
| 10:10–14 Tobiah<br>returns a rich man<br>with Raguel's<br>blessing | 31 Jacob returns a<br>rich man in spite of<br>his uncle's threat | | |
| 11:1–15 Anna<br>embraces her son,<br>ready to die, sees<br>him. Tobiah heals<br>Tobit's blindness.<br>They embrace. | | 31:3–9 Isaac: see<br>son before I die.<br>Rebekah embraces<br>her son. Isaac<br>embraces son.<br>Blindness cured. | |
| | 35:29 Death, burial | | |
| 14:11 Death, burial | | Death and burial | |

# 3

## Homer in Greco-Roman Education

### Ronald F. Hock

Any study of intertextuality in the Greco-Roman world must begin with Homer, whose *Iliad* and *Odyssey* exerted an influence on intellectual life and letters that is difficult to overestimate. One reason for this influence is the central role that Homer's epics played in education. Hence it might be useful to survey Greco-Roman education in order to become more aware of the many ways in which these epics functioned in the schools.

Consequently, this paper will survey, in some detail, the role of Homer in Greco-Roman education, organizing the survey around the curricular sequence of primary, secondary, and tertiary stages. Each stage of this sequence will be briefly summarized before turning to the task of identifying the specific roles that Homer's epics played at that stage, but first some remarks on recent scholarship on education in the Greco-Roman world will help to orient the specific concerns of the following survey.

### GRECO-ROMAN EDUCATION IN RECENT STUDY

The three stages of education in the Greco-Roman world — primary, secondary, and tertiary — have received classic treatment from Henri I. Marrou and Stanley F. Bonner,[1] although recent scholarship has proposed significant modifications and new perspectives. Alan Booth, for example, argues that the primary curriculum, particularly for aristocratic children, may have been taught more informally at home rather

---

1. Henry Irénée Marrou, *A History of Education in Antiquity*, trans. George Lamb (New York: Sheed & Ward, 1956) 142–85; repr. Madison: University of Wisconsin Press, 1982, and Stanley Frederick Bonner, *Education in Ancient Rome: From the Elder Cato to the Younger Pliny* (Berkeley: University of California Press, 1977) 165–249. Still useful are two older treatments, with illustrative texts: Paul Collart, "A l'école avec les petits grecs d'Égypte," *CdÉ* 21 (1936) 489–507, and Erich Gustav Ludwig Ziebarth, *Aus der antiken Schule. Sammlung griechischer Texte auf Papyrus, Holztafeln, Ostraka*, Kliene Texte für Vorlesungen und Übungen 65 (2d ed., Bonn: A. Marcus & E. Weber, 1913).

than in the classroom of a γραμματιστής, or elementary teacher, as is usually assumed; may have required only two years to complete instead of four or five, as is often stated; and may have been taught, on occasion, by a γραμματικός, or secondary teacher of grammar and literature, who thereby insured himself a supply of students for his own curriculum. In fact, the primary school may have served less as the standard institution for primary education than as one used by poor and marginalized children like Kottalos in a mime of Herodas.[2]

In addition, Raffaella Cribiore has provided fuller and more sophisticated control of the numerous and growing number of papyri, ostraca, and tablets that document the actual activities of teachers and students in Greco-Roman Egypt.[3] More important, she has proposed a more systematic typology of school hands, distinguishing four grades: zerograde, alphabetic, evolving, and rapid.[4] This typology of school hands led Cribiore to offer a modification of our understanding of the primary curriculum. She argues that the curricular sequence that scholars have reconstructed, largely on the basis of scattered literary references to education — namely of learning first the letters of the alphabet, then syllables, then words, then sentences, and finally short poetic passages — is not the whole story. Left out, for example, is the importance that was attached to teaching students to write their own names and to do so from the very beginning, that is, already when learning the alphabet.[5] Moreover, Cribiore underscores the emphasis placed on calligraphy, or writing sentences correctly and beautifully, even before learning to read what they were copying; indeed, some students hardly moved beyond the task of copying, whereas those who did learn to read continued to practice and so perfect their copying skills.[6] Thus the primary stage was not focused simply on learning to read but on learning to write beautifully as well.

---

2. Alan Booth, "Elementary and Secondary Education in the Roman Empire," *Florilegium* 1 (1979) 1–14. Kottalos, the son of a blind fisherman, is a poor boy who attends the primary school of a certain Lampriskos in hopes of becoming a clerk (see Herodas *Mime* 3: The Teacher).

3. *Writing, Teachers, and Students in Graeco-Roman Egypt*, American Studies in Papyrology 36 (Atlanta: Scholars Press, 1996) esp. 173–284. This is a comprehensive catalogue of the documentary evidence for education. Where applicable, texts used in this study will be identified by the letter C and her catalogue number.

4. Ibid., 102–18.

5. Ibid., 40 and 139–52.

6. Ibid., 43–44.

Another scholar who has made a full and sophisticated study of the documentary evidence is Teresa Morgan.[7] Her investigation proceeds according to the curricular sequence, but adds a sense of historical development and reality, noting, for example, that the standard curriculum developed shortly after the conquests of Alexander and indeed in response to them;[8] that the study of grammar did not appear until the early Roman period and did so as "an extra rung on the ladder of literate status;"[9] and that the curriculum represented in literary sources like Quintilian's *Institutio* is more ambitious than what the documentary evidence from Egypt suggests students actually learned,[10] a conclusion that prompts Morgan to propose a core and periphery model for Greco-Roman education in which all pupils learned a core of skills and authors, whereas only the most advantaged among them went on to more peripheral ones.[11]

The core-periphery model leads Morgan to her main interest: attempting to establish the function of literate education. Literacy was low, perhaps no more than 15 percent, so that it, along with birth, wealth, and culture, became a measure of identity and status. As she says, "reading Homer is, among other things, a statement of Greek identity," not only for the ethnic Greek aristocracy in Egypt but also for non-Greeks. Each stage of education marked an increase in status; the few students who moved on to the grammatical curriculum could look down on those whose education ended at the primary stage, and even more so on those without education at all, and up to those who had attained even higher levels of education.[12]

Further insights from Morgan's study, as well as from Cribiore's, however, must await the appropriate place in the following analysis. But it should be clear already that our understanding of Greco-Roman education is growing and changing significantly.

---

7. Teresa Jean Morgan, *Literate Education in the Hellenistic and Roman Worlds*, Cambridge Classical Studies (New York: Cambridge University Press, 1998).

8. Ibid., 21–25.

9. Ibid., 57–63.

10. Ibid., 94–104.

11. Ibid., 67–73. The core is rather modest, with students learning their letters and getting as far as reading maxims, and some Homer, and perhaps a little Euripides, whereas the periphery included more authors, such as Menander, as well as grammar and some rhetoric—a far cry from scholars, using the literary sources, imagined as typical of Greco-Roman education.

12. Ibid., 74–89 and 109–10.

## HOMER IN THE PRIMARY CURRICULUM

With this summary of recent work on Greco-Roman education in mind, we turn first to the primary curriculum (Morgan's core) and specifically to the roles that the Homeric epics played at this initial stage of education. The point where one first encounters the use of Homer is after students have learned to identify and write the letters of the alphabet and have copied and pronounced exhaustive combinations of syllables.[13]

The next step was reading proper, as students now copied, from a written model or from dictation, rather long lists of words which were usually arranged alphabetically, if only for the first letter, and organized according to increasing numbers of syllables; that is, the lists moved from one to two, to three, to four, even to five syllables.[14]

We have hints of such lists in Herodas, where the truant and possibly dyslexic schoolboy Kottalos is at the point of reading two-syllable words, but cannot distinguish ΜΑΡΩΝ from ΣΙΜΩΝ.[15] What is of interest to us is that Kottalos's list has proper names and one of them, Μάρων, is Homeric, taken from the *Odyssey* (9.197). That Kottalos's reading assignment is typical is shown by other literary sources as well as by documentary evidence. Epictetus, for example, refers several times to schoolboys writing the name ΔΙΩΝ,[16] and Philostratus recounts a story about the sophist Herodes Atticus who, on learning that his son was having difficulty reading, surrounded him with twenty-four σύντροφοι, "comrades," each named after a letter of the alphabet, and, if I read Philostratus correctly, three of them are identified by Homeric names: Achilles, Polydeuces, and Memnon.[17]

The best evidence for these lists, however, comes from documentary texts. Cribiore has collected and analyzed the known lists of words,[18]

---

13. See further Marrou, *Education*, 150–52; Bonner, *Education*, 166–69; and esp. Cribiore, *Writing*, 37–42 and 175–91. For sample texts, see Ziebarth, *Aus der antiken Schule*, 3–5, and Collart, "A l'école," 497–98. For complete catalogues, see Cribiore, *Writing*, 175–96, which lists 97 texts, designated here and below with the letter C and the appropriate number; hence: C1–97; cf. also Morgan, *Literate Education*, 275–78.

14. See further Marrou, *Education*, 152–54; Bonner, *Education*, 169–72; and esp. Cribiore, *Writing*, 42–43 and 191–96.

15. Herodas 3.24–26.

16. Epictetus 1.12.13, 2.2.23, 13.20, and 3.24.51.

17. Philostratus *Vitae sophistarum* 558.

18. Cribiore, *Writing*, 42–43, 196–203, 269–70, 274–76, 280–81 and 283, citing 38 texts (=C 98–128, 379, 380, 390, 391, 393, 404 and 411). Cf. also the tabulation in Morgan, *Literate Education*, 101–4.

and her tabulation now supersedes the standard collection of edu-
cational texts in Pack²,[19] as well as the more recent one by Janine
Debut.[20]

A perusal of Cribiore's collection confirms the use of proper names in
these lists as well as a consistent and heavy reliance on Homeric names.
For example, one ostrakon from the second century contains a complete
list of one word for each letter of the alphabet; each word, moreover, is
a proper name, and among them we read not only the premier Homeric
name Ἀχιλλεύς but also Kottalos's Μάρων as well as Epictetus's Δίων.[21]
The name Achilles, as well as other Homeric names, appears on other
lists preserved on papyrus and ostraca,[22] but the lists contained in two
notebooks deserve closer attention.

The first notebook, P. Chester Beatty, is a papyrus book from the late
third or early fourth century.[23] The editors regard this notebook as a
student's copy, presumably taken down from his teacher's dictation.[24]
But Cribiore applies her typology of school hands and classifies the
writing as that of a teacher.[25] At any rate, this text originally had six
sheets and, to judge from the preserved fragments, contained a series of
alphabetized lists of words, beginning with one syllable and proceeding
through four. None of the one-syllable words is preserved, and only a
few of the two-syllable words, but of the 216 words that remain 127 are
proper names, and of these 49 names come from Homer.

Among these Homeric names are, not surprisingly, those that figure prominently in the epics, such as Ἑκάβη (line 56), Καλυψώ (l. 95),
Ὀδυσσεύς (l. 128), Σαρπηδών (l. 148), Χρυσηίς (l. 173), and Χάρυβδις
(l. 176). Other names also figure prominently but are not exclusive to
Homer, such as Ἡρακλῆς (l. 76), Ὀρέστης (l. 130), and Ποσειδῶν (l. 132),

19. Roger A. Pack, *The Greek and Latin Literary Texts from Greco-Roman Egypt* (2d ed.,
Ann Arbor: University of Michigan Press, 1965) 137–40.

20. Janine Debut, "Les documents scolaires," *ZPE* 63 (1986) 251–78. Cribiore's collection (*Writings*, 175–284) is obviously more up-to-date, but it is also more informative and
methodologically sophisticated than these previous collections. See also the tabulation of
texts in Morgan, *Literate Education*, 275–87.

21. O.Bodl.Gr. Inscr. 2993 (=C 105), published by Joseph Grafton Milne, "Relics of
Graeco-Roman Schools," *JHS* 28 (1908) 121–32, esp. 122.

22. Cribiore, *Writing*, 200–1 (=C 113, 119).

23. P. Chester Beatty (=390), published by Willy Clarysse and Alfons Wouters, "A
Schoolboy's Exercise in the Chester Beatty Library," *AncSoc* 1 (1970) 201–35 (text: 210–17).

24. Clarysse and Wouters, "Schoolboy's Exercise," 205; cf. 232.

25. Cribiore, *Writing*, 43 and n. 58 and 275. Cf. also Morgan, *Literate Education*,
101 n. 48.

while others are obscure Homeric names, sometimes appearing only once, such as Φέρεκλος, a Trojan slain by Meriones (l. 165; *Iliad* 5.59), or Φαέθουσσα, a nymph herder of Helios's flocks (l. 188; *Odyssey* 12.132).

The second notebook, P.Bour. 1, is, like the Chester Beatty papyrus, a primary school book, although it is a little later, probably from the mid-to late fourth century, and its eleven pages contain much more of the primary curriculum.[26] The Bouriant papyrus is clearly a student's copy, as its first editors, Pierre Jouguet and Paul Perdrizet, recognized (calling it "un cahier d'écolier"). It lacks the first stages of the curriculum — the alphabet and syllables — but it has the remainder of the curriculum: lists of alphabetized words of one through four syllables; beginners' sentences, specifically five chreiai attributed to Diogenes as well as twenty-four monostichoi, one for each letter of the alphabet; and a short poetic passage, specifically the opening lines of the prologue to Babrius's fables.

The lists of words, as in the Chester Beatty papyrus, contain many proper names, and while various Menandrian names from the *Samia, Dyskolos,* and *Aspis* have been the focus of attention lately,[27] the presence of Homeric names is far more pervasive. Indeed, of the 160 proper names 65 derive from Homer, including Μάρων again (line 28) as well as the name of the poet himself (l. 98: Ὅμηρος). The selection of names ranges, as in the Chester Beatty papyrus, from the likes of Αἴας (l. 6), Ἕκτωρ (l. 27), Νέστωρ (l. 34), Θερσίτης (l. 81), Πάτροκλος (l. 103), Πρίαμος (l. 104), and Ἀγαμέμνων (l. 129) to such obscure personages as Ἶφις, a captive whom Achilles gave to Patroclus (l. 28; cf. *Iliad* 9.667); Μέντωρ, the father of a fallen Trojan (l. 31; cf. *Iliad* 13.171); Βιήνωρ, a Trojan slain by Agamemnon (l. 64; cf. *Iliad* 11.92); and Φέρεκλος again (l. 113; cf. *Iliad* 5.59).

The function of these lists of names is debated. At a minimum they provided practice at copying correctly and beautifully, and the presence of a number of words that would be difficult to pronounce — such as the Homeric name Ῥηξήνωρ (l. 110; *Odyssey* 7.63) — has suggested to scholars that practice at pronunciation was another function of these

---

26. P.Bour. 1, now known as P. Sorbonne 826 (=C 393), published by Pierre Jouguet and Paul Perdrizet, "Le papyrus Bouriant no. 1. Un cahier d'écolier grec d'Égypte," *StudPal* 6 (1906) 148–61 (text: 150–56), and by Paul Collart, *Les papyrus Bouriant* (Paris: Édouard Champion, 1926) 17–27 (text: 21–26). The text is also available in Ziebarth, *Aus der antiken Schule,* 21–24, and portions of it are in Morgan, *Literate Education,* 313–14.

27. Alain Blanchard, "Sur le milieu d'origine du papyrus Bodmer de Ménandre," *CdÉ* 66 (1991) 211–20.

lists.[28] But Debut has emphasized a broader function; these lists, she argues, introduced students to elements of Greek history and culture, as the γραμματιστής no doubt would pause to comment on the identity, character, and significance of the many names from the Homeric epics as well as on those from mythology and history.[29] In other words, at the earliest stages of learning to read and write students would be exposed to many of the heroes and deities who figured in the *Iliad* and *Odyssey*. Even minimal familiarity with these figures at this early stage would help students when they began to read Homer's poems later under a γραμματικός.

After the lists of words, however, further exposure to the Homeric epics at the primary stage of education was less assured. What remained of the primary curriculum, reading and writing sentences and short passages,[30] focused on other material, Menandrian monostichoi and chreiai, as in the Bouriant papyrus, for the sentences; and a wide variety of poetic materials for the short passages. In addition, as Cribiore has emphasized, the assignment of sentences was primarily to develop handwriting skills and speed,[31] as is evident from texts like a waxed tablet of unknown provenance and date that contains a maxim written down by the teacher and then copied four times by the student.[32]

Still, lines from Homer appear among these sentences, as a few texts indicate.[33] When the student's hand is sufficiently advanced, "rapid," to use Cribiore's typology, we can be fairly sure that the student could

---

28. Marrou, *Education*, 152–53; cf. Cribiore, *Writing*, 39–40; Collart, "A l'école," 498; and Ziebarth, *Aus der antiken Schule*, 5.

29. Janine Debut, "De l'usage des listes de mots comme fondement de la pédagogie dans l'antiquité," *REA* 85 (1983) 261–74. Cribiore (*Writing*, 42–43) is doubtful of such a function, but Morgan, without citing Debut, sees a similar function (*Literate Education*, 77 and 101–2).

30. Marrou, *Education*, 153–57; Bonner, *Education*, 172–77; Cribiore, *Writing*, 43–47 and 204–27; and esp. Morgan, *Literate Education*, 120–51, who analyzes the ethos of the sentences found in these texts.

31. Cribiore, *Writing*, 43: "The aim of writing exercises was improvement of the handwriting: beginners practiced letter shapes imitating the teachers' hands in the models, while older students attempted to acquire more fluent hands or to learn more elaborate styles."

32. T.Berol. inv. 13234 (=C 134), available in Ziebarth, *Aus der antiken Schule*, 6, and Collart, "A l'école," 495. For a picture of this text, see Bonner, *Education*, 61. The maxim: φιλοπόνει, ὦ παῖ, μὴ δαρῇς ("Work hard, son, so that you do not receive a beating."). See also Cribiore, *Writing*, 127–28.

33. Cribiore lists five such texts: C 132, 146, 159, 168 and 173 (*Writing*, 204, 208, 211 and 213–14).

read what he was copying. Thus one Oxyrhynchus papyrus preserves the first words of the first line of the *Iliad* copied twice by a student with a rapid hand.[34]

Short passages, in contrast, were intended to be copied and learned by heart, and here Homer comes more to the fore, as twenty-four texts contain one or more lines from "the poet," nearly all from the *Iliad* and most of these from the early books. Thus one Byzantine ostrakon contains, in a rapid hand, the first two lines of Book 1 of the *Iliad*,[35] and fifteen other texts have lines from one of the first three books.[36] The importance of Homer is further underlined in two other texts, a waxed tablet and an ostrakon (C 209), on which, among other things, there appears the sentence: Θεός οὐδ᾽ ἄνθρωπος ῞Ομηρος ("A god, not a man, was Homer").[37]

In summary: At the primary stage of education we have various indicators that a familiarity with and an appreciation for Homer had already begun. Students would learn the names of a number of heroes, deities, and other proper names that appear in the *Iliad* and *Odyssey*, and they might also have copied and memorized a few lines from the early books of the *Iliad* and perhaps have already come to view Homer with something akin to awe.

## HOMER IN THE SECONDARY CURRICULUM

Once students had learned to read and write and had gained a rudimentary knowledge of Homer, they moved on, though in fewer numbers,[38] to the secondary curriculum of grammar and literature under the supervision of a γραμματικός. In one sense this curriculum was quite similar to the one they had just completed, in that it also progressed from letters to syllables, to words, and finally to poetic works. But the similarity is merely formal, as this progression is now much

34. P.Cairo 56225 (=C 132), photographed by Cribiore (*Writing*, plate XIV).

35. O.MMA 14.1.139 (=C 225), photographed by Cribiore (*Writing*, plate XIV).

36. C 193, 201, 206, 212, 224, 226, 227, 254, 259, 264, 289, 294, 296, 310, and 315 (*Writing*, 218, 220–22, 225–26, 233, 235–36, 242, 244 and 249–51).

37. T.Bodl.Ms.Gr.class.dl59 (=200), published by D. C. Hesseling, "On Waxen Tablets with Fables of Babrius," *JHS* 13 (1892–1893) 293–314, esp. 296, and P.Mich.inv. 9353 (=C 209), published in *Papyri and Ostraca from Karanis*, Herbert Chayyim Youtie and John Garrett Winter, eds., Michigan Papyri 8 (2d series.; Ann Arbor: University of Michigan Press, 1951) 206–7.

38. On the very small number of students who went on to the secondary curriculum, at least for Egypt, see Morgan, *Literate Education*, 163.

more complex and sophisticated. Thus instead of merely learning the names and shapes of the letters, students began to classify them, distinguishing consonants from vowels and classifying both according to various subcategories, such as vowels into short and long. Likewise, instead of merely pronouncing lengthy lists of syllables, they started to learn the metric values of syllables they would find in their reading. Again, instead of merely reading lists of words of one, two, or more syllables, they began to classify words according to one of the eight parts of speech and to divide them — nouns, verbs, participles, articles, and so forth — into various subcategories. Finally, instead of merely reading sentences or short passages of poetry, they started to read and interpret lengthy literary works, always Homer and principally the *Iliad*, but also other poets, most likely Euripides and perhaps Menander.

The centrality of Homer in the secondary curriculum is thus obvious from this brief summary.[39] To be sure, the *Iliad* was far more popular than the *Odyssey*,[40] and students did not read the entirety of either at this stage,[41] although the first two books of the *Iliad* were almost certainly read.[42] It is nonetheless clear that students greatly increased their knowledge of Homer under the γραμματικός. They read and memorized a set number of lines daily, aided, at least at first, by what are called *scholia minora*, or glosses on words and phrases in which the archaic or poetic Greek of Homer is rendered into its Koine equivalents.[43] Nearly all preserved *scholia minora* (eighteen of nineteen compiled by students) gloss the *Iliad*, and most of these do so for the early books, especially

---

39. For fuller accounts of secondary education, see Marrou, *Education*, 160–85; Bonner, *Education*, 189–249; Robert Henry Robins, *The Byzantine Grammarians: Their Place in History*, Trends in Linguistics, Studies and Monographs 70 (New York: Mouton de Gruyter, 1993) 41–110; and Morgan, *Literate Education*, 152–89.

40. Of the 97 texts containing portions of Homer, 86 come from the *Iliad*, 11 from the *Odyssey* (Morgan, *Literate Education*, 105).

41. Bonner, *Education*, 213.

42. Raffaella Cribiore, "A Homeric Writing Exercise and Reading Homer in School," *Tyche* 9 (1994) 1–8, esp. 4. See also idem, "Literary School Exercises," *ZPE* 116 (1997) 53–60, esp. 57–58. Morgan (*Literary Education*, 107–9) points out that many of these Homeric texts have the quality of lists, such as catalogues of ships, parts of a ship, names of deities and heroes, similes or metaphors, and descriptions of battles and places, not what modern readers would expect; no text, for example, contains Achilles' slaying of Hector (*Iliad* 22) or Achilles' giving up Hector's body to Priam (*Iliad* 24). See also her statistical tables, 320.

43. On the *scholia minora*, see Cribiore, *Writing*, 50–51, 71–72, 253–58, and the valuable new tool: John Lundon, "Lexeis from the Scholia Minora in Homerum," *ZPE* 124 (1999) 25–52.

Books 1 and 2.[44] Thus one papyrus from the late first or early second century glosses the first nine lines of Book 1 and presents a nearly word for word translation of the Homeric language.[45] For example, for line 1 we have:

| | |
|---|---|
| μῆνιν | χόλον ὀργήν θυμόν |
| ἄειδε | ὕμνει |
| θεά | Μοῦσα |
| Πηληϊάδεω | Πηλέως υἱοῦ λέγει |
| <Ἀχιλῆος> | τοῦ Ἀχιλλέως |

Students also increased their grasp and appreciation of the Homeric epics through paraphrases of books of the *Iliad* or through catechisms with questions and answers about characters and relationships in the story. One paraphrase, part of a third-century grammatical notebook written on a wooden tablet, summarizes, if that is the word, *Iliad* 1.1–21 in prose that is four times longer than the original.[46] For the catechetical form of question and answer one can cite documentary evidence,[47] as well as a brief example in Epictetus who assumes that his students are familiar with questions that had been put to them by the γραμματικός:

Q: Who was the father of Hector?

A: Priam.

Q: Who were his brothers?

A: Alexander and Deiphobos.

Q: Who was their mother?

A: Hecuba.[48]

The role of Homer in the secondary curriculum did not end, however, with reading and interpreting the *Iliad* and the *Odyssey*. Homer was also a part of grammatical instruction, usually through illustration.

---

44. C 325, 330, 331, 332, 338, 339, and 343 (*Writing*, 253, 255 and 257–58).

45. P.Mich.inv. 1588 (=C 325), published by Timothy Renner, "Three New Homerica on Papyrus," *HSCP* 83 (1979) 311–37, esp. 313–21(complete text: 315–16). For a similar text, see P.Berol.inv. 5014 (=C 343), available in Ziebarth, *Aus der antiken Schule*, 13–14, and photographed by Cribiore (*Writing*, plates LIV–LV).

46. T.Bodl.Gr.Inscr. 3019 (=C 388), published by P. J. Parsons, "A School-Book from the Sayce Collection," *ZPE* 6 (1970) 133–49, esp. 135–38.

47. Esp. P.IFAO inv. 320 (=C 406), published by J. Schwartz, "Un manuel scolaire de l'époque byzantine," *ÉdP* 7 (1948) 93–109; cf. Marrou, *Education*, 166–69.

48. Epictetus, 2.19.7.

Whether one looks at the standard grammar of Dionysius Thrax[49] or at the grammatical texts preserved on papyri and collected by Wouters,[50] it is clear that Homer figured frequently in the teaching of grammar. For example, a central concern of Dionysius's grammar is his classification of the Greek language into eight parts (μέρη) of speech: noun (ὄνομα), verb (ῥῆμα), participle (μετοχή), article (ἄρθρον), pronoun (ἀντωνυμία), preposition (πρόθεσις), adverb (ἐπίρρημα), and conjunction (σύνδεσμος).[51]

A scholiast commenting on Dionysius at this point illustrates these eight parts of speech by citing a line from Homer whose eight words included all eight parts of speech, as follows: πρὸς δ᾽ ἐμὲ τὸν δύστηνον ἔτι φρονέοντ᾽ ἐλέησον (Iliad 22.59; "Have pity on me, the unfortunate one, while I am still alive"). The scholiast explained: "The word πρός is a preposition, δ᾽ is a conjunction, ἐμέ a pronoun, τόν an article, δύστηνον a noun, ἔτι an adverb, φρονέοντα a participle, and ἐλέησον a verb."[52]

Dionysius, however, does use Homer for illustrative purposes elsewhere and particularly in his analysis of the noun (ὄνομα). He says, for example, that there are two sub-types (εἴδη) of the noun (ὄνομα): original (πρωτότυπον) and derived (παράγωγον). The latter are those nouns that derive from another word, as, for example, Γαιήιος, which comes from Homer (Odyssey 6.324) and derives from Γῆ.[53] There are also seven sub-types (εἴδη) of derived nouns: patronymic, possessive, comparative, superlative, diminutive, and so on, and illustrations of these are sometimes taken from Homer: patronymic (πατρωνυμικόν) nouns like Πηλείδης for Achilles (cf. Iliad 1.1); possessive (κτητικόν) nouns like Νηλήιοι ἵπποι (Iliad 11.597) or Ἑκτόρεος χιτών (Iliad 2.416).[54] In addition, when Dionysius discusses the three numbers — singular (ἑνικός), dual (δυικός), plural (πληθυντικός) — he uses the name "Homer" as his il-

---

49. For the text, see *Dionysii Thracis Ars grammatica*, G. Uhlig, ed., Grammatici graeci 1.1 (Leipzig: Teubner, 1883) 3–100; for English translation, see Alan Kemp, "The *Tekhnê Grammatikê* of Dionysius Thrax: English Translation with Introduction and Notes," *The History of Linguistics in the Classical Period*, ed. Daniel J. Taylor (Philadelphia: John Benjamins, 1987) 169–89.

50. Alfons Wouters, *The Grammatical Papyri from Graeco-Roman Egypt: Contributions to the Study of the 'Ars Grammatica' in Antiquity* (Brussels: Paleis der Academiën, 1979).

51. Dionysius Thrax *Ars grammatica* 11 (23, 1–2 [Uhlig]).

52. See *Commentarius Melampodis seu Diomedis in artis Dionysianne* 11 (in *Scholia in Dionysii Thracis artem grammaticam*, A. Hilgard, ed., Grammatici graeci 3 ([Leipzig: Teubner, 1901] 58 and 16–19); cf. also Robins, *Byzantine Grammarians*, 59.

53. Dionysius Thrax *Ars grammatica* 12 (25, 3–26, 1 [Uhlig]).

54. Dionysius Thrax *Ars grammatica* 12 (26, 7–27, 1 [Uhlig]).

lustration: Ὅμηρος, τὼ Ὁμήρω, and οἱ Ὅμηροι.[55] Finally, there are five cases for nouns: nominative (ὀρθή), genitive (γενική), dative (δοτική), accusative (αἰτιατική), and vocative (κλητική) (31, 5–6), and, although Dionysius gives no illustrations, one papyrus of the fifth or sixth century declines the Homeric names ὁ Πρίαμος and ἡ Ἑκάβη in all cases and numbers.[56]

Many other documentary texts confirm the illustrative use of Homer in grammatical instruction. To cite but one example: a third-century wooden book, made up of eight tablets,[57] contains, among various grammatical subjects, a lengthy classification of nouns (ὀνόματα) and many Homeric names as illustrations, for example lines 281–89:

> Proper noun (κύριον ὄνομα): for example, Ἀγαμέμνων, Ἀλέξανδρος, Μενέλαος, Ἀχιλλεύς, Ὀδυσσεύς, Σθενέλαος.
>
> Patronymic noun (πατρωνυμικὸν ὄνομα): for example, Πηλείδης, Πηλείων, Ἀτρείων, Νεστορίδης, Πριαμίδης, Δευκαλίδης, Τελαμώνιος.
>
> Possessive noun (κλητικὸν ὄνομα): for example, Νηλήιος ἵππος, Ὀδυσσήιος οἶκος, Ἀχιλλήια ὅπλα

To sum up: As in the primary curriculum, so also at the secondary stage Homer played an important role, and not only as the principal text for reading, memorization, and exposition but also as a ready source of illustrations for grammatical analysis. What is more, the grammatical use of Homer, like the literary, carried over into adulthood where facility with Homer was expected and frequently demonstrated. For the literary use I am reminded of Lucian's *Symposium* in which the Cynic philosopher Alcidamas came uninvited to Aristaenetus's symposium and tried to smooth over the awkwardness of his arrival by citing part of a line from Homer: "But Menelaus came on his own" (*Iliad* 2.408). The narrator Lycinus adds, however, that no one else at the symposium was amused by this citation, for he notes that another part of that very line was also applicable, namely, that Alcidamas, like Menelaus, was "good at the war-cry" (*Iliad* 2.408), referring to the Cynic's unwelcome barking on virtue. In addition, the other guests quoted other lines from

---

55. Dionyisus Thrax Ars *grammatica* 12 (30, 5–31, 1 [Uhlig]).

56. PSI inv. 479 (=C 372), published by Giorgio Zalateo, et al., "Papiri Fiorentini inediti," *Aegyptus* 20 (1940) 12–14, esp. 13.

57. Brit.Mus.Add. 37533 (=C 385), published by F. G. Kenyon, "Two Greek School-Tablets," *JHS* 29 (1909) 29–40, esp. 32–39; cf. Ziebarth, *Aus der antiken Schule*, 24–29, esp. 27–28.

Homer to express their disapproval of his arrival that were appropriate or at least witty. One guest quoted part of another line: "You are a fool, Menelaus" (*Iliad* 7.109), and another guest added yet another, "But Agamemnon, Atreus's son, was sorely vexed" (*Iliad* 1.24).[58] Alcidamas' lack of welcome and acceptance is made apparent with Homeric tags.

The culture of secondary or grammatical education, however, is nowhere more apparent than in Athenaeus's *Deipnosophistae*. The host in Athenaeus's work is the Roman aristocrat Larensis, himself a keen lover of Homer;[59] indeed, he was nicknamed Asteropaeus after his Homeric namesake because, as Asteropaeus could throw spears with either arm (cf. *Iliad* 21.163–64), so Larensis could cite Greek and Latin literature with equal facility.[60] Larensis' symposia included nine γραμματικοί, and the conversations that fill Athenaeus's pages are primarily grammatical, concerned with questions about spelling, accent, gender, case, and etymology, with many questions settled by appeal to Homer.[61]

But Larensis also refers to grammatical matters of a more lighthearted nature. He speaks of one guest reciting a line from Homer at random and the one reclining next to him having to recite the next line, he in turn doing the same for the one next to him, and so on.[62] In another instance guests were asked to recite Homeric lines beginning and ending with α (*Iliad* 4.92; 5.226, 543), or beginning and ending with ε (*Iliad* 4.89; 5.686), or with η (*Iliad* 5.133, 370), or with ι (*Iliad* 6.60, 206), and so forth;[63] or they were asked to cite lines where the first and last syllables formed a proper name, as in *Iliad* 2.557: Αι plus Αἴας= (10.458d); or a utensil (*Iliad* 8.202: ολ plus μος = ὅλμος [mortar]), or a food (*Iliad* 1.538: αρ plus τος = ἄρτος [bread]).[64]

In short, this facility with Homer — varied, profound, and nearly absolute — had started with lists of words at primary school, was broadened throughout the secondary curriculum, and then was displayed throughout life at symposia like those of Aristaenetus and Larensis.

---

58. Lucian *Symposium* 12.
59. Athenaeus 14.620b.
60. Athenaeus 1.2c; 4.160c and 6.273a-274e.
61. For details on the character and pervasiveness of grammatical discussions in Athenaeus, see Ronald F. Hock, "A Dog in the Manger: The Cynic Cynulcus among Athenaeus' Deipnosophists," in David L. Balch et al., eds., *Greeks, Romans, and Christians: Essays in Honor of Abraham J. Malherbe* (Minneapolis: Fortress Press, 1990) 20–37, esp. 28–31.
62. Athenaeus 10.457e.
63. Athenaeus 10.458a-d.
64. Athenaeus 10.458d-f.

Clearly, such facility was a social marker, separating, as Morgan puts it, "the better from the less well educated,"[65] not to mention the opportunities to turn facility with Homer into a way of bettering even one's social superiors, as shown in a schoolroom chreia in which Alexander rebuked a sleeping Diogenes with a Homeric line: "To sleep all night ill-suits a counselor" (*Iliad* 2.24), to which the Cynic philosopher turned the rebuke around by quoting the next line when barely awake: "On whom the folk relies whose cares are many" (*Iliad* 2.25).[66] Now that's grammatical facility, to have Homer on one's lips on awakening!

## HOMER IN TERTIARY EDUCATION

To return to the classroom: Once students had finished their studies under a γραμματικός and had increased and deepened their knowledge of the Homeric epics, they moved on to the tertiary stage of education, usually rhetoric or philosophy.[67] Their study of literature was expected to continue, however, in part because having quotations from Homer and other poets readily at hand would prove useful when making speeches, as Quintilian says, and hence his confidence that students will read Homer more than once.[68]

At any rate, most young men chose rhetoric — indeed, overwhelmingly so[69] — and went to a ῥήτωρ or σοφιστής to learn the rules and study the models for composing and delivering the three types of public speech: the judicial speech (δικανικός), the advisory speech (συμβουλευτικός), and the celebratory speech (ἐπιδεικτικός).[70] Skill at delivering these speeches, it was presumed, was paramount in preparing them for carrying out their eventual adult responsibilities of managing households and governing cities.[71]

---

65. Morgan, *Literary Education*, 170–71.

66. P.Osl. III, 177 (not in Cribiore), restored and published by Jean Lenaerts, "Fragment d'Analecta sur Diogène (P.Osl. III, 177)," *CdÉ* 49 (1974) 121–23. This chreia also shows up in Epictetus's schoolroom (3.22.92).

67. On tertiary education, see further Marrou, *Education*, 186–216.

68. Quintilian 1.8.5, 12.

69. On the dominance of rhetoric over philosophy, see Marrou, *Education*, 194–96. Note that even students at Epictetus's Stoic school in Nicopolis are assumed to have had prior instruction in rhetoric (see 2.2.7, 24.24–26, and 3.1.1 and 34).

70. The division of speeches into three γένη goes back to Aristotle (see *Rhetoric* 1.3.3–5) and the Stoics and soon became conventional.

71. On rhetorical education, see further Marrou, *Education*, 194–205, and Bonner, *Education*, 277–327.

For students to begin immediately to compose judicial, advisory, or celebrative speeches, however, would be, to use Theon's apt comparison, much like learning the potter's craft by starting with a πίθος, or huge storage jar.[72] Better to begin with shorter, simpler compositions that nonetheless taught the basics of rhetorical argumentation and style. Such pre-rhetorical compositions, called προγυμνάσματα, provided this intermediary step and hence prepared students for the greater complexities of rhetorical composition.[73]

We thus begin our discussion of the rhetorical curriculum with the *progymnasmata*, paying special attention to any role that Homer might have had at this stage of education. Four examples of *progymnasmata* are extant, written from the late first to the fifth century, those by Theon of Alexandria, Hermogenes of Tarsus, Aphthonius of Antioch, and Nicolaus of Myra.[74] Aphthonius's became the standard text with fourteen exercises, arranged in a graded series of increasing length, complexity, and difficulty. Students began with the easiest *progymnasmata*, the μῦθος, the διήγημα, the χρεία, and the γνώμη. But even here students were already learning specifically rhetorical lessons. As John Doxapatres, a Byzantine commentator on Aphthonius, says, the various *progymnasmata* provide preliminary instruction in the three types of speech. Specifically, he says that the skills learned in composing μῦθοι or chreia elaborations will be useful later when writing advisory speeches; the skills learned in composing an ἀνασκευή or κατασευή will be helpful when writing judicial speeches; and the skills learned in composing an ἐγκώμιον, ψόγος, or κοινὸς τόπος will aid in writing celebratory

---

72. Theon *Progymnasmata* 1, *Rhetores graeci*, Christian Walz, ed. (9 vols.; Stuttgart: Cottae, 1832–1836) 1.146, 3–6.

73. The best discussion of the *progymnasmata* is Herbert Hunger, *Die hochsprachliche profane Literatur der Byzantiner*, Handbuch der Altertumswissenschaft 12.5.1–2 (Munich: Beck, 1978) 1.92–120. See also Otmar Schissel, "Rhetorische Progymnasmatik der Byzantiner," *BNGJ* 11 (1934–35) 1–11, and George Alexander Kennedy, *Greek Rhetoric under Christian Emperors* (Princeton: Princeton University Press, 1983) 54–66.

74. For the text of Theon, see Walz, *Rhetores graeci*, 1.145–257; for Hermogenes, see *Hermogenis opera*, Hugo Rabe, ed., Rhetores graeci 6 (Stuttgart: Teubner, 1913) 1–27; for Aphthonius, see *Aphthonii progymnasmata*, Hugo Rabe, ed., Rhetores graeci 10 (Leipzig: Teubner, 1926) 1–51; and for Nicolaus, see *Nicolai progymnasmata*, Joseph Felton, ed., Rhetores graeci 11 (Leipzig: Teubner, 1913). For introductory discussions of these *progymnasmata*, see Ronald F. Hock and Edward O'Neil, eds., *The Chreia in Ancient Rhetoric. Vol. 1. The Progymnasmata*, SBLTT 27 (Atlanta: Scholars Press, 1986) 10–22 (on *progymnasmata*), 63–66 (on Theon), 155–60 (on Hermogenes), 211–16 (on Aphthonius), and 237–39 (on Nicolaus).

speeches.[75] Likewise, the *progymnasmata* prepare students to compose the four parts of a speech. For example, Doxapatres says: "Just as the task of the introduction is to make the audience attentive to what will be said in the narrative, so the task of (composing) a μῦθος is to prepare the audience for accepting the ἐπιμύθιον, or moral, of the μῦθος."[76]

But while the focus in the *progymnasmata* was thus rhetorical, it is also clear that literature and Homer in particular were not forgotten. Indeed, a perusal of the four extant *progymnasmata* shows that Homer was once again very much in use for illustrations, models, and subject matter. A brief review of the *progymnasmata* will clearly demonstrate the continuing use of Homer in the tertiary curriculum.

Students made special use of Homer in three individual *progymnasmata*: the διήγημα, the γνώμη, and the ἠθοποιία. First, in the διήγημα-chapter Homer is regularly used to illustrate a distinction between διήγημα and διήγησις. Students were already familiar from their secondary training with a distinction between διήγημα and διήγησις. Hence they knew that a ποίημα is a portion of a ποίησις, or a larger poetic work, so that the preparation of Achilles' weapons in *Iliad* 18 is a ποίημα of a larger poetic work, or ποίησις, namely the *Iliad*. Accordingly, a διήγημα is a specific incident and a διήγησις the entire narrative.[77]

Theon's discussion of the διήγημα also refers to Homer, but now as a model of narrative style. For example, he illustrates the rule that a speaker should narrate concisely whenever events are likely to distress an audience by referring to the brevity of Homer's narration of a distressful occasion — Achilles' learning of Patroclus's death. Homer merely says: "Patroclus lies dead (κεῖται Πάτροκλος)" (*Iliad* 18.20). The converse, Theon says, is also true, that a speaker should be expansive when events are cheerful, a rule illustrated again by Homer, who has Odysseus narrate his adventures after leaving Troy in great detail and at leisure for the Phaeacians (*Odyssey* 7–13).[78] Finally, Theon says that it is possible to begin a narrative in the middle, return to the beginning and then move to the end, as Homer does in the *Odyssey*.[79]

---

75. Doxapatres 2.125, 3–126, 6 (Walz).
76. Doxapatres 2.125, 15–19 (Walz).
77. Aphthonius *Progymnasmata* 2 (2.16–18 [Rabe]). See also Nicolaus *Progymnasmata* 3 (12.2–6 [Felten]), and Hermognenes *Progymnasmata* 2 (4.10–13 [Rabe]); the latter identifies three ποιήματα: the ἀσπιδοποιία (*Iliad* 18), the νεκυομαντεία (*Odyssey* 11), and the μνηστηροφονία (*Odyssey* 22).
78. Theon *Progymnasmata* 4 (1.184, 4–9 [Walz]).
79. Theon *Progymnasmata* 4 (1.193, 3–15 [Walz]).

Homer is especially prominent in a second *progymnasma,* the γνώμη, where he is often cited to illustrate various kinds of maxims. Aphthonius, for example, uses lines from Homer to illustrate five of the eight kinds of maxims in his classification system:

> Protreptic (προτρεπτικόν): "One should welcome a stranger when he arrives and send him on when he wishes to go" (*Odyssey* 15.74).
>
> Apotreptic (ἀποτρεπτικόν): "To sleep all night ill-suits a counselor" (*Iliad* 2.24).
>
> Simple (ἁπλοῦν): "The one best omen is to fight for one's country" (*Iliad* 12.243).
>
> Compound (συνεζευγμένον): "Many kings is not a good thing; let there be one king" (*Iliad* 2.204).
>
> Hyperbolic (ὑπερβολικόν): "The earth nourishes nothing weaker than a human" (*Odyssey* 18.130).[80]

Hermogenes likewise cites the same apotreptic γνώμη (*Iliad* 2.24), but he also goes on to make this γνώμη the subject of his sample elaboration, and in the process refers again to Homer, specifically to Hector's refusal to sleep while Dolon is sent to spy out the Greek ships (*Iliad* 10.299–336) in the παράδειγμα-section of this elaboration.[81] Likewise, Aphthonius refers to the beggar Irus (*Odyssey* 18.1–116) in the παράδειγμα-section of his sample elaboration of a line from Theognis.[82] In other words, the Homeric epics were an important source for students both when they classified the γνῶμαι and when they elaborated them.

The third *progymnasma,* an advanced exercise called ἠθοποιία, offered students even more scope for displaying their knowledge of the Homeric epics. Students were asked in this exercise to write a speech that might have been spoken by someone on a certain occasion.[83] Theon, for example, says that many subjects for this exercise are taken from Homer.[84] A check of the extant *progymnasmata* proves Theon right. In Hermogenes, for example, one finds these suggested topics: What words Andromache might say to Hector and what words Achilles might say to

---

80. Aphthonius *Progymnasmata* 4 (7.7–8, 2 [Rabe]). See also Hermogenes *Progymnasmata* 4 (8.18–19, 9.15 and 17 [Rabe]), and Nicolaus *Progymnasmata* 5 (26.10–12, 27.8–9 and 20–21, 27.22–28.1, and 28.5–6 [Felten]).

81. Hermogenes *Progymnasmata* 4·(9.18–10.21, esp. 10.18–20 [Rabe]).

82. Aphthonius *Progymnasmata* 4 (9.16–10.2 [Rabe]).

83. For full discussion of this exercise, both the theoretical aspects of it and the many sample ἠθοποιίαι, see Hunger, *Literatur,* 1.108–16.

84. Theon *Progymnasmata* 2 (1.164, 6–7 [Walz]).

Deidamia as he was about to go out to war.[85] Aphthonius suggests these: What words Hecuba might say as Troy lay in ruins and what words Achilles might say over a dead Patroclus as he deliberates about going to war.[86] And Nicolaus adds these: What words Agamemnon might say as Troy fell, what words Andromache might say when Hector died, what words Achilles might say after Patroclus's death, and what words Peleus might say on hearing of Achilles' death.[87]

But in addition to these suggested topics for composing ἠθοποιίαι that involve Homeric subjects, there are also many fully worked out ἠθοποιίαι in the various collections of sample progymnasmata. The earliest collections that we possess are those from the late fourth century by Libanius of Antioch[88] and, shortly afterwards, by his student, Severus of Alexandria.[89] Libanius's sample ἠθοποιίαι include several on Homeric subjects, and while not all twenty-seven ἠθοποιίαι in the Libanian corpus are genuine,[90] six of the eight genuine ones do treat Homeric subjects: What words Andromache might say to Hector, what words Achilles might say over a fallen Patroclus, what words Achilles might say as the Greeks were being out-fought, what words Achilles might say after losing Briseïs, what words Menelaus might say on learning of the death of Agamemnon, and what words Odysseus might say while held in the cave of the Cyclops. Incidentally, those not by Libanius but still addressing Homeric topics are: What words Odysseus

85. Hermogenes *Progymnasmata* 9 (20.7–8, 22–23 [Rabe]).

86. Aphthonius *Progymnasmata* 11 (35.3–4, 8–9 [Rabe]).

87. Nicolaus *Progymnasmata* 10 (64.10–12 and 16–18, and 65.21–66.1 [Felten]).

88. For Libanius's extensive collection of sample *progymnasmata*, see *Libanii opera* 11 vols.; Richard Foerster, ed., Bibliotheca scriptorum graecorum et romanorum teubneriana (Leipzig: Teubner, 1903–1927) 8.1–571. For discussion of them, especially regarding the question of authenticity, see Richard Foerster and Karl Münscher, "Libanios," *RE* 12.2 (1925) 2485–551, esp. 2518–22.

89. A collection of six διηγήματα and eight ἠθοποιίαι attributed to a Severus (see Walz 1.537–48) had long been assigned to a Roman of this name who was *consul ordinarius* in 470 (so, e.g., Wilhelm von Christ and Wilhelm Schmid, *Geschichte der griechischen Literatur*, Handbuch der Altertumswissenschaft 7.2.2 [Munich: Beck, 1924] 1027). Then, thanks to the detective work of Otmar Schissel, this collection has been reassigned to another Severus, Libanius's student Severus of Alexandria ("Severus von Alexandreia. Ein verschollener griechischer Schriftsteller des IV. Jahrhunderts n. Chr.," *BNGJ* 8 [1929–30]: 1–13, esp. 1–3). This identification has been accepted (see, e.g., K. Gerth, "Severos von Alexandreia," *RE Sup* 8 [1956] 715–18, and Hunger, *Literatur*, 1.110). See also Paul Petit, *Les étudiants de Libanius* (Paris: Nouvelles Éditions Latines, 1956) 25, 62, 64, 81, 155, and 187.

90. Foerster and Münscher, "Libanius," 2520–21.

might say as he watched Cyclops eating his comrades and what words
Odysseus might say while he was slaying the suitors.[91]

Severus follows his teacher's lead with four of his eight ἠθοποιίαι on
Homeric subjects: What words Menelaus might say when Alexander ab-
ducted Helen, what words Briseïs might say as she was being led away
by the heralds, what words Hector might say in Hades on hearing that
Priam was eating with Achilles, and what words Achilles might say in
Hades on hearing that Pyrrhus was plundering Troy.[92]

Clearly here, if anywhere among the *progymnasmata*, students needed
to have a broad and detailed knowledge of Homer, for the temporal
structure of an ἠθοποιία required knowledge not only of the immedi-
ate circumstances that prompted the speech, but also of the events that
preceded it and the consequences that might follow from it.[93] Hence students might well have to make use of several passages from Homer and
perhaps related material in other literature and tradition.

One example should suffice to illustrate the familiarity with Homer
that was needed to compose an ἠθοποιία. Indeed, even the shortest of
the ἠθοποιίαι by Severus — the one referred to above in which he imagines what Briseïs might have said as she was being led away by the
heralds — will display this familiarity. But first a translation of this
ἠθοποιίαι to aid in the analysis.[94] Briseïs says:

> After the destruction of my country, after the slaying of my king, after
> so great a series of misfortunes I am a captive again for the second time.
> The Greeks waged war against us, and I became a captive. Greeks turned
> against Greeks, and so I am being led away to slavery. And if, it seems,
> only death will liberate me, my life as a slave will never cease.

This ἠθοποιίαι follows the temporal structure prescribed in the *progymnasmata* in which the basic structure is temporal and in this sequence: present, past, future.[95] Thus Briseïs' speech begins with the
present situation of her being made a captive for the second time. She

91. For the texts of these ἠθοποιίαι, see Foerster, *Libanii opera* 8.376–84, 408–11, 421–23
and 425–34.

92. Severus 1.543–46 (Walz).

93. For the formal structure of the ἠθοποιίαι, see Aphthonius *Progymnasmata* 10 (35,
13–14 [Rabe]), and Hunger, *Literatur*, 108–9.

94. For the text, see 1.544, 11–19 (Walz). A new critical edition of this text, though
it is unchanged from Walz's, was made by one of Schissel's students: Fr. P. Karnthaler
("Severus von Alexandreia," 327–30, esp. 327).

95. The temporal structure is indicated by the shift in the tenses of the principal verbs from present (γίνομαι) to past (ἐστρατεύετο, γεγόνασι) to future (ἐλευθερώσει,

is referring to the moment when the heralds of Agamemnon, Talthybius and Eurybates, come to Achilles' tent to take her away to become Agamemnon's concubine (cf. *Iliad* 1.320–48).

Then Briseïs turns to the past when she was made a captive for the first time, recalling when the Greeks, led by Achilles, had attacked her city of Lyrnessus; killed her husband, king Mynes, and her family; and led her off as a captive (cf. 19.291–96). Then she recalls the more recent past when Greeks turned against Greeks. Agamemnon, forced by Achilles to return Chryseïs to her father Chryses, a priest of Apollo, in order to end a plague caused by Apollo in reaction to Agamemnon's arrogant dismissal of his priest's offer of ransom, tries to recoup his loss of Chryseïs by demanding that Achilles give him Briseïs in her stead (cf. 1.8–474), a turn of events, as everyone knows, that initiates the main events of the *Iliad* as a whole: Achilles, in anger, refuses to fight any longer against the Trojans and consequently sits idly while the Greeks are nearly overrun and defeated.

Finally, Briseïs looks ahead to a grim future of slavery where only death can emancipate her. This emphasis on slavery reflects her assumption that she will be merely a slave-concubine of Agamemnon, whereas previously Patroclus had told her that Achilles was planning to marry her on his return home from Troy (19.298–99). Short as it is, this ἠθοποιία uses various parts of the *Iliad* and alludes to even more.

Elsewhere in the *progymnasmata* Homer is less in evidence, or missing altogether (as in the chapters on the μῦθος, ἀνασκευή, κατασκευή, and νόμου εἰσφαρά). Still, a few more references will help to underscore the presence of Homer at this point in the tertiary curriculum. In addition, Theon illustrates a form of elaboration called ἐπιφώνησις, in which a chreia is confirmed by four arguments that establish its truth, nobility, advantage, and conformity with what other men of distinction have said. The example is: The poet Euripides said that the mind of each of us is a god, and Homer is cited as being in conformity with this sentiment, in these lines: "The mind of earthly men is like the day / Which the father of men and gods brings on" (*Odyssey* 18.136–37).[96]

We have now seen that the compositional skills taught in the *progymnasmata* looked ahead to the skills needed to compose speeches, but

---

παύσεται). For fuller analysis of this ἠθοποιία, see Hunger, *Literatur*, 1.110, and esp. Karnthaler, "Severus von Alexandreia," 328–30.

96. Theon *Progymnasmata* 5 (1.212, 12–213, 2 [Walz]).

the *progymnasmata* also required students to continue to look back to their grammatical training by having to reread Homer for lines to cite and subjects to treat.

When students finished the *progymnasmata,* they turned to rhetoric proper, to the task of learning to compose and deliver the three kinds of speeches. In the rhetorical handbooks, however, familiarity with, and admiration of, Homer are assumed, whether we look at Aristotle or at Hermogenes,[97] with the latter calling Homer not only the best of poets but also the best of orators.[98] Still, it must be admitted, at least for later rhetorical handbooks, that Demosthenes is far more important than Homer as a model for style and subject matter. Indeed, in the rhetorical handbook of Rufus of Perinthus, late second century C.E., Demosthenes is quoted 20 times, Homer never.[99] In addition, a perusal of the themes for declamation among Philostratus's sophists, for example, shows that historical rather than heroic subjects were preferred.[100] To cite only one example, Polemo is reported to have declaimed on a number of themes, all historical: Demosthenes swears that he did not accept a bribe of fifty talents, as Demades had alleged; the Greeks should take down their τρόπαια after the Peloponnesian war; Xenophon decides to die after the execution of Socrates; and Demosthenes advises the Athenians to flee on their triremes at the approach of Philip.[101] Polemo's two extant declamations are likewise historical, being burial speeches for two Greeks who died at Marathon, Cynegrius and Callimachus.[102]

Still, the role of Homer is far from absent among rhetors and sophists, for, to judge from anecdotes in Philostratus, Homer was often on their lips, as the example of Polemo will again show. Thus when Smyrna

---

97. See Aristotle *Rhetoric* 1.6.20–25, 7.33, 11.9 and 12, and 15.13, passim; and Hermogenes *On Ideas* 1.11 (279.23–26 [Rabe]), 2.10 (392.7–395.2) passim.

98. Hermogenes *On Ideas* 2.10 (389.25–27 [Rabe]).

99. For the text of this rhetorical handbook, see *Rhetores graeci,* Leonardi Spengel and C. Hammer, eds. (3 vols.; Leipzig: Teubner, 1884) 1.2.399–407. On Rufus and his handbook, see Otmar Schissel, "Die rhetorische Kunstlehre des Rufus von Perinthos," *RhM* 75 (1926) 369–92, and Walter Ameling, "Der Sophist Rufus," *EA* 6 (1985) 27–33. Demosthenes clearly dominates Homer in two other Roman handbooks, that known as the Anonymous Seguieranus and that by Apsines, whose texts have been recently edited and translated (see *Two Greek Rhetorical Treatises from the Roman Empire,* Melvin R. Dilts and George A. Kennedy, eds., Mnemosyne Supplementum 168 [Leiden: Brill, 1997]).

100. On sophistic declamation, see Donald Andrew Russell, *Greek Declamation* (New York: Cambridge University Press, 1983).

101. Philostratus *Vitae sophistarum* 542–43.

102. William Reader, *The Severed Hand and the Upright Corpse: The Declamations of Marcus Antonius Polemo,* SBLTT 42 (Atlanta: Scholars Press, 1996).

needed to send an ambassador, and the city's principal sophist Scopelian was too old to go, a young Polemo was elected. The latter prayed that the persuasion of Scopelian might become his, then hugged Scopelian before the assembly, and aptly added two lines comparing himself to Patroclus's going to fight in place of Achilles: "Allow me to put your armor on my shoulders, so that the Trojans may take me for you" (*Iliad* 16.40–41).[103] Years later, when the sophist Herodes Atticus was asked by Marcus Aurelius what he thought of the now mature Polemo, Herodes quoted Homer: "The sound of swift-footed horses strikes me on both ears (*Iliad* 10.535)," indicating thereby how resonant and far-echoing were Polemo's speeches.[104] Finally, long after Polemo had died, the sophist Hippodromus, when he was being praised and even being compared to Polemo, recoiled from the comparison with a Homeric line: "Why do you compare me with the immortals?" (*Odyssey* 16.187).[105] In other words, whether it was his self-concept, his oratory, or his subsequent reputation, Polemo presented himself or was regarded by others in Homeric terms. What is more, Hippodromus expanded the Homeric mantle to all sophists when he, after some sophist had said that the mother of sophists was tragedy, corrected him by saying that Homer was their father.[106]

## CONCLUSION

The Homeric epics, then, were part of the curriculum in all three stages of Greco-Roman education. Indeed, Homer's role in education was varied, continuous, and profound: names from Homer were some of the first words students ever learned, lines from Homer were some of the first sentences they ever read, lengthy passages from Homer were the first they ever memorized and interpreted, events and themes from Homer were the ones they often treated in compositional exercises, and lines and metaphors from Homer were often used to adorn their speeches and to express their self-presentation. Indeed, for the rest of their lives, those who had been educated, πεπαιδευμένοι, were expected to have Homer on their lips for capturing and articulating the essence of a moment or the character of a person, even when half asleep.

---

103. Philostratus *Vitae sophistarum* 521.
104. Philostratus *Vitae sophistarum* 539.
105. Philostratus *Vitae sophistarum* 616.
106. Philostratus *Vitae sophistarum* 620.

# 4

## Pagan Traditions of Intertextuality in the Roman World

### Ellen Finkelpearl

As the sole conference participant trained solely in classics and not in the study of early Christian texts, but as someone who has been thinking about what this conference calls "intertextuality" for most of my academic career, I feel that my role is to discuss the classical backgrounds of the process of literary appropriation. I will not discuss so much the persistence and universality of imitation, which I take as a given, as the particular ways that imitation is played out in just four passages in Apuleius. Apuleius is an appropriate classical non-Christian point of reference since he was born around 123 C.E. and writes about philosophy and religion, even if he does so in often comic and problematic ways. His novel, the *Metamorphoses,* is subtly intertextual with a wide variety of works, both Greek and Latin.[1] Yet, before discussing these examples of literary borrowing, I will step back and ask some of the questions that I first asked myself about allusion and that others constantly ask me. Some attention to methodology is needed as a supplement to our various discussions of particular passages.

Therefore, I would like to revisit various points of view in current classical scholarship, mostly those of Latinists, on such questions as how one distinguishes an "allusion" from "mere" topos or commonplace; what sorts of terms are used for the practice and what nuances of critical approach are implied by the variation in terms; what sorts of issues do we need to consider when poetry is transferred into prose; and, finally, what sorts of interrelationships can we expect between the source text and its descendant? Throughout my discussion, my aim is to

---

1. For a full discussion of Apuleius's use of his Latin literary models in the *Metamorphoses,* see Ellen Finkelpearl, *Metamorphosis of Language in Apuleius: A Study of Allusion in the Novel* (Ann Arbor: University of Michigan Press, 1998) with bibliography. Other discussions may be found in Stavros A. Frangoulidis, "Epic Inversion in Apuleius' Tale of Tlepolemus/Haemus," *Mnemosyne* 45 (1992) 60–74, and Stephen J. Harrison, "Some Odyssean Scenes in Apuleius' *Metamorphoses.*" *Materiali e discussioni,* 25 (1990) 193–201.

complicate and disorient rather than to clarify. I begin with three examples from Apuleius's *Apology* and *Florida* in which the author is explicit about literary appropriation, and move on to a more intricate instance from the Isiac portion of the *Metamorphoses*. I have deliberately chosen examples from Apuleius involving philosophy and religion in the hope that I will better intersect with the rest of the papers in the conference.

In the first place, and this is a more elusive process than it might first appear, the critic must locate and defend each instance of alleged literary borrowing. How do we distinguish between an author's conscious evocation of a particular source and a chance combination of words, images, or concepts? If the author of the Gospel of Mark mentions sea voyages, how do we really know whether he is referring to the *Odyssey* or rather to the many sea voyages that humans everywhere commonly take? On a linguistic level, if Apuleius uses the phrase *validis viribus*, "with great strength," how do I decide whether he is referring to a particular place in the *Aeneid* or whether this was simply a common phrase used all over Latin literature or even was common in the streets of the Roman world? When do "flames of love" become an allusion to a specific text rather than a generic part of the tradition of love poetry? Many classicists, perhaps the vast majority, who work on literary influence are strict philologists who argue that allusions have to be proved. An often cited proponent of this approach, Kathleen Morgan, in a book on Ovid's imitations of Propertius says: "Only by establishing philological criteria for imitation can the pitfalls created by the thematic traditions of the genre be avoided."[2] Among classicists, the criteria tend to be linguistic. Critics therefore scour concordances, grammars, and the *Thesaurus linguae latinae* for concrete evidence that vocabulary, grammatical or rhetorical construction, or confluence of words is unique to the source text and imitator to be sure that they have located a "true" allusion.

More recently, scholars have asked whether writers and language work in quite this way. The Italian scholar, Gianbiagio Conte, in *The Rhetoric of Imitation*, has addressed these questions in particular through the concept of "poetic memory," that is, language itself, and especially literary or poetic language, already contains within it the memory of previous texts:

---

2. Kathleen E. Morgan, *Ovid's Art of Imitation: Propertius and the Amores*, Mnemosyne Supplementum (Leiden: Brill, 1977) 3.

Readers or imitators (also a type of reader) who approach the text are themselves already a plurality of texts and of different codes, some present and some lost or dissolved in that indefinite and generic fluid of literary language. Intertextuality, far from being a matter of merely recognizing the ways which specific texts echo each other, defines the condition of literary readability.[3]

Conte emphasizes the relationship between texts and downplays the role of the writer as conscious imitator. It is this approach that should properly be called "intertextuality," in which one examines the texts and not the writer's assumed intent. I will discuss the different terms below.

Another scholar, Stephen Hinds, in a new book that faces these contradictions head-on, particularly reacts against what he calls "philological fundamentalism." Hinds pushes the boundaries of what he sees as defensible as an allusion by examining especially its context and the relationship of source text and imitating text. At his most provocative, he argues that the phrase "me miserum!" although frequent in literature and on the streets of Rome, may be an allusion to Catullus by Propertius given the centrality of Catullus's work for the later poet. The fact that Propertius is constantly and self-consciously aware of Catullus changes the way these common words may be read.[4] Conte, in a similar vein, supports the centrality of the "code model"; e.g., Homer for Vergil, in consideration of intertextuality, perhaps not an issue for Christian appropriation of non-Christian texts.[5] Hinds agrees with Conte to a degree on the limitations of philological proof in the investigation of allusion, but he emphasizes the role of the author: "There is no getting away from the fact that the production of a poetic text is, in some very important ways, a private, self-reflexive, even solipsistic activity; and even the poet's dialogue with the work of other poets can be a very private, solipsistic kind of dialogue."[6]

There is often little agreement, then, on the methodology behind identifying an allusion. In my own view, however, all of the approaches here summarized must be taken into account. One must make some at-

---

3. Gian Biagio Conte, *The Rhetoric of Imitation: Genre and Poetic Memory in Vergil and other Poets,* Charles Segal, ed., Cornell Studies in Classical Philology 44 (Ithaca: Cornell University Press, 1986) 29.

4. Stephen Hinds, *Allusion and Intertext: Dynamics of Appropriation in Roman Poetry,* Roman Literature and Its Contexts (New York: Cambridge University Press, 1998) 29–34.

5. Conte, *Imitation,* 29.

6. Hinds, *Allusion,* 49.

tempt to distinguish allusion from accidental confluence, yet one must also consider literary memory. I find myself more in agreement with Hinds about the role of the author than with Conte's insistence on the irresistible memory of poetic language, yet it seems to me both can occur in different instances. Surely, at times the author wishes allusions to be recognized, yet at other times he unconsciously evokes the language and motifs from the sources he has read.

Critics' approaches to allusions, or whatever they choose to call them, are intimately connected with the names by which they designate the process. None of these terms is really value-neutral; the term used in the title of our conference, "intertextuality," is, as I have said, one that emphasizes the interrelationships between texts rather than any putative authorial intent. At the other end of the critical spectrum stands the term "reference" coined by Richard Thomas to describe the very scholarly Latin use of a borrowed phrase to refer consciously back to its source and to comment implicitly upon it.[7] Thomas imagines the Latin writer quite deliberately crafting a response, perhaps with an open book beside him, to particular arcane details in the Greek source. In this vein, classicists often speak of "programmatic allusion"; an author evokes a particular earlier author's version of events with a word or two to announce allegiance to his poetics. My favored term, "allusion," similarly implies that the author was conscious of what he was doing, but permits more leeway in the interpretation; while Thomas' "reference" is a scholarly and solemn activity, "allusion" implies literary play and clever manipulation of the earlier text. "Imitation," ancient *imitatio*, is often used as a neutral term, as is "borrowing," but may imply a desire to emulate or equal the source text. In short, even in our choice of terms, we are implying something about our approach.[8]

Finally, and following on the previous questions, what are some of

---

7. Richard F. Thomas, "Catullus and the Polemics of Poetic Reference," *American Journal of Philology* 103 (1982) 144–64.

8. I have been randomly selective in my choice of representative writings on allusion by Latinists. Other important and useful discussions include Wendell Clausen, "Callimachus and Latin Poetry," *Greek, Roman and Byzantine Studies* 5 (1964) 181–96, David O. Ross, Jr., *Style and Tradition in Catullus*, Loeb Classical Monographs (Cambridge: Harvard University Press, 1969), Giuseppe Giangrande, " 'Arte allusiva' and Alexandrian Poetry," *Classical Quarterly* n.s. 17 (1967) 85–97, Alessandro Barchiesi, *La traccia del modello. Effetti omerici nella narrazione virgiliana*, Biblioteca di materiali e discussioni per l'analisi dei testi classici 1 (Pisa: Giardini, 1984), and Joseph Farrell, *Vergil's Georgics and the Traditions of Ancient Epic: The Art of Allusion in Literary History* (New York: Oxford University Press, 1991) 3–25.

the effects of "intertextuality" or "allusion"? If appropriation is conscious, why does one do it; if it is unconscious, what are its effects? It is here that I often find among classicists simplistic solutions and easy formulas applied to complex literary situations. One of the standard answers is that the new text is in constant competition with the old and is attempting to exceed its achievement; the ultimate goal of the referential poet is to create his own superior version. Harold Bloom, of course, is known for his eccentric formulation of the "anxiety of influence"; each new poet is in a kind of familial competition with the poets before him, and his poetry represents the anxiety of being constantly belated and attempting to swerve from the precursor text.[9] Another frequent explanation for the use of epic language is as ornament that demonstrates the learning of the borrowing writer.[10]

In the case of Apuleius, because his text follows the often comic travels of a donkey, his engagement with epic material is frequently seen as parodic. One critic calls Apuleius's practice of incorporating Homeric and Vergilian material "epic inversion," focusing on the comic reapplication of elevated themes.[11] There is no doubt that Apuleius and others who import epic into a lower literary medium can be parodic and that deflation and contrast can be the result, but I prefer a more nuanced reading that asks also how the new text permanently reshapes the old, and how the new text may reveal hidden correspondences and may involve a destabilization of the worlds both of the new and the old text. One non-classicist, Thomas Greene, in *The Light in Troy,* paradoxically emphasizes the dependence of the *old* text on the *new* to interpret it and reshape it for the present day. Literary allusion becomes a kind of literary criticism, exploring meanings available in the source text beyond the obvious. This notion of new texts incorporating and negotiating their way through the old texts is suggestive in the case of Christian narratives; does the new text altogether discard the values of the old, or does it not sometimes reshape and redefine those values and events in a non-oppositional way?

I would like to touch briefly on the ancient testimony about *imitatio* or *mimesis,* inasmuch as students of allusion always hope that the ancients themselves will offer some guidance about how to read literary appro-

---

9. Harold Bloom, *The Anxiety of Influence* (Oxford: Oxford University Press, 1973).
10. Harrison, "Odyssean Scenes," 193–201.
11. Frangoulidis, "Epic Inversion," 60–74.

priation. Others have already discussed the importance of imitation in rhetorical training as well as early education.[12] Dennis MacDonald has also mentioned the ancient distinction drawn between hidden and advertised imitation, a distinction raised in an often-cited anecdote in the Elder Seneca, describing Ovid's use of Vergil: "non surripiendi causa, sed palam mutuandi, hoc animo ut vellet agnosci" (Seneca *Suasoriae* 3.7: "not for the sake of stealing, but borrowing, with this intent: that he wanted it to be recognized"). The anecdote brings up both possibilities: theft and deliberate evocation. Quintilian and others recommend imitation and the transference of poetic language into prose, both as a way to improve one's own writing and as a way better to prove one's point; Horace refers to flitting around and gathering all the best models to patch together into a better whole (*Odes* 4.2).

Yet, all these references to the importance of imitation are of little use when it comes to examining a particular instance of borrowing, and here, as elsewhere, I find ancient literary criticism lagging behind the sophistication of their practice. In the Younger Seneca, however, one finally finds an admission that the process and effects of literary borrowing are much less concrete and definable than earlier discussions would have one believe. It is worth taking a close look at this passage because Seneca deliberately mystifies from several angles. In *Epistle* 84 Seneca imagines the writer wandering about like the bee who gathers material suitable for making honey, but then he enters a long digression in which he speculates on how bees make honey; some say they find it lying around in flowers or on the grass, but others say that the bees transform the delicate flower-substance by a kind of fermentation: "non sine quodam, ut ita dicam, fermento" (Seneca *Epistle* 84.3). One ought to imitate the bees, he concludes, taking ideas from reading, but also applying one's own genius. He compares the digestion of food: what one eats is transformed into sinew and blood, and so it should be also with those things "quibus aluntur ingenia...concoquamus illa" (*Epistle* 84.7: "those things by which our intellects are nourished...let us digest them"). Finally, Seneca advises the writer that he should be like the writer he emulates, as a son, not a copy, a "clone" we might say ("similem quomodo filium, non quomodo imaginem"). These images stress mysterious transformation, or metamorphosis, rather than copy-

---

12. See especially the discussions of Dennis MacDonald and Ronald Hock in this volume.

ing or stealing. In the case of the bee-image, it is significant that Seneca says that he does not know what is happening in the bee's innards. In this later period, then, there is greater emphasis on the ability of the individual to transform his models in indefinable ways and much more admission that intertextuality works in mysterious ways.[13]

I turn now to a few examples of linguistic appropriation in Apuleius's rhetorical works, the *Apology* and *Florida,* that represent an interesting middle ground between the kind of discussion above and the subtle and even questionable allusions seen in his *Metamorphoses* and in many of the works we have been discussing.[14] Here Apuleius, in a practice more associated with oratory, is overt about his borrowings, but in so doing he gives a glimpse into what he considers a legitimate transformation of another author's words. It turns out that he gives himself a broad license.

At *Florida* 2, an excerpt (as all of the *Florida* are) whose larger context is unknown, Apuleius describes Socrates sitting next to a beautiful but silent youth. Socrates turns to him and says, "Say something so that I can see you," indicating Socrates' interest in mental acuity rather than what is immediately before the eyes. Apuleius goes on to say that Socrates would not have agreed with the soldier in Plautus who said, "pluris est oculatus testis unus quam aurati decem" ("one eyewitness is worth more than ten earwitnesses"; *Truculentus* 489), but would have rewritten the line (converterat) to say, "pluris est auritus testis unus quam oculati decem" ("one earwitness is worth more than ten eyewitnesses"; *Florida* 2.3–4). He goes on to say that if the judgment of the eyes were the most important, the eagle would be the wisest creature on earth. In the rest of the excerpt he describes the eagle's flight and its ocular powers.

This excerpt is interesting in several, perhaps obvious, ways. First, Apuleius imagines Socrates rewriting Plautus and hence takes intertextuality out of all genre-boundaries or indeed time-boundaries; the earlier writer rewrites the later one. Moreover, he gives the fictionalized Socrates the right to misinterpret and metaphorize the original meaning

---

13. Much of the discussion of Seneca *Epistle* 84 is heavily indebted to Thomas M. Greene, *The Light in Troy: Imitation and Discovery in Renaissance Poetry* (New Haven: Yale University Press, 1982) 70–74.

14. Apuleius's *Apology* is a speech of self-defense against his in-laws' accusations that he attracted his wife, a wealthy widow, through magic. The speech is full of quotations from poetry and playful references to, e.g., the crocodile's tooth-cleaning habits. The *Florida* is a collection of flowery excerpts from Apuleius's entertaining speeches.

of Plautus's line. What the soldier in *Truculentus* said was quite straight-forward, but is bent to conform to Socratic philosophy. Apuleius goes on in the same part of the *Florida* to cite a line of Homer (*Iliad* 3.10) about dense fog, turning it into a statement about human short-sightedness: "profecto verissime poeta egregius dixit velut nebulam nobis ob oculos offusam nec cernere nos nisi intra lapidis iactum valere" (*Florida* 2.7: "Very truly the great poet said there is a cloud in front of our eyes and we cannot see farther than a stone's throw").

Apuleius also performs a radical yet explicit transformation on a Homeric phrase in his *Florida* excerpt discussing Pythagoras' expedition to the East (*Florida* 15). In this interesting passage, Pythagoras travels to Egypt and India and meets with sages who include the Brahmin (Bracmani) and Zoroaster, and he returns to his pupils with an appreciation of the importance of restrained silence:

> vir praesertim ingenio ingenti ac profecto super captum hominis animi augustior, primus philosophiae nuncupator et conditor, nihil prius discipulos suos docuit quam tacere, primaque apud eum meditatio sapienti futuro linguam omnem coercere, verbaque quae volantia poetae appellant, ea verba detractis pinnis intra murum candentium dentium premere. (*Florida* 15.23)

> (This man of particularly great genius and of an intelligence beyond human capacity to comprehend, the first founder and inventor of Philosophy, taught his pupils nothing before being silent, and his first exercise for those hoping to be wise was to restrain all their speech; the words which poets call "winged" he made them tear off their wings and keep them contained within the walls of their white teeth.)

In this passage, Apuleius combines and reinvents two Homeric phrases through someone else. Pythagoras (not Apuleius) is imagined as ma-nipulating the images of the winged word and the barrier of teeth (ἔπεα πτερόεντα and ἕρκος ὀδόντων) literalizing the meaning so that the words have physical wings that can be removed, resulting in si-lence — they can't fly out of the barrier of teeth (a very graphic and horrifying image). In other words, Apuleius feels free to attribute to Pythagoras an appropriation of epic material in a way that will support eastern-influenced Pythagorean philosophy.

Finally, another similar example occurs at *Apology* 22 where the phi-losopher Crates is described as giving up all his possessions in exchange for "peram et baculum," the satchel and staff associated with Cynic philosophers. He even made up a song (poem) about it, says Apuleius, "flexis ad hoc Homericis versibus" (bending/turning the Homeric verses to this use). The song goes: πήρη τις πόλις ἔστι μέσῳ ἐνί οἴνοπι τύφῳ (*Apology* 22.5: "a satchel is a city in the middle of the wine-dark smoke," i.e., the smoke which clouds our vision). Apuleius has changed the line from the description of Crete in the *Odyssey* ("Crete is a city in the midst of the wine-dark sea"; *Odyssey* 19.172).

All this is still quite straightforward and yet, I think, not exactly covered by the ancient critical descriptions of what happens in the process of literary appropriation. Theft versus open borrowing, making one's model better, making one's own work better by using models, parody of the source — none of these is an apt way to look at the process here represented. Only the idea of digestive metamorphosis seen in Seneca applies. In each of these three cases, Apuleius quite freely and openly represents a philosopher with an ideological agenda rewriting, reshaping, reinventing a poetic line in ways that comically, yet polemically, redesign the world in which these philosophers live. As the author controlling the mechanism of appropriation, Apuleius represents each philosopher as appropriating according to his own agenda; these philosophers do not even try to preserve the original meaning but feel free to make the lines say what they wish to say. The source text remains a visible sign of the norm against which the imitating text emphasizes its difference. Earlier literature remains an authority, if only a literary one, to be exploited by each of these imagined authors, yet the intersections of old and new represent the tension between the everyday bourgeois values implicit in the norm and the radical positions assumed by the philosophers. Surely this is the way much Christian appropriation of pre-Christian texts operates. It is rarer for pre- or non-Christian intertextuality to present such a difference in ideologies; more often the tensions are literary.

In my final example, one sees a more nuanced example of what Apuleius achieved in his allusive practice. Rather than wholesale irresponsible appropriation of another's words, here he employs a more subtle mixture of the literary and ideological, the acceptance and the rejection of the source text. An entirely different sort of appropriation is at work here; no longer does one find explicit borrowing and rewriting, but the more elusive type of alluding that I discussed at the beginning.

In Book 11 of the *Metamorphoses*, after Lucius has been transformed from a donkey into a human being and has been initiated into the rites of Isis, he lies prostrate, "murdering his speech and devouring his words," as he claims (11.24). Nonetheless, he speaks an eloquent alliterative and measured prayer to Isis, in which he claims to be inadequate to sing the magnitude of her majesty, and, in so doing, he alludes perhaps to Homer, Vergil, and others: "nec mihi vocis ubertas ad dicenda, quae de tua maiestate sentio, sufficit nec ora mille linguaeque totidem vel indefessi sermonis aeterna series" ("nor do I have the richness of voice to say what I feel about your majesty, nor are a thousand mouths enough and the same number of tongues or an endless succession of tireless speech"; 11.25).

The motif of the writer who could not express adequately the vastness of the material at hand even if he had many mouths is familiar from Homer onward. Homer, in the catalogue of ships, had said he could not, without the help of the Muses, name the multitude of ships even if he had "ten tongues and ten mouths" (*Iliad* 2.489). The motif appears again most prominently in Vergil in both the *Aeneid* and *Georgics*, but by now Homer's mouths have been multiplied by ten: "not if I had a hundred tongues and a hundred mouths, an iron voice" (*Georgics* 2.43–44; *Aeneid* 6.625–26).[15] Vergil appears to have multiplied Homer's inadequate mouths by ten, and, if Apuleius is imitating Vergil with an eye also to Homer, the motif seems to involve the belated writer needing more voices by a factor of ten in order to express himself.

The picture is more complicated yet. While Vergil may have imitated Homer, it is not at all clear that Apuleius was alluding rather than using a widespread motif. Issues brought up at the beginning of this paper arise: Is this a topos or a more direct allusion? Persius makes fun of the poets who employ it: "Vatibus hic mos est, centum sibi poscere voces / centum ora et linguas optare in carmina centum" ("This is the habit of poets: to ask for a hundred voices and a hundred mouths and a hundred tongues for their songs"; *Saturarum Liber* 5.1–2). Despite his insistence on the exhaustion of the image, Persius goes on to appropriate it and revivify it by reflecting on the gastronomic implications of having a hundred mouths; satire, ever mindful of the body, rereads the lines on its own terms. Ovid, likewise using the motif in accordance with his genre, tells us in the *Ars amatoria* that not if he had ten mouths and ten tongues could he tell all the devious arts of the *meretrix* (1.435–36).[16] As in the previous examples, the later writers do not simply borrow but

---

15. *Iliad* 2.489: οὐδ' εἰ μοι δέκα μὲν γλῶσσαι δέκα δὲ στόματ' εἶεν. *Aeneid* 6.635–36: "non mihi si linguae centum sint, oraque centum/ferrea vox."

16. Discussion of Persius's and Ovid's use of the many-mouths motif here is heav-

appropriate; each crafts the image, or the allusion, to his own design. What of Apuleius?

The particular ways that Apuleius has made this text his own revolve around the way the large number of mouths is linked to something numerous. Homer finds himself unable to enumerate the vast quantity of ships without the Muses' help; the Vergilian Sibyl finds herself unable to tell the crimes of those in the underworld even if she had a hundred mouths, and so on. In Apuleius's case, it is the vastness of Isis' majesty, the variety of her forms, and the multiplicity of her powers that are indescribable. Isis is known as the goddess of many forms and many names, and Lucius's expression of inability follows upon an earlier enumeration of her powers: "The gods above worship you, those below render you homage, you turn the globe, light up the sun, rule the world, trample hell" (*Metamorphoses* 11.25.3). The homage continues in this vein, enumerating more and more of Isis' powers. Moreover, Apuleius's specific linguistic changes on the motif concentrate attention on the richness of Isis' traits; he lacks the *vocis ubertas* ("richness of voice") to tell her greatness. The epic tone of the "bronze voice" or "iron voice" seen in Vergil and others is modified in Apuleius to "indefessi sermonis aeterna series" ("a tireless discourse continuing into eternity"). What was martial in the epic poems becomes an expression of Isis' eternity and multiplicity. What was previously a literary expression is recontextualized to have nearly theological implications.

I do not wish to stress only the departures and appropriation involved in such literary play. Apuleius also links himself to the literary tradition of which he is a part and exploits it as a means of self-expression. Rather than defining this intertextual moment as either a specific allusion to Homer and Vergil or as a commonplace, I suggest that Apuleius is following a number of sources at once and is evoking the fraternity of writers who, through the ages, have all struggled with words and wished for more tongues with which to speak. In a sense, the thousand mouths themselves suggest that all those writers and their texts serve as sources for Apuleius. The motif suggests a complex mixture of humility and arrogance: both a sense of decline in each writer's need to multiply the number of inadequate mouths by ten and also a boast that the subject matter is more complex and needs more

ily indebted to Hinds, *Allusion*, 39–46. See Hinds passim for further discussion of the complex question of topos versus imitation.

tongues to describe it. The multiformity of Isis is difficult to express and needs more mouths, hence the achievement is by implication greater. Yet, at the same time, Lucius maintains a state of religiously appropriate humility.

Finally, Apuleius's use of the many-mouths motif is contextually linked up with the function of Isis in his book as both literary and religious inspiration. Isis transformed Lucius back into human form early in Book 11, and his worship of her is primarily predicated on her role as a goddess who provided him a port of safety from the whims of cruel Fortune.[17] However, there is also much emphasis in his descriptions of the goddess on her power to restore his voice.[18] At 11.2, upon sensing the presence of the goddess who turns out to be Isis, Lucius speaks, although still a donkey. After his metamorphosis back into humanity, his first thought is what to say with his newly regained voice. In sources outside Apuleius, it is clear that some credited Isis with the invention of writing.[19] She becomes not only a savior goddess but a kind of Muse as well. Lucius's human voice and his literary eloquence both come from Isis. The evocation of the thousand- mouths motif, then, has both literary and cultic meaning; in making Lucius use the motif, Apuleius aligns himself literarily with other writers, but the context summons images of Isis's cultic characteristics of multiformity and her status as inventrix of writing. The allusion, then, to Homer, Vergil, and other struggling writers is many-edged. It does not simply reject earlier literature; in fact, the more overt message is one of humility before its greatness. Yet, like any good appropriation, Apuleius's use introduces new meanings already available in the motif. The religious overlay does not negate the self-conscious literary subtext but twists its terms to express particular Isiac cult characteristics. My point here is that literary and religious meanings are not mutually exclusive and may even be intertwined. In Apuleius, in any case, the transference of literary material

---

17. Anyone who has studied the scholarship on Apuleius will be aware that there are those who read Book 11 as satiric, a parody of religious conversion. I am ignoring those questions for the purposes of my discussion. For a lengthy discussion of the *Metamorphoses* as serious conversion narrative, see Nancy Shumate, *Crisis and Conversion in Apuleius's Metamorphoses* (Ann Arbor: University of Michigan Press, 1996). There is no room here for a full discussion, but an examination of literary allusion is not entirely dependent on the interpretation of Book 11.

18. For fuller discussion, see Finkelpearl, *Metamorphosis*, 184–217.

19. For Isis as the inventrix of writing, see the Kyme Isis Aretalogy 3c, Augustine *De civitate dei* 18.3, 37, 39 and 40, and Plutarch *De Iside et Osiride* 2, 3.

into a religious context does not involve an outright rejection of the old material but allows both to coexist.

In this somewhat diffuse paper, I have been trying to suggest the complexity of the problem of intertextuality in terms of some of the issues that I imagined would arise in this volume. What is intertextuality? What are its effects? How did ancient critics seem to understand the process? How does Apuleius, as a second-century "pagan," represent in fictionalized form the appropriation of poetry by philosophers? How does he then transform a literary motif into a religious context? My sense is that Christian texts work in many of the same ways, given that their writers are living in the same world and working within the same traditions.[20]

---

20. I would like to thank Karen Torjesen and Dennis MacDonald for inviting me to be a part of the conference from which this volume was derived. While many participants have expressed the need for those working on early Christian texts to take more account of the classical backgrounds in philosophy and literature, it is also true that classicists who work on material from the imperial period could stand to be more aware of contemporary writings in the Christian and Jewish traditions.

# 5

## Mimesis of Classical Ideals
## in the Second Christian Century

*Gregory J. Riley*

The theme of this volume, "Mimesis and Intertextuality in Early Christian Literature," is intimately related to another topic, the rise of Christianity itself. The subjects are connected because the first, mimesis, was in no small way a means to the other. It was the appeal of the early Church to the wider Greco-Roman society that fueled its rise, and that appeal was very much a result of its success in modeling the ideals of the culture as a whole. The early Christians imitated and copied the fundamental values found in the literature and stories of its wider culture as it formed its self-image and presented itself to the world.

Christianity began as a small sect among the several Judaisms of Palestine; eventually it became the largest and most important religious movement in the Roman world. This conversion of the ancient world from paganism to Christianity is one of the more remarkable developments in human history. Yet direct investigation of the reasons for this spectacular success too rarely occupies scholars and interested researchers. In the field of New Testament Studies we are more often drawn to matters such as "righteousness in the apostle Paul," or what Jesus meant by "the Son of Man," or whether one should read "Let us have peace" or "We do have peace" in Rom 5:1, and the like. One of the largest and most important questions of all, however, worthy of the most intense discussion and investigation, has received by comparison little attention. The question is: why did the number of Christians go from zero in the year zero to become the numerical majority of persons in the Roman world by about the year 350?[1] How does one account for its dramatic success? That, I submit, is a larger and more interesting question than "righteousness in the apostle Paul." A fundamental contributing cause to the rise of Christianity is the subject of this volume:

---

1. Statistics may be found in Rodney Stark, *The Rise of Christianity: A Sociologist Reconsiders History* (Princeton: Princeton University Press, 1996) 7–13.

Christianity took hold in the empire as no foreign cult could (for example, Judaism, the Isis cult, and Mithraism) precisely because it was not foreign, but an expression and imitation of the best the empire had to offer. In Tertullian's words, "we are from you" (*Apol.* 18.4).

If one asks why the subject of Christian mimesis of classical ideals and its importance for the rise of Christianity has received comparatively little attention, one learns much about the inheritances and presuppositions of our field. According to the greatest writer and historian of the New Testament, the writer of Luke/Acts, the rise of the Church was inevitable. It was not the product of human choices or historical events that can be studied; it was God's will, and the growth of the Church was supported at each step by the intervention of the Holy Spirit and the exemplary behavior of the faithful original apostles. No opposition, however successful for a season, could have stood against the purpose and power of God and the single-minded faithfulness of those who were called to be saints. The persecution associated with the stoning of Stephen, for example, only succeeded in moving the numbers of disciples outside of Jerusalem, as they were commissioned to do, to begin the mission to Judea and Samaria. The attempted assault and arrest of Paul only fulfilled God's vision to him, that he must bear witness in Rome. The Church grew because God added to its numbers day by day. Eventually and inevitably, it would reach the heart of the empire and the uttermost parts of the earth. Its success was guaranteed and could not be stopped. This view of Luke and many other early Church writers, most notably Eusebius, has been held throughout the history of the Church and is still to be found as a dominant view in many places. It was inevitable that the Church would win. It was not a historical process but the divine will, so why should (or how could) one investigate the issue?

Another similar inheritance from the early Church is the claim that Christianity, despite its appearance to observers in antiquity, was in reality based wholly upon and organically grown from "the root of the tree of Jesse," like the trunk or branches of a tree sprouting from the ancient roots of Judaism. This is classed in scholarly language under the general heading of the "Jewish backgrounds of Christianity." We live in a culture that creates a Bible by attaching the Old Testament to the New Testament as though this, the Old Testament, were the proper and sufficient introduction to the Christian faith. The implication is that there is really no difference between the Testaments; they are one revelation from one and the same God. The effect of this claim has been more far reaching than the triumphalism of Luke and Eusebius. Far too often, those scholars who have observed that Christians spoke and wrote in Greek and were fundamentally influenced by Greco-Roman literature and culture have been dismissed as though they were not part of the same conversation. What is Jewish, we have by Bible and tradition been taught to believe, is good and from God, while what is Greco-Roman is pagan. To make things even more difficult, we can observe that as both Jews and Christians turned to the wider society to present their views, they rejected large parts of biblical tradition and recast other parts into Greco-Roman forms in order to gain a greater hearing. There were a number of embarrassing aspects that needed rethinking, for how could a genuine monotheistic God show his hand and back to Moses, and lead one nation to battle against another?

On the other hand, we have inherited the equally unconscious idea from the field of Biblical Studies that what is Greco-Roman is pagan and not from God, even though so many good ideas found among Christians come from Homer and Plato and the Greco-Roman tradition. The biblical texts and early Christian writers speak relentlessly about the evils of paganism, pointing especially to the immorality of the pagan gods as told in myths. Their gods are either mute idols or demonic spirits. "What harmony has Christ with Belial?" (2 Cor 6:15), or again in the words of Tertullian, "What has Athens to do with Jerusalem?" The rhetoric has convinced us. Did not the military standards of Constantine and his successors, bearing the symbols of Christ, overcome and overturn with impunity the forces and images of Jupiter? Here the triumphalism of Luke-Acts and the anti-pagan rhetoric come together.

Yet the rhetoric has led us away from what many Christian writers knew well, that very many good ideas found among Christians came from Greek tradition. Greek-speaking Christians defended the use of classical literature as foundational for good character, ethical behavior, and a proper education, well into the fourth century and beyond. Christians in antiquity never developed their own school texts to replace the classics until forced to do so by Emperor Julian in the mid-fourth century. Christians raided the classical tradition for its good ideas and then condemned pagan authors for their immoral myths; Julian finally took offense and made the Christians face their own hypocrisy.

Further proof of this, that many of the best ideas came from the Greeks, is the fact that both Christians and Jews worked long nights inventing various theories how Plato and others had in fact stolen their admirable spiritual and scientific concepts from Moses, since their re-defined Moses predated Plato by centuries. By this both Christians and Jews admitted that many of their own most dearly held concepts were really those of the Greeks. History shows us that Moses knew nothing about the advantages of Greek science or Greek philosophy with its dualism of body and soul. Moses, so far as he was aware, lived on a tiny, flat earth, and worshipped a fifteen-foot high god with a material body, and had no immortal soul. Later Jews and Christians obscured much of this by recasting Moses into something he never was. They accommodated their texts and ideas to Greco-Roman tradition to such an extent that they masked the great differences between a Canaanite prophet and a Greek philosopher.

These differences are often missed today because of a basic unfamiliarity with Greek and Roman culture. How can one see the "Mimesis and Intertextuality in Early Christian Literature," that is, the obvious dependence of ancient Christian authors upon the texts of their own Greek schooling, without a thorough familiarity with the classics? Without an education similar to that of our ancient authors, one cannot recognize when and if they allude to, or imitate, or model a story after Homer or the tragedians. Many today are experts at finding allusions to the Old Testament because we read the Old Testament. But we have little facility in the texts fundamental to all who learned to read and write in Greek. The ancients had no such thing as our Bible, but, if they could read and write at all in Greek, were versed in Homer and the tragedians because these were their school textbooks. Their models for how stories should be told were those of Greco-Roman literature. If, like Philo or Josephus, they retold stories of Jewish characters they found in the Septuagint, they told them according to the standards of the wider culture, with values that were based on and appealed to the larger world.

So mimesis and intertextuality, as I understand the terms, were part of the means that Christians used both to form their own self-image and to present themselves to the Roman empire. They told their stories and wrote their literature not as though they were Israelites in Canaan, even though they often used those ancient Israelite texts, but as members of the empire who shared the ideals of the philosophers and classics.

The substance and basic stance of Christianity cannot, in fact, be derived from the Old Testament. We might do better to attach the collected works of Plato to the front of the New Testament than to do as we do now. Christianity cannot be derived from Plato alone either, of course, but we would go much farther in understanding its basic message using Plato than we do using Moses and the Deuteronomists. Consider how different were David the warrior-king and Socrates the gadfly. Yet how much closer was Jesus, Son of David, to Socrates in lifestyle, career, message, and death than he was to David! "What does it profit if you gain the world and lose your soul?" That statement is perfectly appropriate to Socrates and meaningless for David. How can one understand the cross of Christ and the willing martyrdom of so many Christians from the viewpoint of a book that curses the crucified and praises long life, peace and prosperity? Yet tragic deaths and martyrdoms are the very substance of Greek literature, and the examination of the soul facing such a fate is its driving spirit. Had Christians preached long life, peace and prosperity in the name of a crucified Christ, there would have been no converts and no subsequent Christianity. The Romans really would have ceased persecution, as admonished by Justin to do, and merely thought Christians insane (*First Apology* 68).

We are told that the cross was "to the Jews a stumbling block, and to Gentiles foolishness" (1 Cor 1:23). Yet the Christians filled the cross with enough power to convert the empire by assimilating it to its natural background: a righteous and powerful Son of God is persecuted by unjust authorities, divine and human, faces his own horrible death with courage, and overcomes. This is not an Israelite story, but it is the oldest and most inspiring plot-line in Greco-Roman literature. The ability of Christians to understand and present the story of Jesus according to this model, and then to encourage each other to live and die, if necessary, in the same way, gave them a self-confidence and respectability that was grudgingly admired even by the Roman elite. Christians made it their purpose to live like the heroes, as had their captain.

We cannot dispense with the Old Testament or with "Jewish backgrounds." What would "Son of David" or the like mean to Greeks without the Septuagint to help explain such terms and concepts? But the fact that readers of the New Testament today frequently ignore Greek tradition when confronting the question of the rise of Christianity is another inheritance from the early Church that needs to be examined. Early Christian writers quoted often and directly from the Old Testament whenever it suited their purposes, usually in the context of moral exhortation or threats of judgment. Jesus had done so, and so had the earliest Christian teachers and communities. They had inherited the Old Testament as authoritative "scripture," a concept nearly totally absent in the Greco-Roman world. Christians almost never quote directly from the classical tradition. Of the three such cases in the New Testament, two are proverbial expressions used disapprovingly. The third is from the poet Aratus, who was in the mind of Greeks "inspired," but certainly not "scripture."[2] Christians could not possibly quote Homer or the tragedians or Plato as "scripture" without legitimizing the inspiration and authority of those texts. Think of the difficulties such legitimation would have produced for a writer like Tertullian, and yet how such a case is in fact made by someone like Basil. Both of these authors illustrate their doctrines and quote the Septuagint liberally, yet the substance of what they believed and taught came not in the main from the Old Testament, but from Greek literature, science, theology and philosophy. This they gained not only through the Hellenistic synagogue, but also directly, through their own upbringing and Greek education.

Let me review in reverse order the reasons outlined above why the question of Christian mimesis of Greek literature and ideals is so seldom addressed. (1) Christian writers seem to quote directly only the Old Testament and seem largely to ignore Greek literature. (2) Few readers of the New Testament today would recognize an allusion or dependency anyway, since few are well-versed in Greek literature. (3) Greek literature is neglected because many read little beyond the Old and New Testaments, since the phrase "Biblical Studies" defines rather well the *de facto* literature of the field. (4) That is because we have inherited a Bible that combines these two texts alone as "holy" and excludes all else as "profane." (5) This supports the fact that Christianity is Jewish and not Greek, for what is Jewish is good and from God, while what is Greek is pagan and from the Devil. (6) Finally, we need not look for Greek or Roman causes for the rise of Christianity, since it grew from the roots of Israel alone according to God's inexorable will and brought about the downfall of the religion and culture of the Romans. All this leads to a kind of inability to see that there ever was Christian mimesis of classical ideals, even when it is before our eyes, in our own New Testament and subsequent Christian literature.

---

2. Cf. Robert Renehan, "Classical Greek Quotations in the New Testament," in David Neiman and Margaret Schatkin, eds., *The Heritage of the Early Church: Essays in Honor of Georges Florovsky,* Orientalia christiana analecta 195 (Rome: Pont. Institutum Studiorum Orientalium, 1973) 37–42.

Greek tradition had developed to a very sophisticated degree a world-view often called "Greek pessimism." The literature they held in most high regard is termed "Greek tragedy." From the Latin version of the name of one of their most powerful and ubiquitous deities, the one who had determined the career of Zeus himself, comes the English word "fatal." It has been said that if one has no hope, at least one has no false hope. Greek thinkers were even more sophisticated and understood that not only did humans have no hope, it was one of the joys of the gods to disabuse people of their false hopes, hopes for long life, health, wealth, offspring, peace, even intelligence. Yet these were the very kinds of things that the Deuteronomists promised to those who would follow the Law of Moses. Periods of blessing and curse were seen to depend on obedience or disobedience to the Law in Israel.

No such notion distracted the Greeks. Periods of blessing were transitory, regardless of one's piety, and dangerous, tempting one to *hubris* and the neglect of *dikē*, the proper balance of justice in one's soul that brought forth respect for one's companions, hospitality for the stranger, and courage in the face of the inevitable change in fortune. "Such is the way," Homer tells us, "the gods spun life for unfortunate mortals, that we live in unhappiness, but the gods themselves have no sorrows" (*Iliad* 24.525–6). Zeus, we are told in the following lines, had two great urns, an urn of evils (note that this urn is mentioned first) and an urn of mixture of evils and blessings, from which he meted out the fortunes of each individual. He may mix good and evil for one person, with the result that this life would move back and forth between blessing and curse over time, or he may mete out only evil for another, whose life would then be a complete failure, without sustenance or respect. No one is granted pure blessing; the possibility did not exist. Such was the background of the conversation in the first book of Herodotus's *History* between Solon, the wisest of the Greeks, and Croesus, the barbarian king of Lydia. Croesus was the richest man of his era, and in his *hubris* asked the visiting Solon who was the happiest man on earth. Solon answered with examples of people who had died heroically and with honor, for, we learn, no wise Greek would ever consider a man still alive and prosperous blessed, but merely temporarily lucky. Croesus dismissed Solon as a fool, and immediately thereafter, we learn in a telling sentence, "Nemesis fell upon Croesus"; the gods' vengeance punished his *hubris*, and he lost everything.

In such a world, virtue is something quite different from obeying a set of rules defining sin and righteousness for which one earned earthly and material blessings. In Israel, obedience to the Laws of Moses was seen by the Deuteronomists as the basis for virtue, with blessing as its reward, while disobedience brought calamity, suffering, and early death. In Greece, disobedience to the *nomos* of Zeus would certainly bring one's downfall, but obedience was little better: the time would come, pious or not, when one would have to face the dictates of Fate alone. The stories teach us that Greek life was short and harsh, even for the highly placed, and that suffering was the fundamental human experience. And worse: for the innocent or especially pious, suffering unjustly was inevitable.

There was no hope of escape from one's inevitable and painful fate, but there was a certain profit: *pathei mathos*, "by suffering comes learning." Unfortunately, but typically, this line from Aeschylus's *Agamemnon* (177) describes Agamemnon's tragic death. The word "suffering" here means the suffering of death, and the learning comes too late for Agamemnon; it is we who should learn from his tragic example. *Pathei mathos:* what is it that the ancients were supposed to learn from the scores of heroic figures depicted in the classical Greek tradition?

One clear example is found in Xenophon's *Symposium.* At the dinner, Socrates and others are asked to declare what useful knowledge each possesses. Niceratus, one of the banqueters replies, when it comes his turn, "My father was anxious to see me develop into a good man, and as a means to this end he compelled me to memorize all of Homer" (Xenophon *Symposium* 3.6). What one learned from the classical tradition was what it meant to be a respected person in the larger context of the Greek cosmos, a world controlled by the jealousy of the gods and the vicissitudes of Fate. One learned piety toward the gods, to respect the rights of others, especially the unfortunate, the suppliant, and the stranger. But what one learned above all was how to face the ultimate test, unjust suffering, the inevitable suffering unto death, with courage and integrity. The texts display a remarkable sophistication on this point, using vocabulary and concepts drawn from the military, athletic, and philosophical arenas. One "practices self-control in all things," "endures to the end," "fights the good fight," "runs the course," "arms oneself with the weapons of righteousness," "receives the crown," and many other such ideas. These are expressions of Paul and other Christian writers, but all can be found in scores of variations in the Greek tradition. The point is that one is engaged in a battle or contest that one cannot win except by courageous death. From the health-and-wealth point of view of Deuteronomy, this type of victory was a defeat: the enemy killed you and took your armor. From the Greek point of view, however, you nevertheless won if you held on to your courage and integrity to the end. It did not matter that you went down under your enemy's sword, because now was your fated time. For you there was no escape from destiny in any case, and your opponent's time would come soon enough in turn. Odysseus, for example, caught all alone in a near fatal situation in the Trojan war, declares, "I know it is the cowards who walk out of the fighting, but if one is to win honor in battle, he must by all means stand his ground strongly, whether he be struck down or strike down another" (*Iliad* 11.408–10). One could in fact lose a fight and be killed, yet still win a moral victory.

The Deuteronomists on the one hand and Jesus and the early Christians on the other were radically at odds. Poverty and suffering and early tragic death were either a curse from God, as the Deuteronomists would have it, or the will of God no matter who one was, as the Greek tradition taught. Getting crucified or the like was either a curse from God (so Deuteronomy) or the fundamental requirement for entrance into the kingdom of God (so Mark 8). One cannot have it both ways. Although many contradictory uses were made of the Septuagint in illustrating the story of Jesus and the proper mode of discipleship, the early Church did not try to make Jesus into the eminently successful, long-lived, wealthy, warrior king David; they let him remain crucified and resurrected. They took from the Old Testament what they could use and side-stepped the rest through allegory, spiritualization, and silence. They understood and told the story of the Son of God on earth not according to the Deuteronomists but according to the tragedians.

This was what made the Christian Gospel something familiar and alluring, even captivating, for the masses of the people of the Roman world. It was a story they had heard long before and had learned to admire and respect. Stories of the endurance of suffering and courage in the face of overwhelming fate had prepared them to hear the same story again, but now one in which they themselves were included in a new way: they themselves were invited to participate individually as protagonists and main characters. In the Christian story, each individual was required to repeat the story of the captain, to take up his or her own cross and follow to the end of life, whatever that end might be. For a few it was also crucifixion, or the arena and the lions; for the majority it was faithful Christian service and commitment of resources until death, often in the face of rejection and criticism from their own families and friends. In no case was it a promise of health and wealth and long earthly life.

As an illustration of this, that the substance of the Christian understanding of Jesus and proper discipleship fits more the pattern of Greek literature than that of the Old Testament, let us look at a few texts from the end of the first century to the beginning of the third. Please keep in mind the notable examples within the New Testament for favorable comparison: the Gospel of Mark, the life story of Paul as reflected in his letters, the Book of Hebrews, and the Book of Revelation, all of which depend heavily on Old Testament passages and images and are full of quotations and allusions from the Old Testament, but whose substance likewise is the call to endure with faithfulness to the death in language straight out of the Greek tradition.

1 Clement has been dated traditionally in the year 96, written from Rome to Corinth in order to quell a schism that had arisen in Corinth. Certain younger members, "one or two persons," we are told (47.6), had deposed the presbyters in office, causing a division in the church. Clement had only the Septuagint to use as an authoritative text, as the "word of God"; he could not use Homer in the same way. His argument is a wonder of artful quotations from the Septuagint and New Testament passages woven together to encourage the recalcitrant to repentance and to heal the strife between factions. Although he quoted scores of passages from the Septuagint, his primary examples and the substance of his message are something of a surprise. He wants the younger members who had rebelled against the older (possibly unjust) authorities to submit in humility, much like the ambassadors asked the young Achilles to submit to the authority of Agamemnon. But Clement seemed conscious that the many examples he marshaled from the Bible were hardly cogent or persuasive. He reminded the Corinthians that they had once "kept the sufferings of Christ before their eyes" (2.1). Then, as negative examples of sedition, he brought up Cain and Abel, Jacob and Esau, Joseph, Moses, Aaron and Miriam, Dathan and Abiram, and finally David. But his most persuasive models are the martyrs in his own city, Peter and Paul and the many anonymous Christians who were forced to suffer death in the arenas of Rome. To conclude this section he admonished his readers to "fix our gaze on the blood of Christ" (7.4). He used the Old Testament examples to show that the schismatic un-

righteous suffer judgment, and then used the martyrs for the opposite purpose to show that the righteous suffer the jealousy that produces persecution and even death. He did not seem to be aware of the fundamental contradiction that the righteous heroes in the Old Testament killed their persecutors or watched God destroy them, while the Christian heroes of the church at Rome were tortured to death or eaten by animals. The virtues of the martyrs, of course, are those of Homer, even given in the language of Homer: they endured humiliation and suffering, kept courage in the face of death, strove for the spiritual victory, gained the prize, and now enjoyed the fame, all of which can be traced to Homer. He tells us, "We are in the same arena, and the same struggle is before us.... Let us fix our gaze on the blood of Christ" (7:1–4). Here we see an example of the window dressing of the Old Testament on the framework of Greek heroic tradition.

Another interesting example is found in the work of Justin Martyr. His *Dialogue with Trypho* recounts a conversation he had with Trypho, a Jew, concerning the Christian faith, probably in the 130s. When the conversation begins and Trypho discovers that Justin is not a normal philosopher as he appears but a Christian, he tells Justin, "It would be better for you still to remain in the philosophy of Plato or some other man, cultivating endurance, self-control, and moderation, rather than be deceived by false words and follow the opinions of men of no reputation" (8), by which he means Christians. Trypho then admonishes Justin to follow, if not Greek philosophy, then Trypho himself, and "first be circumcised, then observe what ordinances have been enacted with respect to the Sabbath and the feasts and the new moons of God, and, in a word, do all the things that have been written in the Law; then perhaps you will find mercy from God." If Justin is to be trusted at this point, then we have a second-century text that shows that the language of endurance and self-control, that is, the basic language of the Gospel, is said to be characteristic of Greek philosophy, not Trypho's Judaism.

Justin in a later work, his *Second Apology* (written to the Senate after the accession of Marcus Aurelius, ca. 161), outlined what attracted him first to the Christian faith. He wrote: "When I was delighting in the doctrines of Plato and heard the Christians slandered, and then saw them fearless of death and of all other things that are counted fearful, I perceived that it was impossible that they could be living in wickedness and pleasure" (12). This he had just illustrated by reference to the old story (from Xenophon *Memorabilia* 2.1.21ff.) of Herakles' choice at the crossroads between personified Virtue and Vice, the one promising trial, trouble and suffering, the other pleasures and ease. Herakles, of course made the choice for Virtue. One of the lines in this story, by the way, clearly stands behind Paul's statement in 1 Cor 9, "I buffet my body to make it my slave." Justin declares that "every sensible person ought to think of this story when regarding Christians and athletes and those who did what the poets relate of those thought to be gods [by which he means the heroes like Herakles], concluding as much from our contempt of death" (11). So here Christians are heroes like Herakles, striving on the hard road of virtue, practicing the endurance, self-control, and moderation that Trypho had mentioned, and holding death in contempt. These were the Christian ideals that had attracted Justin to the sect in the first place and showed the slanders against them to be lies; these were the classical virtues of the poets of Greek tradition.[3]

2 Clement also makes an interesting use of the story of virtue and vice, without, however, mentioning Herakles. 2 Clement is a later work, perhaps written as late as the third century, and brackets the time set by the title of this essay. It is a treatise much like the Epistle to the Hebrews, enjoining ethical purity and faithful endurance under persecution. The recipients are told not to fear death (5), and later to "follow after virtue, but give up vice as the forerunner or our sins" (10). Here Virtue and Vice are personified, just as in the story of Herakles, as those who lead one to good or evil. Moral purity and the penalties for vice are illustrated over and over again by repeated quotations from both Testaments and even a few agrapha, but the substance is again the ideals of the Greek classics, presented in language of the heroic tradition. "Let us contend," we are told, "knowing that the contest is close at hand, and that many make voyages for corruptible prizes, but not all are crowned, save those who have toiled much, and contended well. Let us run the straight course, the immortal contest. . . . " (7). And as a conclusion, we learn that "we are contending in the contest of the living God, and we are being trained by the life that now is, that we may gain the crown in that which is to come" (20). *Pathei mathos,* much like Jesus in Hebrews, who learned obedience by what he suffered and then endured the cross, despising the shame (Heb 5:8; 12:2).

---

3. Tertullian makes the same point in his *Apology* with his famous line, "The blood of Christians is seed" (*Apology* 50.13). His point is that as the crowds watched the remarkable courage and grace of the martyrs, they were drawn toward what the martyrs died so bravely for: "We grow more numerous whenever we are cut down by you."

Such was the Christian *ethos*, according to Epictetus. The word *ethos* refers to "what is customary or habitual." Epictetus, a pagan Stoic philosopher of the early second century, discussed in one of his discourses a particular set of virtues, courage in the face of death and detachment from material wealth, that he wanted his fellow philosophers to emulate. If they did so, they would be, he said, "free, serene, happy, unharmed, high-minded, reverent." He used as examples a man seeking death, who therefore feared nothing from the swords of the Imperial guard, or a madman who cared nothing about his family or possessions, and had "reckoned the material things of life as nothing" (*Diss.* 4.7.6). The madman is like a child playing with potsherds, who after the game has no attachment to the shards themselves. "What kind of tyrant," he asked, "or guards, or swords in the hands of guards, can anymore inspire fear in the breast of such a man?" The answer is of course none. "If, therefore," he continues, "madness can produce this attitude of mind toward the things which have just been mentioned, and also *ethos*, as with the Galilaeans, cannot reason and demonstration teach a man" such things? (*Diss.* 4.7.6). Recall that the goals set by the Deuteronomists were wealth, long life, and the like. Here in the Greek tradition they are a disregard for possessions, contempt of death, fearlessness in the face of the swords of tyrants. There were, apparently, three ways to achieve these ideals of Greek philosophy: insanity, training by reason and demonstration, and Christian *ethos*.

# 6

## Towards Tracing the Gospels' Literary Indebtedness to the Epistles

### Thomas L. Brodie

As is generally agreed, earliest Christianity produced two major waves of extant writings: first Paul's epistles, and then the gospels, including Acts. The epistles belong to the broad genre of epistolography; and the gospels may be called biographical historiography or historiographical biography. This paper argues that the second wave of earliest Christian writers built on the first; the evangelists used the epistles. Before developing this thesis, it is necessary to make some preliminary observations and to summarize criteria.

### PRELIMINARY OBSERVATIONS

The first commandment of exegesis is that the literary question comes first, before history and theology. History and theology may be more important, and they have rightly been the basic goals of exegesis for centuries, but the first task is to attend to what is certain, to the words on the page, and to the relationships among the words.[1] The possible

---

1. In comparison to theology and history, the literary aspect is more tangible and verifiable. No one has ever seen God, and therefore one is careful in speaking about theology. Furthermore, the origin of Christianity is two thousand years away, so one is careful also in speaking about the events of the first century. But the text is here. This means that on an issue such as the evangelists' possible use of the epistles, the primary guide is not theology, such as the difference in theology between Luke and Paul. Nor is the primary guide history, such as a picture of Jesus and of early communities. Rather, it is appropriate to concentrate first of all on the texts and on the relationship between them.

In understanding the texts and the relationship between them the primary guide again is not history or theology: it is literature. Many introductions to the New Testament do not understand this basic principle: they discuss history, sociology, and theology, but not literature. *The Anchor Bible Dictionary*, for instance, is a wonderful publication — I treasure it — and one might expect it to be a good source from which to learn about one of the greatest writers of all antiquity, someone whose work was essentially complete before the Pentateuch: Homer. The *Anchor Bible Dictionary* does indeed have an entry under Homer:

HOMER [Heb homer]. See WEIGHTS AND MEASURES.

dependence of the gospels on the epistles is just one of the literary tasks that needs to be undertaken before embarking on a quest for the historical Jesus.

The gospels may be compared to something woven. The very word "text," coming as it does from the Latin *texere*, "to weave," suggests something woven, and in ancient Greece and Rome, composition was sometimes compared to weaving a fabric.[2] Even if one starts, not with the Greco-Roman world but with New Testament scholarship, the metaphor of weaving and fabric still applies. Most New Testament researchers see the gospels as involving a complex process of blending, a process approximate to the weaving of fabric.

The proposal that the evangelists used the epistles is quite limited. Within the gospels' complex fabric, the epistles constitute just one thread or series of threads. Much of the basic narrative, the plot, comes from other sources and from other literature, particularly from epic, biography, and historiography (especially biblical historiography, above all, the Elijah-Elisha narrative).[3] The role of the epistles, therefore, while important, is not necessarily dominant. Their threads have been subjected to the requirements of a new fabric; they are but one component.

## CRITERIA OF LITERARY DEPENDENCE

In judging whether one document depends on another, one may employ three kinds of criteria: (1) external plausibility, (2) similarities significant beyond the range of coincidence, and (3) intelligible differences.

## FIRST CRITERION: EXTERNAL PLAUSIBILITY

At first sight the idea of a literary link between the gospels and epistles may seem implausible. For instance, on the question of Luke's possible use of Paul, what frequently happens is that, instead of following the

That entry, in so magnificent a work, is a symptom of the degree to which, as a group, we have lost our way. We have forgotten the priority of the literary.

2. John Scheid and Jesper Svenbro, *The Craft of Zeus: Myths of Weaving and Fabric*, Carol Volk, trans., Revealing Antiquity 9 (Cambridge: Harvard University Press, 1996) 141–55.

3. See Thomas L. Brodie, *The Crucial Bridge: The Elijah-Elisha Narrative as an Interpretive Synthesis of Genesis-Kings and a Literary Model for the Gospels* (Collegeville: Liturgical Press, 2000).

first commandment of exegesis (the literary question comes first), there is a preemptive intervention by history and theology. History poses a question as to whether Luke really was Paul's traveling companion, and theology observes that the viewpoints of Luke and Paul are quite different, even incompatible.[4] Hence on grounds of history and theology it seems unlikely that Luke followed Paul.

On closer inspection, however, the objections of history and theology are not convincing. The decisive historical question here is not whether Luke was with Paul, whether he was a traveling companion, but whether Luke had access to any of Paul's epistles. Whether Luke was Paul's companion is essentially irrelevant; it serves mainly as an example of a historical conundrum which, when posed prematurely, blocks progress on other questions.

Theological differences, too, are essentially irrelevant. The issue is not whether there are theological differences but whether the differences are intelligible. On the question of Luke and Paul, J. C. Beker implied that in fact the theological gap *is* intelligible. Luke "redesigned" Paul's theology in view of a later situation: "Within the overall perspective of Luke's salvation history and the problems he needs to address, his portrayal of Paul becomes intelligible."[5] Luke Timothy Johnson's brief comparative study of "salvation" tends to confirm continuity between Paul and Luke.[6] The issue, then, is not difference per se but its intelligibility.

Having laid aside the red herrings of traveling companionship and theological differences, it is now possible to look more clearly at the question of external plausibility. At least two basic arguments provide plausibility to the idea that the evangelists used the epistles. These arguments focus on the literary context and the developed state of communications.

---

4. For discussion, see Joseph A. Fitzmyer, *The Gospel According to Luke (I–IX)*, AB 28A (Garden City: Doubleday, 1981) 47–51. On Luke's portrait of Paul as theologically incompatible with the epistles, see Paul Vielhauer, "On the 'Paulinism' of Acts," in Leander E. Keck and J. L. Martyn, eds., *Studies in Luke-Acts* (London: SPCK, 1968) 31–50, and Ernst Haenchen, *The Acts of the Apostles*, Bernard Noble and Gerald Shinn, trans. (Oxford: Blackwell, 1971) 112–16.

5. J. Christiaan Beker, "Luke's Paul as the Legacy of Paul," in Eugene H. Lovering, Jr., ed., *SBL 1993 Seminar Papers* (Atlanta: Scholars Press, 1993) 511–19, esp. 517 and 519.

6. Luke Timothy Johnson, "The Social Dimensions of *Soteria* in Luke-Acts and Paul," in Eugene H. Lovering, Jr., ed., *SBL 1993 Seminar Papers* (Atlanta Scholars Press, 1993) 520–36.

The Literary Context

In ancient composition as a whole, writers studiously reworked previous writers. The most prestigious writing of the Roman Empire, Vergil's *Aeneid*, involved a thorough reworking of Homer. Roman literature as a whole was largely built on that of Greece. Literary dependence occurred not only within particular genres, as when one epic poet imitated another, but also between genres that were quite diverse. Homeric epic, for instance, was imitated and adapted by both historiography and drama. In a very different mode of crossing from one genre to another, Vergil's Latin epic poetry was summarized into Greek prose.[7]

Likewise in biblical composition; there are many well-known instances of literary dependence within particular genres. Within the broad realms of historiography and biography, for instance, the Chronicler reworks part of Genesis-Kings, and some gospels are built on others. Within the genre of the epistles also, some epistles depend on others.

In biblical composition, as in the broader world of writing, literary dependence is not confined within a particular genre. Within the Old Testament, Deuteronomy transformed various materials into its own special form of wisdom-legislation;[8] and Michael A. Fishbane has chronicled several instances of literary influence crisscrossing between the Pentateuch and the prophets.[9] Within the New Testament, it is becoming increasingly clear — especially through Dietrich Alex Koch, Richard B. Hays and Carol K. Stockhausen — that the epistles are heavily indebted to the Torah, in other words, to ancient biblical historiography.[10]

This context — the general reworking of existing texts and the epistles' reworking of biblical historiography — lends external plausibility to the idea that the evangelists used the epistles. If the evangelists were recasting materials from earlier texts, they were doing what many of their contemporaries were doing. More specifically, it would allow one

---

7. See Marianne Palmer Bonz, *The Past as Legacy: Luke-Acts and Ancient Epic* (Minneapolis: Fortress Press, 2000) 61–86.

8. See, for instance, Calum M. Carmichael, *Women, Law, and the Genesis Traditions* (Edinburgh: Edinburgh University Press, 1979).

9. Michael A. Fishbane, *Biblical Interpretation in Ancient Israel* (Oxford: Clarendon Press, 1985) esp. 132 and 139.

10. For references and evaluation, see Kenneth D. Litwak, "Echoes of Scripture? A Critical Survey of Recent Works on Paul's Use of the Old Testament," *Currents in Research. Biblical Studies* 6 (1998) 260–88.

to propose that (biographical) historiographers did to the epistles what some of the epistles had done to older historiography: they converted them to their own purposes.

## The Developed State of Communications

The evangelists lived in a world of communication. The legacy of form criticism has tended to isolate individual evangelists, particularly John, within the confines of one community, but this theory of isolation is being radically revised. An analysis of early Christian data and of first-century travel and communications has led Michael B. Thompson to conclude:

> The churches from A.D. 30 to 70 had the motivation and the means to communicate often and in depth with each other....News and information could spread relatively quickly between the congregations in the great cities of the empire, and from there into the surrounding regions....Many churches were less than a week's travel away from a main hub in the Christian network.[11]

Communication among Christians was such that Thompson's governing image is not that of isolated communities but of what he calls "the holy internet."[12]

In the course of arguing that the gospels were written not for specific communities but for all Christians, Richard Bauckham reaches a similar conclusion: "The early Christian movement was a network of communities in constant communication with each other, by messengers, letters, and movements of leaders and teachers — moreover, a network around which Christian literature circulated easily, quickly, and widely."[13] The details of how ancient books were produced and circulated has been spelled out by Loveday Alexander.[14] Given this background of written communication, it is plausible that the evangelists knew of the epistles and that, if they wished, they could get copies of them.

The author of Luke-Acts again provides an example. Only with difficulty could one construct a credible scenario in which Luke, while

---

11. "The Holy Internet: Communications Between Churches in the First Century Generation," in Richard Bauckham ed., *The Gospels for All Christians: Rethinking the Gospel Audiences* (Grand Rapids: Eerdmans, 1998) 49–70, esp. 68.

12. Ibid.

13. Richard Bauckham, "For Whom Were the Gospels Written," in Bauckham, ed., *All Christians*, 9–48, esp. 44.

14. Loveday Alexander, "Ancient Book Production and the Circulation of the Gospels," in idem, 71–105.

writing about Paul, would not bother trying to acquire copies of Paul's epistles. Luke was no self-taught scribbler marooned on a distant desert island. Even if one locates Luke as far west as Rome or as far east as Antioch, he is still within a few weeks of Corinth. If one locates him in Greece, as some do, then his distance from Corinth is just a matter of days. Furthermore, he was a *littérateur*; he dealt with writings and used sources (Luke 1:3). In chronicling Jesus, he searched for sources on Jesus; he used the works of other evangelists. Would he do less for Paul? Would he write so much about Paul and never bother getting a copy of any of Paul's own writings?[15]

1 Corinthians would have been particularly useful for Luke. Among all the New Testament epistles its implied picture of a community is uniquely vibrant, and its ideas are foundational, "part of the foundations of Christian theology."[16] If Luke, in searching for sources (Luke 1:3), wanted an authoritative sense of an early community, he could hardly do better than consult 1 Corinthians. Other evangelists, too, were aware of the basic conventions of their day — including the use of existing writings — and they had access to an effective system of communication. It is therefore externally plausible that they used epistles.

## SECOND CRITERION:
## SIMILARITIES BEYOND THE NORMAL RANGE OF COINCIDENCE

This criterion is so widely recognized that it can be dealt with quickly. Similarities may include theme, motif, plot/action, detail (including linguistic details), order, and completeness. Similarity of theme, though helpful, is not decisive, but similarities of motif, action, and details — particularly when numerous — provide strong evidence. Order also is significant: if two people are asked to arrange five random elements,

---

15. The problem of the relation of Luke to the epistles touches another puzzle, that of the sources of Acts. Despite much research, these sources have remained unidentified: see Jacques Dupont, *The Sources of the Acts: The Present Position*, Kathleen Pond, trans.; (London: Darton, Longman and Todd, 1964); Haenchen, *Acts*, 24–34, 81–90; Erich Grässer, "Acta-Forschung seit 1960," *ThR* 41 (1976) 141–94 and 259–90, and 42 (1977) 1–68, esp. 41 (1976) 144–46, and 186–94; Gerhard von Schneider, *Die Apostelgeschichte*, HTKNT 5/1 (Freiburg: Herder, 1980) 82–89; Hans Conzelmann, *The Acts of the Apostles*, James Linburg et al., trans.; Eldon Jay Epp and Christopher R. Matthews, eds., Hermeneia (Philadelphia: Fortress Press, 1987) xxxvi–xl.

16. Jerome Murphy-O'Connor *1 Corinthians*, New Testament Message 10 (Dublin: Veritas, 1979) ix.

the chance that they will follow the same order is less than one in a hundred. With ten elements, the chance is less than one in a million. Completeness also can be an important clue: the likelihood that a text was used by an author is all the greater if every section of the text is echoed or varied in the finished work.

## THIRD CRITERION: INTELLIGIBLE DIFFERENCES

There is a tendency, especially in New Testament studies, to consider literary dependence only in those cases where differences are quite limited. Thus it is generally accepted that Mark was used by Matthew and Luke, but on the use of Mark by John, many say no; the differences between John and Mark are too great. Implicitly the Mark-Matthew relationship has become the model. Instead of dealing with the complexity of diverse kinds of literary relationship, scholars too often have accepted the tyranny of one model — that of Mark and Matthew — which governs the Aland synopsis and shapes the study of the gospels.

But differences between two texts do not decide the issue of their relationship. One must allow for the whole range of relationships found in ancient mimetic rivalry (*imitatio/aemulatio*). The issue is not whether the differences are small or great but whether they are intelligible, whether, for instance, instead of being hodgepodge, they form a coherent pattern, whether one can account for them in view of the writer's larger purposes.

## EVANGELISTS' USE OF THE EPISTLES:
## SOME INITIAL CLAIMS

The basic idea of a link between the epistles and the evangelists is not new. M. E. Boismard, for instance, maintains that Mark uses Pauline words and themes.[17] Likewise Wolfgang Schenk: "Mark shows familiarity with Paul's epistles."[18] Philippe Rolland seems to go further:

---

17. M. E. Boismard and Paul Benoit, *Synopse des quatre évangiles en français avec parallels des apocryphes et des Péres* (Paris: Cerf, 1972) 23–24.

18. Wolfgang Schenk, "Sekundäre Jesuanisierungen von primären Paulus-Aussagen bei Markus," in F. Van Segbroeck et al, eds., *The Four Gospels,* Festschrift Frans Neirynck. BETL 100 (3 vols.; Louvain: Louvain University Press, 1992) 2.877–904, esp. 903.

"Mark has nourished himself on the letters of Paul and Peter."[19] In 1989 Michael D. Goulder indicated a close literary connection between the text of Luke and some of Paul's epistles, especially 1 Corinthians.[20] I, too, have made some proposals, four altogether, one for each of the evangelists:

1. Mark 10 distills the practical admonitions at the center of 1 Peter;[21]

2. Matthew 1–7, especially the Sermon on the Mount, draws on Romans;[22]

3. John 17, with its broad vision of unity, synthesizes much of Ephesians;[23]

4. Acts 1–5, on community unity, reverses the disunity in 1 Corinthians 1–5.[24]

The kernel thesis of this essay is simple: Luke reversed and reshaped the account of abuses at supper (1 Cor 11:16–34) to form one component for the account of Jesus' last supper (Luke 22:14–30). The elements of Paul's version have been adapted to a new context, and the process of reversal means that at times the relationship between the texts is one of sharp contrast.

For practical purposes of analysis the texts may be outlined in five sections (see the table on the following page). The order of the two texts is essentially the same. However, in section 4 the square brackets indicate a variation: Luke's reshaping *combines* two kindred passages, namely, the initial reference to problems (11:16–19, including, curiously, the preceding reference to contentiousness, 11:16) and the later reference to further problems (11:30–32). Also, there are some minor variations of order within sections 2 and 3. The overall process of reversal and contrast is particularly acute in section 1.

---

19. Philippe Rolland, "Marc, lecteur de Pierre et de Paul," idem, 2.775–78, esp. 778.

20. *Luke: A New Paradigm,* JSNTSup 20 (Sheffield: Sheffield University Press, 1989) 129–46. See also the review of the discussion in Morton Scott Enslin, "Once Again, Luke and Paul," *ZNW* 61 (1970) 253–71.

21. Thomas L. Brodie, "Mark 10:1–45 as a Creative Rewriting of 1 Peter 2:18–3:17," *PIBA* 4 (1980) 98 (an abstract of a paper given at the annual meeting of the Irish Biblical Association at Bellinter Conference Center, near Tara, April 27, 1979).

22. "Vivid, Positive, Practical: The Systematic Use of Romans in Matthew 1–7," *PIBA* 16 (1993) 36–55.

23. *The Quest for the Origin of John's Gospel: A Source-Oriented Approach* (New York: Oxford University Press, 1993) 128–34.

24. "Luke's Redesigning of Paul: Corinthian Division and Reconciliation (1 Corinthians 1–5) as One Component of Jerusalem Unity (Acts 1–5)," *IBS* 17 (1995) 98–128.

## The Supper Texts in Paul and Luke

**1 Cor 11:16–19**                                **Luke 22: 14–30**

### 1. Coming Together

Coming together to eat.                     Reclining together to eat.
Each for himself.                           Desiring to eat with others.
Regarding the church of God as nothing.     Fulfillment in the kingdom of God.
No praise (11:20–22)                        Giving thanks (22:14–17a)

### 2. Eucharist

Eucharist.                                  *Eat this ... I clearly imply my death
*Do this ... declaring the death of the Lord   **"until the kingdom of God comes."
**until he comes (11:23–26)                 Eucharist (22:17b–20).

### 3. Guilty Participant

Guilty eater.                               Treacherous table companion.
Examine yourself.                           **Woe
**Condemnation (11:27–29).                  Examining themselves (22:21–23).

### 4. Problems of contentiousness and worldliness

[Problems: Contention; divisions (11:16–19).]   Problems: Contention. Who is greater?
Judgment: not like the world (11:30–32).    Do not be like the kings (22:24–27).

### 5. Solidarity. Not judged, but judging

Solidarity in waiting.                      Solidarity in staying.
Eating and not being condemned (11: 33–34). Eating and judging (22:28–30).


## ANALYSIS

The following section-by-section analysis is not meant to be exhaustive.
Rather it is a preliminary step for further research.

### 1. Coming together (1 Cor 11:20–22: Luke 22:14–17)

Both Paul and Luke begin by telling people to eat (1 Cor 11:20; Luke
22:14), yet the scenes they describe are opposites:

- The Corinthian coming together is *not* for the Lord's Supper (1 Cor 11:20),
  but Luke, in contrast, has a sense of appropriate timing and decorum, a
  sense of harmony (Jesus "reclined," "when the hour had come," and "the
  apostles with him," Luke 22:14).

- In Corinth each gives preference to his own supper, so that while one is
  hungry, another gets drunk (1 Cor 11:21); but Luke is precisely the opposite: Jesus has a deep desire to eat with the others, and his readiness is
  not for drunkenness but for suffering (Luke 22:15).

- The Corinthian eaters regard "the church of God" as nothing (καταφρονέω,
  "despise/regard as nothing") (1 Cor 11:22a), but Jesus, as he eats, has
  an opposite attitude: he looks towards a fulfilling (πληρόω, "fulfill") in

"the kingdom of God" (Luke 22:16). Luke's use of "kingdom" rather than "church" is part of a larger pattern of emphasizing the imagery and language of kings and kingdoms.

- Given the Corinthian situation, Paul refuses to give praise ("In this I do not praise," ἐπαινέω, 1 Cor 11:22b), but Jesus does give a form of praise: taking the cup, he gives thanks (εὐχαριστέω, Luke 22:17a). Luke's version of praise is thus more elevated, and furthermore he adapts this thanksgiving ("And . . . having given thanks . . . ") so that it flows into what follows: concerning the eucharist.

## 2. Eucharist (1 Cor 11:23–26; Luke 22:17b-20)

As is well known, Paul's account of the institution of the eucharist (1 Cor 11:23–25a) occurs also in Luke (22:19–20). The verbatim similarity, while explainable through a common liturgy, is also consistent with a form of imitation known in secular contexts as sacramental.[25] Paul's preliminary reference to the night Jesus was betrayed (1 Cor 11:23) finds an elaborate counterpart in Luke's pre-supper account of the plot to betray Jesus (Luke 22:1–6). Paul's subsequent reference to the eucharist as declaring the death of the Lord ("you *declare the death of the Lord* until he comes," 1 Cor 11:26) finds a Lucan counterpart in Jesus' declaration, implicit but solemn, of his own death ("*For I tell you, I shall not drink . . . until the kingdom of God comes,*" Luke 22:18). Luke's further phrasing — looking forward not to *the coming of the Lord* but to the *coming of the kingdom of God* — is a further illustration of his preference for the language of kings and the kingdom. Luke also avoids repeating "in memory of me," and he adapts the order slightly: he places the declaration of death before rather than after the basic eucharistic account. Part of the effect of this adaptation is to build a narrative that flows smoothly.

## 3. Self-Examination and Condemnation (1 Cor 11:27–29; Luke 22:21–23)

Having spoken of sharing the eucharist, both Paul and Luke turn to a specific problem: eucharistic sharing that is unworthy. Paul does not specify any individual: "whoever eats unworthily" is "guilty of the body and blood of the Lord" (1 Cor 11:27). Luke gives a particular instance but without giving a name: "the hand of my betrayer is with

---

25. Richard B. Hays, *Echoes of Scripture in the Letters of Paul* (New Haven: Yale University Press, 1989) 173–75.

me at the table" (22:21). The single word "betrayer" captures both the unworthiness and the guilt.

The topic of the unworthy eater leads Paul to two remarks: the participant's need for self-examination (1 Cor 11:28); and condemnation of the unworthy ("he eats...condemnation to himself," 1 Cor 11:29). These two features — self-examination and condemnation — likewise appear in Luke, in reverse order: "woe to that man..." (Luke 22:22); and the participants began to examine themselves ("they began to debate among themselves which of them it might be," 22:23). Luke's text is more specific and dramatic; and the adaptation of order again helps to build a smooth narrative. The picture of the apostles in debate leads easily to the next development — contentiousness.

### 4. Problems (1 Cor 11:16–19 and 11:30–32; Luke 22:24–27)

In the context of the eucharist, Paul focuses on various problems at two main points. First, near the account's beginning, he refers to contentiousness, aggravation and division (1 Cor 11:16–19). Second, in the aftermath of condemning the unworthy eater, he evokes people who are variously laid low ("weak/sick, ill, sleeping/dead") and speaks of the need not to be like the world ("that we may not be condemned with the world [11:30–32])." In reworking these problems Luke conflates them and thus concentrates most of the problems into a single brief scene in which the disciples debate who is greater (Luke 22:24–27). Without attempting to trace all the details of Luke's adaptation, it is possible to indicate some main correspondences:

- Contentious/contentiousness (φιλόνεικος, 1 Cor 11:16; φιλονεικία, Luke 22:24). Neither of these words occurs elsewhere in the NT.

- The Corinthian tendency, when people are together, to become *worse* (rather than *better*, 1 Cor 11:17) seems partly reflected in the way the apostle's discussion leads to a focus of who is the *greater*. In both texts this slide towards trouble ("worse," "greater") is offset implicitly by setting the negativity within the framework of two opposing comparative adjectives ("better," "younger"): Not better but worse (1 Cor 11:17); not so, but let the greater be like the younger (Luke 22:26a).

Two elements are particularly elusive:

- The Corinthian tendency towards divisions and factions (1 Cor 11:18–19) may, perhaps, be part of the background for Luke's contrasting picture of leaders as servants (Luke 22:26b). Divisions are generally led by people who somehow set themselves above others. One of the opposites for such a leader is a servant.

- Likewise, Paul's reference to people laid low — weak/sick, ill, asleep/ dead (1 Cor 11:30) — may, perhaps, be part of the background for Luke's contrast between the servant and the one who is reclining (22:27).

The need to be unlike the world — to avoid being judged with the world (1 Cor 11:32) — finds a fairly elaborate counterpart in Luke's reference to the need not to be like the kings of the nations (22:26). Luke has kept the basic idea of being unlike the world, but he again employs the imagery of kings/kingdoms. And, instead of being focused on the final judgment, he is focused on conduct here and now, on an ongoing historical reality. While Paul sets this contrast with the world in a part of his text that is climactic, Luke uses it in an opposite but complementary way — as a beginning (the beginning of Jesus' brief speech). Paul's brief reference to self-judgment (1 Cor 11:31) apparently has been conflated with the apostles debating among themselves (Luke 22:23) and with the final emphasis on judgment (Luke 30). The overall impression concerning the presentation of the problems is that Luke has rendered Paul's many diverse images into a form that is simpler, clearer, and more vivid.

## 5. Conclusion (1 Cor 11:33–34; Luke 22:28–30)

Paul goes on finally to call for solidarity in waiting (that brothers wait for each other in eating, 1 Cor 11:33), and Luke also gives an image of solidarity: staying with Jesus in his temptations (22:28). Then, while Paul speaks of eating so as to avoid condemnation (1 Cor 11:34), Luke shows eating and the avoidance of condemnation as occurring in a kingdom: in the kingdom the apostles eat, and far from being condemned, they are the judges (22:29–30). In other words, the picture of eating and escaping judgment (Paul) is adapted to become a picture of eating and judging (Luke).

There are many clear differences between the two supper accounts (1 Cor 11:16–34; Luke 22:14–30). Yet there are also strong reasons for seeing a literary link between the two texts.

First, there is the extrinsic plausibility: Luke, as someone interested in sources, in the early church, and in Paul, could have sought access to a copy of 1 Corinthians. Given the ease of first-century communications, acquiring such a copy would have been relatively easy.

Second, there are the consistent similarities. Both texts deal not only with the same broad theme but also with several of the same specific motifs. Furthermore, they do this with completeness: for every significant portion of the Pauline texts there is a potentially corresponding feature in Luke. In addition, they follow essentially the same order. As indicated earlier, the chance that five elements will occur in the same order in two unrelated texts is less than one in a hundred. Variations of order, when they occur in the supper texts, are minor, yet precise. Finally, there are several correspondences of detail.

Third, there is the intelligibility of the differences. The idea of transforming an existing text — however alien to modern procedure — finds plausibility in the context of literary imitation and theological redesigning. The imitator could change the earlier text and could also vary the modes of transformation. On the one hand, Luke's verbatim similarity concerning the words of institution corresponds to what has been called the sacramental mode of imitation. On the other hand, the major differences in describing the larger supper scene correspond to the need to adapt the rather negative Corinthian account to the context of the life of Jesus and to Luke's general practice of setting out a positive vivid ideal.

In the end there are two possible explanations of the data: either an extraordinary series of coincidences, or, more simply, that Luke the *littérateur* used a literary method. The chronicler of the church used one of Paul's letters to a specific church. It is reasonable then to conclude that the Corinthian account constituted one of Luke's sources, and that it provided him with one component for his account of the last supper.

Luke's use of the supper text is not an isolated phenomenon. As already indicated (see note 24), there is evidence that Acts 1–5 uses 1 Corinthians 1–5. Taken together, these systematic links raise the question of whether Luke used the entire epistle. However, rather than embark on such a project it seems better for the moment to leave that question to further research.

# 7

## Space, Place, Voice in the *Acts* of the Martyrs and the Greek Romance

### *Judith Perkins*

Some years ago I made a case for the evolution of a new self-understanding of the human subject in the early Roman Empire, a new "subjectivity" — the self as sufferer.[1] In his excellent article, "Body/Power/Identity: Passion of the Martyrs," Brent Shaw added support to my position in his delineation of an important shift in values in the first centuries before and during the Common Era. From a range of discursive examples covering a wide cultural spread — the ancient novel, 4 Maccabees, the Testament of Job, the writings of Cicero, Seneca, Tertullian, Cyprian, and *Acts* of the Martyrs among others — Shaw demonstrated how the "sheer ability of the body to resist, to endure the application of any force to it: endurance or *hypomonē* (ὑπομονή)" came to be endorsed as a virtue.[2] Moreover, according to Shaw, this shift indicated a moral revolution of sorts. In this new economy of the human body, passivity, suffering, endurance — attributes that had previously been thought of as weak, womanish, and slavish behaviors — were translated into positive values that even men might embrace.[3] Shaw posed this altered value scheme as a necessity within "the longer term duration of new institutional changes . . . that compelled a newly negotiated view of the body: a civil body under trial and test in a civic regime of power."[4] This newly elaborated ideology of *hypomonē* (Latin: *patientia*) took a "commanding presence" in Christian perceptions of the body and provided their "primary modes of identification and resistance." As Shaw says, "In the truth of identity which

---

1. Judith Perkins, *Suffering Self: Pain and Narrative Representation in the Early Christian Era* (London: Routledge, 1995).
2. Brent D. Shaw, "Body/Power/Identity: Passions of the Martyrs." *Journal of Early Christian Studies* 4 (1996) 278.
3. Ibid., 295.
4. Ibid., 311.

they [Christians] wished to assert, an inverted image of the body had become the quintessential weapon of the weak"[5]

Shaw's article is comprehensive, well-argued, and persuasive, but its conclusion somewhat understates the institutional implications established by its argument. Christianity, I suggest, was able to construct itself as a competing institutional locus of power within the "civic regime of power" precisely through its usurpation and manipulation of this circulating discourse around and through the body that Shaw has indicated. In his conclusion Shaw seemingly moves from the institutional implications of this discourse to focus on the individual:

> But those bodies were still finite, mortal, isolated and weak; and they faced the long term durability of institutional power.... The residual problem was that.... It [the body] alone could not subvert institutions or corporate bodies which had their own, much greater endurance. Only new incorporations could do that. From the perspective of the individual human body, all of this was a terrible hypocrisy. As even the martyrs themselves confessed, their passivity remained a paradox — in order to win, one had to lose.[6]

In this paper I wish to emphasize that the cultural discourse around tortured and imprisoned bodies was in fact a central element in forging a new incorporation whose endurance long outlasted that of the Roman state, namely, the Christian community: Christian practice was not hypocritical, if, as in all corporate endeavors, Christian winning was never to be viewed from the perspective of the individual human body but in the enlarged perspective of the body social. Christianity won because it co-opted the contemporary cultural discourse around the tortured and constrained body and redirected it to its own ends — the defining and strengthening of a corporate body, the Christian community, described by Paul as "the body of Christ."

In my examination I will look once more at how competing social institutions used the image of the tortured and constrained body to define and to locate themselves in the larger social context of the early Roman Empire. I will focus primarily on the interconnections between the Greek romance and the Christian *Martyr Acts*, as I did in my earlier study, but with new examples and a clearer focus on the corporate implications of this dialectic. By its very nature my project must be intertextual. Intertextual investigation locates meaning not "inside"

5. Ibid., 312.
6. Ibid., 312.

texts but in the space "between" them.[7] As Michel Foucault explains, "there are only reciprocal relationships. . . . What is interesting is always interconnections, not the primacy of this over that which never has meaning."[8] In the discursive space of the early empire, the cultural dialectic between texts and around tortured bodies will display, I suggest, the tactics through which competing institutions made claims for social power. First I will demonstrate some connections between these two sets of texts and, secondly, show how their respective positioning of the represented tortured bodies indicates a basic contestation over the locus of social power. I am going to be particularly attentive to representations of spaces and the space of representation, topics much in vogue in contemporary discussions of "identity politics."[9] A basic premise of my discussion is that in the dialectic between the romance and the *Acts*, historians are offered a glimpse of the dynamics of some "identity politics" in the early empire.[10]

One commonality between the romance and the *Acts* is that both genres arose in the same time frame, around the beginning of the Common Era. At first glance the genres do not look to have much in common. Four of the ideal romances (those of Chariton, Xenophon, Achilles Tatius, Heliodorus) treat the falling in love of a beautiful and well-born couple, their separation and tribulations, until their final reunion at the

---

7. George Aichele, Jr. and Gary A. Phillips, "Exegesis, Eisegesis, Intergesis," *Semeia* 69/70 (1995) 14.

8. Michel Foucault, "Space, Knowledge, Power,"in Paul Rabinow, ed., *The Foucault Reader* (New York: Pantheon,1984) 254.

9. See Henri Lefebvre, *The Production of Space,* Donald Nicholson-Smith, trans. (Oxford: Blackwell, 1991) 40. Lefebvre refers to the "the three moments of social space," the "preceived, conceived, lived" triad. In spatial terms the three are spatial practice, representation of spaces, and representational spaces. Cf. Derek Gregory, *Geographical Imaginations* (Oxford: Blackwell, 1994) 403. Gregory quotes Lefebvre's triad:

> (1) spatial practices, which refer to the time space routines and the spatial structures — the sites and circuits — through which social life is produced and reproduced. (2) Representations of space, which refer to the conception of space — or more accurately perhaps, to constellations of power, knowledge, and spatiality — in which the dominant social order is materially inscribed (and, by implication, legitimated). (3) Spaces of representation, which refer to counterplaces, spatial representations that 'arise from the clandestine or underground side of social life' and from the critical arts to imaginarily challenge the dominant spatial practices and spacialities.

10. For a consideration of the roles of martyrs in forging Christian identity against "the other two 'nations,' Greeks and Jews," see J. W. Van Henten, "The Martyrs as Heroes of the Christian People," in M. Lamberigts and P. Van Deun, eds., *Martyrium in Multidisciplinary Perspective* (Louvain: Louvain University Press, 1995) 303–22.

end of the narrative, where they are reinstated in their home city to live, it is assumed, happily ever after. The *Martyr Acts* portray the confrontation of the early Christians with Roman authority, describing the suffering, imprisonment, trials, and death of Christian martyrs. For all the differences between the genres, mere coincidence is unlikely when two new forms develop in the same space in close chronology. Rather, the emergence of new forms and new subject matters in a culture generally tokens some cultural exchange taking form.[11] In this instance once the striking surface differences between the genres are minimized, their shared attentiveness toward suffering emerges.

Achilles Tatius's narrative is framed explicitly as the hero's, Clitophon's, answer to the question "what have you suffered? (τί πέπονθας).[12] The sufferings are those inflicted by Eros. Chariton similarly offers his romance as a tale of suffering. At the romance's conclusion, Callirhoe, at long last safely returned to Syracuse, offers thanks in the temple of Aphrodite. She prays, "Thank you, Aphrodite!" she said. "You have shown Chaereas to me once more in Syracuse, where I saw him as a maiden at your desire. I do not blame you, my Lady, for what I have suffered; it was my fate. I beg you never again part me from Chaereas, but grant us a happy life, and death together."[13] With that, the narrative ends. A thanksgiving for sufferings endured also concludes Xenophon's romance. When the loving couple, Habrocomes and Anthia, finally return to Ephesus, their first act is to visit the temple of Artemis and erect an inscription to the goddess, as the text states, commemorating all that they had suffered and done (πάντων ὅσα τε ἔπαθον καὶ ὅσα ἔδρασαν).[14] The *Ephesian Tale* itself could be described as a similar inscription. Heliodorus opens his romance, the *Ethiopian Tale*, *in medias res* on a scene of horrific carnage and death. The only people still alive are the heroine and the hero, grievously wounded. Captured by another band of pirates, Charikleia laments to Apollo: "Apollo, you punish us too much and too harshly for our sins. Do you not think we have already endured punishment enough — separation from our families, capture by pirates, a thousand dangers at sea, now a second capture by bandits on land and

11. John B. Bender, *Imagining the Penitentiary: Fiction and Architecture of Mind in Eighteenth Century England* (Chicago: University of Chicago Press, 1987) 7.
12. Translations of the romance, with modifications, are from Bryan P. Reardon, ed., *Collected Ancient Greek Novels* (Berkeley: University of California Press, 1989). Achilles Tatius *Leucippe and Clitophon* 1.2.2.
13. Chariton *Chaereas and Callirhoe* 8.8.16.
14. Xenophon of Ephesus *An Ephesian Tale* 5.15.4.

a future even more bitter than the past."[15] Four of the ideal adventure romances define themselves as narratives of sufferings endured before their final happy ending.

The romances, like the *Martyr Acts*, are remembrances of suffering; also like the *Martyr Acts*, they present their readers graphic depictions of their characters' afflicted bodies. In Xenophon, for example, a bandit chief's daughter accuses Habrocomes of rape when he spurns her sexual overtures. Her father "gave orders to his slaves to tear off Habrocomes' clothes, bring fire and whips, and flog the boy. It was a pitiful sight. For the tortures disfigured his whole body, unused to servile tortures, his blood drained out and his handsome appearance wasted away."[16] The *Letter of the Churches of Lyons and Vienne* similarly notes the particular difficulty of torture for those unused to it, describing the death of certain young people who "had not suffered bodily torture before" and "could not support the burden of imprisonment and died in the jail."[17] In Xenophon, another rejected lover accuses Habrocomes, this time of murder, and the prefect of Egypt orders him to be crucified. Habrocomes is led away and tied to his cross and the text states (exposing an interest in torture) that this was the customary method of crucifixion for the Egyptians. Habrocomes prays for help, and the god sends a gust of wind to topple his cross into the Nile. When he washes ashore, Habrocomes is again sentenced to death, this time by fire. The Nile rises and sends a wave of water to put out the fire. Believing they have seen a miracle, the onlookers led Habrocomes back to the prefect "who was amazed . . . and ordered Habrocomes kept in prison, but to be well looked after till they could find out who he was and why the gods were caring for him like this."[18]

A letter sent by a group of martyrs to their Carthaginian church in the middle of the third century supplies another account of an angry governor and a similar reprieve from death by fire.[19] The group has learned from the soldiers guarding them that they are to be burned alive. But like Habrocomes, their prayers gain them a reprieve:

---

15. Heliodorus *An Ethiopian Story* 1.8.2.

16. Xenophon of Ephesus *An Ephesian Tale* 2.6.4–5.

17. *Letter of the Churches of Lyons and Vienne* 1.28. Translations of the *Martyr Acts* are from *The Acts of the Christian Martyrs*, Herbert Musurillo, ed., Oxford Early Christian Texts (Oxford: Clarendon Press, 1972).

18. Xenophon of Ephesus *An Ephesian Tale* 4.2.10.

19. See Joseph W. Trigg, "Martyrs and Churchmen in Third-Century North Africa," *Studia Patristica* 15 (1984) 242–46.

But the lord alone can rescue his servants from fire...he it was who averted from us the insane savagery of the governor. Earnestly devoting ourselves to constant prayer with all our faith, we obtained directly what we had asked for: no sooner had the flame been lit to devour our bodies when it went out again: the fire of the overheated ovens was lulled by the Lord's dew. And it was not difficult for those of faith to believe that modern marvels could equal those of old.[20]

In the *Martyrdom of Polycarp* the narrator describes another miraculous fire: "A great flame blazed up and those of us to whom it was given to see beheld a great miracle.... For the flames, bellying out like a ship's sail in the wind, formed into the shape of a vault and thus surrounded the martyr's body as with a wall. And he was within it not as burning flesh but rather as bread being baked.... "[21] Even when the fires successfully killed their victim, Christian witnesses could abstract something marvelous. In the *Martyrdom of Pionius,* fellow Christians take note and are heartened that "after the fire had been extinguished...his [Pionius's] ears were not distorted; his hair lay in order on the surface of his head; and his beard was full as though with the first blossom of hair."[22]

Many such overlaps exist between the depictions of tortured bodies in the *Acts* and the romances. In Achilles Tatius, Clitophon is imprisoned and the narrative describes him positioned for torture: "my arms had been tied and the clothes had been stripped from my body and I was hanging in the air on ropes and the torturers were bringing on the whips and fire and rack."[23] At that moment, the fortuitous arrival of a priest of Artemis and Leucippe's father interrupts the proceedings. Marian, a mid-third-century martyr in Carthage, is not so lucky. Like Clitophon, suspension is part of his torture.

As he hung, the thongs that bore his weight were bound not about his hands but the joints of his thumbs, so that these because of their slightness and weakness might suffer all the more in supporting the rest of his body. Moreover, unequal weights were fastened to his legs, so that the whole structure of his body, torn as it was two ways at once by unequal pain and weakened by the wrenching of his viscera, thus hung supported by his muscles.[24]

---

20. *Martyrdom of Montanus and Lucius* 3.3–4.
21. *Martyrdom of Polycarp* 15.1–2.
22. *Martyrdom of Pionius* 23.2–3.
23. Achilles Tatius *Leucippe and Clitophon* 7.12.2.
24. *Martyrdom of Marian and James* 5.6–7.

Representations of tortured and imprisoned bodies intersect in the romances and *Acts*.

If Heliodorus's depiction of Theagenes imprisoned by a Persian eunuch were removed from its context, one would have difficulty determining whether it referred to a romance hero or a Christian martyr: "He immediately loaded him with chains and enclosed him in a gloomy cell and oppressed him with hunger and injurious treatment... though his body was in torment his soul was strengthened by virtue (σωφροσύνη)."[25] This focus on the tortured and constrained body in such different narrative contexts alerts us to important cultural exchanges, to a social dialectic around the body with repercussions for social identity and power. Shaw's hint that this dialectic relates to larger changes in the political sphere ("a civil body in a civic regime of power") is pertinent. In fact, I offer that these representations display the struggle between different social entities for control of the tortured "self" for their own social and political ends.

Attention to the notion of space will help to explicate the poles of the competition around this evolving discursive formation. As Foucault has pointed out, interpretations consistently undervalue space: "as the dead, the fixed, the undialectical, the immobile."[26] Space is the taken for granted, the transparent. But contemporary theory, if not contemporary events, have reminded us that space, in the words of Edward W. Soja, is never just an innocent backdrop: "it is filled with ideology and politics."[27] Space is neither natural, nor an absolute domain; it is the product and the producer of social relations. Space and identity are intimately tied. As Walter Benjamin noted, "Knowing oneself is primarily an exercise in mapping where one stands," and central to this mapping is staking out the boundaries between oneself and the "others."[28] Nor do all groups within a society share equally in this mapping process; not all social locations enjoy equal access to enunciating their perspective. Where one speaks from and whose voices are sanctioned has important ramifications in a society. Economic, political, status, and gender

---

25. Heliodorus *An Ethiopian Story* 8.6.4.

26. Michel Foucault, *Power/Knowledge: Selected Interviews and Other Writings*, Colin Gordon et al., eds. and trans. (New York: Pantheon Books, 1972) 70.

27. Edward W. Soja, *Postmodern Geographies: The Reassertion of Space in Critical Social Theory* (London: Verso, 1989) 6.

28. Quoted by Michael Keith and Steve Pile, "Introduction: Part 2, The Place of Politics," in Michael Keith and Steve Pile, eds., *Place and the Politics of Identity* (London: Routledge,1993) 26.

locations affect groups' opportunities and possibilities for social enunciation.[29] In the spatialities associated with the tortured body, one can see the strategies of different social groups for manifesting their social identity and for inscribing their perspective on the cultural discourse of the period. In the romance Greek urban elite used the image of the tortured and constrained body to build social cohesion and solidify their social identity. In the *Acts* Christians co-opted the same representation as a focus of resistance to the dominant social power and as an opening of a new site for social enunciation.

Elsewhere I have argued that the Greek romance, with its emphasis on marriage and chastity, celebrated the revitalized social identity within the cities of the Greek east.[30] Through the trope of the loving couple, separated, suffering hardship and tribulation, until finally reunited, the Greek urban elite offered an ideal representation of the bonds of their social structure and of the individual's devotion to the social. The four ideal romances are specifically works of social mapping. Each romance begins and ends in a city, and the extensive traveling that separates that beginning and ending demonstrates how the city provides individuals their only security and safety. Within the home city, love, civic festivals, and social rituals such as marriage predominate; outside, pirate attacks, reduction to slavery, imprisonment, torture, and near death. The Greek romance presumes boundaries and legitimated social spaces. Once the loving couple leave their city — its streets, homes, and temples — they encounter danger and destruction.

A speech of Anthia to Habrocomes after her safe return to Ephesus demonstrates how the romance equates separation from the city and foreignness with danger and assaults upon social union as imaged by chastity:

> I have found you again after all my wanderings over land and sea, escaping robbers' threats and pirates' plots and pimps' insults, chains, trenches, stocks, drugs and tombs. But I have reached you, Habrocomes, lord of my heart, the same as when I first left you in Tyre for Syria. No one persuaded me to go astray; not Moeris in Syria, Perilaus in Cilicia, Psammis or Polyidus in Egypt, not Anchialus in Ethiopia, not my master in Terentium. I remain chaste.[31]

---

29. Cf. Caren Kaplan, *Questions of Travel: Postmodern Discourses of Displacement* (Durham, North Carolina: Duke University Press, 1996) 159.

30. Perkins, *Suffering Self,* 44–76.

31. Xenophon of Ephesus *An Ephesian Tale* 5.14.1–2.

Anthia's speech gives evidence both of the extent of her travels and her understanding of them as travails.

Romance characters stress the suffering that separation from their home city gives rise to. On her way to Babylon Callirhoe laments her entrance into barbarian territories and her distance from home. As the narrator describes: "As far as Syria and Cilicia, Callirhoe found her journey easy to bear: she heard Greek spoken.... But when she reached the Euphrates beyond which there is a vast stretch of unending land... then longing for home and family welled up in her and she despaired of ever returning."[32] Greek romance is about displacement and the dangers inherent in it; the genre serves to idealize social cohesion and its security for the individual. All of the characters' imprisonments, sufferings, and torture take place outside the social boundaries. If creating social identity is mapping where one stands, the romance plays a central role, for it erects rigid boundaries between the dangers outside and the security within. Jean Alvares recently provided maps of the travels depicted in the Greek romance, and they display the extent and frequency of such journeys all across the Mediterranean world and beyond as far as Babylonia and Ethiopia.[33] The function of this traveling illustrates how powerfully the home city is the haven and protector of social existence.

The embodiment of the danger outside the city is precisely imaged in the characters' tortured and imprisoned bodies as depicted in the narrative. Xenophon of Ephesus, for example, carefully offers the torture of Habrocomes as a barbarian infliction. Manto, the daughter of the Phoenician bandit chief Apsytus, whose thwarted love is the cause of his torture, is clearly labeled as a barbarian.[34] Theagenes suffers his imprisonment and torture at the hands of a Persian princess' eunuch. Both Chariklea and Theagenes languish in Persian captivity. Chaereas, a Syracusan, suffers imprisonment in Caria and Ephesus. The prefect of Egypt, a Roman official, imposes a death sentence on Habrocomes. The narrator places the prison — the ultimate bad social space — outside the characters' city.[35]

---

32. Chariton *Chaereas and Callirhoe* 5. 1.3–6.

33. Jean Alvares, "Maps," in Gareth Schmeling, ed., *The Novel in the Ancient World* (Leiden: Brill, 1996) 801–14.

34. Xenophon of Ephesus *An Ephesian Tale* 2.3.5 (twice); 2.3.8; 2.4.2; 2.4.5; cf. Heinrich Kuch, "A Study on the Margins of the Ancient Novel: Barbarians and Others," in Gareth Schmeling, ed., *The Novel in the Ancient World* (Leiden: Brill, 1996) 209–20, especially 218.

35. Charikleia is held captive in her native Ethiopia, but only until she is recognized

In their home cities the narratives refer to the social spaces that foster social identity and cohesion, in particular, the sacred spaces where
divine affirmation pervades human society. Chaereas and Callirhoe,
Habrocomes and Anthia, Theagenes and Chariclea all first see each
other at festivals.[36] It is in temples that the heroes marry or reunite in
the novels of Chariton, Achilles Tatius, and Xenophon. The romances of
Chariton and Xenophon end with prayers offered in their city's temple.
In Heliodorus, the gods receive sacrifices before the couple's culminating entrance into the city. As Suzanne Saïd has pointed out, "towns [in
the Greek novel] are evoked by the very places that represent the proper
setting for urban life according to the Greeks of the imperial age." The
romances commend those same places mentioned by the Greek sophists
in their encomia of the cities: the temples, squares, streets, and houses.[37]
The romances, like these orations, are equally encomia of the Greek city
and part of the instrumentality of their political power; for in their
displacement of the prison and the tortured body outside the city's
boundaries, they project a reiterated warning of what can happen to the
individual's body separated from the protective strength of the united,
civic, social body. Every metaphor of displacement includes a reference
to placement and power. The emblematic formulation for authority is
boundaries,[38] and the Greek romance's project is to emphasize the inherent danger of transgressing the boundaries of the Greek city for
its inhabitants. The genre promotes the social structures of the urban
centers in the Greek east.

While the image of the tortured body had a different goal in Christianity, it functioned analogously, as part of the Christian apparatus for
forging a social identity and social cohesion and power. It also allowed
Christianity to claim a new site for social enunciation, introduced new
speakers, and projected a perspective that interrupted the elitism of the
surrounding Greco-Roman culture. In regimes of sovereign power, the
language of the tortured body imparts a set message. As Elaine Scarry
has noted, "Real human pain is to be converted into the regime's fiction

and the whole community votes to release the couple from her father's vow to sacrifice
them to the native gods.

36. Chariton *Chaereas and Callirhoe* 1.1.4; Xenophon of Ephesus *An Ephesian Tale* 1.1.2;
and Heliodorus *An Ethiopian Story* 2.34.1–3.

37. Suzanne Saïd, "The City in the Greek Novel," in James Tatus, ed., *The Search of the
Ancient Novel* (Baltimore: Johns Hopkins University Press, 1993) 219 with citations.

38. Bender, *Imagining the Penitentiary*, 44.

of power."[39] The body of the condemned at the very public spectacles of torture and death signifies the power of the sovereign state for both the condemned and for the spectators. The action of criminals violated the social body and challenged its power. Through the torture and destruction of the criminals' bodies, the social body can see itself reconstituted and its ineluctable power reiterated. In Roberta Culbertson's words, "The carrier of the weapon is also the carrier of social messages."[40] In the discourse around martyrs' tortured bodies, however, Christians refused to follow this script. The Christian rhetoric of endurance and victory through suffering deconstructed the Roman language of power.[41] I will now examine how the rewritten script of the *Martyr Acts* explicitly reclaims and redirects the power that was supposed to inhere in the state to empower an alternate social body, the Christian community.

Space is never natural, and this holds particularly for the space of representation. The authorial space of the Greek romance is typical of third person omniscient narrative.[42] The author is unlocated, expressing authorship not just from a position outside the action but in a sense above the action; not just exterior, but superior. Consider Chariton's statement in Book 8: "I think that this last book will prove the most enjoyable to my readers, as an antidote to the grim events in the preceding ones....How then the Goddess brought the truth to light...I shall now relate."[43] The author, without claiming it, holds a hierarchical position; he not only knows what is going to happen, he knows how his readers are going to respond to it. The same perspective informs Heliodorus's commentaries as he interprets events for his readers: "So it is that genuine affection and wholehearted love disregard all external pains and pleasures and compel the mind to concentrate thought and vision on one object, the beloved."[44] The narrator of the romance

---

39. Elaine Scarry, *The Body in Pain: The Making and Unmaking of the World* (New York: Oxford University Press, 1985) 18.

40. Roberta Culbertson, "Embodied Memory, Transcendence and Telling: Recounting the Trauma, Re-establishing the Self," *New Literary History* 26 (1995) 169.

41. Shaw, "Body/Power," 307–9; Perkins, *Suffering Self*, 15–40.

42. This is the case even in Achilles Tatius's romance where there is a pretense of first person narrative. See Bryan P. Reardon, "Achilles Tatius and Ego-Narrative," in J. R. Morgan and Richard Stoneman, eds., *Greek Fiction: The Greek Novel in Context* (London: Routledge, 1994) 80–96.

43. Chariton *Chaereas and Callirhoe* 8.1.14.

44. Heliodorus *An Ethiopian Story* 1.2. 9. See J. R. Morgan,"Heliodorus," in Gareth Schmeling, ed., *The Novel in the Ancient World* (Leiden: Brill, 1996) 417–56. Morgan offers

abrogates the traditional position of authority — external, hierarchical, and hegemonic; he speaks from the universalized and unlocated position of the dominant culture and his position and right to speak go unquestioned.

In contrast to this, many *Martyr Acts* locate the authorial space specifically. For example, an author may locate his position — a prison — and claim his right to speak on the basis of this location. A number of the *Acts* are offered as the autobiographical writings of the imprisoned martyrs themselves. As Suzanne Saïd noted, both the romance and civic oratory featured the same social spaces. In contrast, the *Acts* aggressively open a new social space for social praxis and enunciation: the prison.[45] The romance displaced prisons and torture outside the city; the *Martyr Acts* locate them in the very center of the city and the narrative. Moreover, they posit subjects speaking from the prison and the location empowers their voices. As Glen Bowersock has noted, *Martyr Acts* are quite specifically an urban phenomenon: "The early martyrdoms provide a checklist of the most prosperous and important cities of the eastern empire: Pergamum, Smyrna, Caesarea, Carthage, and Alexandria."[46] Rather than a secure haven for inhabitants, the martyr narratives project the city and its social structure as a prison and place of torment. Elsewhere I have suggested that Christian writing scripted the Christian subject as a sufferer. If identity is, to some extent, knowing where one stands, the *Acts* define the Christian subject as not only a sufferer but explicitly as a prisoner of the surrounding social structures. It is from this location and because of it that the martyr's voice gains authority.

Who gets to speak and which voices are sanctioned by societies regulate the possibilities for social enunciation. Status, gender, and economic

---

that Heliodorus has dispensed with the omniscient narrator, but his description of Heliodorus's riddling narrator suggests a narrator with an equally superior stance toward the narrative.

45. Two recent books examine the non-legal evidence for prisons. See Brian Rapske, *The Book of Acts and Paul in Roman Custody*, The Book of Acts in Its First-Century Setting 3 (Grand Rapids: Eerdmans, 1994), and Craig S. Wansink, *Chained in Christ: The Experience and Rhetoric of Paul's Imprisonments*, JSNTSup 130 (Sheffield: Sheffield Academic Press, 1996). Much of our ancient evidence on prisons seems to come from the early Common Era, which may suggest an evolving cultural discourse. Not only the *Martyr Acts*, but also the Acts of the Apostles, Paul's epistles, the Apocryphal Acts, the *Life of Apollonius of Tyana*, and Lucian's *Toxaris* feature prison narratives.

46. Glenn Warren Bowersock, *Martyrdom and Rome* (Cambridge: Cambridge University Press, 1995) 41.

position often determine who gets to write, and who gains. Discursive silences become political and cultural exclusions.[47] By opening new social space, Christianity empowered new voices. The *Martyrdom of Perpetua and Felicitas* is an example. So few women's voices issue from the ancient world that is rather a shock to read Perpetua's vivid first-person narrative of her experiences in prison before her martyrdom in 203 C.E. But the narrator of the larger document in which her words are embedded vouches for their authenticity: "From this point on the entire account of her ordeal is her own, according to her own ideas and in the way she herself wrote it down."[48] Perpetua is explicit about the basis for her ability to speak: "I knew that I could speak with the Lord whose great blessings I had come to experience."[49] As often in Christian rhetoric, the Lord's blessings are her sufferings. They both empower her to speak with the Lord and to tell (write) what she hears. The voice empowered through her suffering overcomes the silence of her gender.

Ignatius's voice also issues from a subordinate social location. It was unusual in the ancient world for the writings of a condemned, noncitizen to get a readership. Ignatius stresses his act of authorship. He repeatedly employs variations on the expression "I write to you."[50] Again it is his suffering that lends him prestige. As he says: "Am I not able to write to you . . . though I am in bonds and can understand heavenly things . . . ?"[51] His bonds confer benefits. He wants above all things to complete his suffering in martyrdom, when, in his view, he will finally become a real disciple ("hoping by your prayers to attain to fighting the beasts in Rome that by attaining I may be able to be a disciple").[52] Ignatius describes his suffering as a goal. Thus he writes to the Roman community pleading with them not to impede the sufferings: "obey this which I write to you; for in the midst of life I write to you desiring death."[53] "I no longer desire to live after the manner of men. . . . I beg you by this short letter believe me . . . if I suffer, it was your favor."[54] Narrative patterns script human beings as subjects, as certain

---

47. Kaplan, *Questions of Travel*, 153.

48. *Martyrdom of Perpetua and Felicitas* 2.3.

49. *Martyrdom of Perpetua and Felicitas* 4.2

50. See Rapske, *Book of Acts*, 344 with citations.

51. William R. Schoedel, *Ignatius of Antioch*, Helmut Koester, ed., Hermeneia (Philadelphia: Fortress Press, 1985); Ignatius *Trallians* 5.1.

52. Ignatius *Ephesians* 1.2.

53. Ignatius *Romans* 7.2.

54. Ignatius *Romans* 8.1–3.

kinds of subjects. These first-person letters again and again script the Christian subject as a prisoner and potential sufferer. In this Christian context, Ignatius, as he enacts this Christian subjectivity, guarantees himself an audience. When Ignatius arrived in Smyrna, he received comfort not only from that community but also from the churches of Ephesus, Magnesia, and Tralles.[55]

Another group of otherwise unknown and seemingly undistinguished men were empowered by their sufferings to write of their experiences in prison. These men proclaimed their identity, as they named themselves in their group letter from prison to the Church at Carthage around 258: Lucius, Montanus, Flavian, Julian, Victoricus, Primolus, Renus, and Donatianus. Their letter opens with a recognition of the link between Christian solidarity and the record of their suffering: "For to servants of God . . . there is no other duty than to think of the multitude of the brethren. It is by force of this reasoning that love and a sense of obligation have urged us to write this account, that we might leave to all future brethren . . . a historical record of our labors and our suffering for the Lord."[56] The enthusiasm of these martyrs for their suffering matches that of Ignatius. They described the day they were brought before the procurator: "Oh, what a happy day. Oh, the glory of being in bonds. Oh the chains that were the object of our prayers. Oh, the clanking of the chains as they were drawn over one another."[57] Again, the importance of suffering for the Christian community ensured that their text — no matter what the status of those writing it — would be heard and treasured. As in all these autobiographical martyr texts, the suffering of the martyrs insured that their voice would be heard. Christianity privileged suffering as the site of social enunciation and thereby privileged speakers from some new social locations.

Emerging from new locations, these martyr texts rewrote the surrounding society's value system. Instead of the usual tokens of status — money, rank, education — it was suffering that generated prestige. Another African text made this point explicitly. This text was not written by a martyr but by a companion to the martyrs in prison who was later released. He explained why his friends asked him to write: "not because they wanted the glory of their martyr's crown to be arrogantly

55. Ignatius *Romans* 8.9. See Schoedel, *Ignatius,* 12.
56. *Martyrdom of Montanus and Lucius* 1.1.
57. *Martyrdom of Montanus and Lucius* 6.2.

broadcast, but rather that the multitude of common people who are the people of God could be strengthened."[58] One of the episodes in this text has overt social implications. The narrator opens an episode with a comment on the novelty of the status of a martyr: "A man named Aemilianus, who enjoyed equestrian rank among the pagans, was nonetheless himself one with the brethren in prison."[59]

This man, himself elite, had a dream that articulated the Christian status system replacing the wider, contemporary system. In his dream, Aemilianus met his brother, whom he described: "Very curious about our affairs, he asked in a taunting voice how we were getting on with the darkness and the starvation of prison." His brother further asked whether all of the Christians "who condemn this life" would receive equal rewards in heaven. Aemilianus tried to answer, but his brother kept probing; " 'If there is some distinction,' he said, 'which of you is higher in meriting the good will of the Lord?' " At last annoyed with his questions, Aemilianus answered him "those whose victory is slower and more difficult, these receive the more glorious crown." Then he quoted the gospel saying, "it is easier for a camel to go through the eye of a needle than a rich man to enter the kingdom of heaven."[60] In the Christian paradigm the new token of riches and status is suffering.

*Martyr Acts* so often stressed their autobiographical origin because it was precisely this site of enunciation that conferred their authority. Unlike the romances, martyr texts did not take a universalized perspective, but precisely located themselves as the writings of suffering and constrained human beings. This explains why so many *Acts* claimed to have been written by martyrs in prison or by those with access to written testimony. The *Acts of Pionius* are introduced with the comment: "When he was finally called to the Lord and martyred, he left us this writing for our instruction that we might have it even to this day as a memorial of his teaching."[61] Pionius includes his teachings and sermons delivered in prison. Eusebius testified that his description of the martyrs' experiences in Egypt were from the very words that Bishop Phileas sent to his diocese from prison before his death around 305 C.E. These

---

58. *Martyrdom of Marian and James* 1.3.

59. *Martyrdom of Marian and James* 8.1.

60. *Martyrdom of Marian and James* 8.11.

61. *Martyrdom of Pionius* 1.2. See L. Robert, *Le martyre de Pionios prêtre de Smyrne* (Washington: Dumbarton Oaks Research Library, 1994), and Robin Lane Fox, *Pagans and Christians* (New York: Alfred A. Knopf, 1987) 462–83 on this text. Both accept a date around 250 and that the text may incorporate Pionius's prison writings.

texts are first-person narratives because they are central documents in the creation of the Christian subjectivity that to be a Christian is to suffer; the first person is the quintessential subject position. By positing an "I" who speaks out of his or her own experiences as the place of enunciation, the *Martyr Acts* display and mark the authenticity of this subjectivity. Christian emphasis on suffering empowered new speakers and opened a new position for cultural enunciation. Christians cherished and circulated texts that confirmed their oppressed subjectivity. It was through such circulating texts and through the public performance of this subjectivity in the arena that the corporate Christian community manifested its social presence and staked out its ideological territory.

It is my contention that martyrdom was constitutive not only for the individual Christian subject but also for the incorporation of the Christian Church. The martyr texts themselves demonstrate that martyrdom was much more of a corporate enterprise than moderns tend to think, and that martyrs themselves consciously invested it with a corporate purpose. In *Discipline and Punish*, Michel Foucault showed that modern prisons, with their segregating practices and emphasis on reformation, arose alongside the modern subject — an autonomous reflective individual — both as a product and as a producer of this subjectivity. Ancient prisons did not share this model, as our martyr texts display; martyrs often experienced prison as part of a group and used the time of imprisonment to strengthen their group solidarity.[62]

Perpetua referred to the group prayers in prison. The *Acts of Pionius* depict the martyrs strengthening one another with psalms and prayers and notes, "they were at liberty to discourse and to pray night and day."[63] Confessors imprisoned in Rome wrote Cyprian of studying the Bible, and Lucian portrays Peregrinus bolstered in prison by the reading aloud of sacred books.[64] Not even torture interrupted this group participation. In the *Martyrdom of Marian and James*, Marian returned to the prison after his grievous torture and celebrated the Lord's victory (won by his bodily suffering) in "repeated prayer" with the rest of his group of martyrs.[65] The *Letter of the Churches of Lyons and Vienne* simi-

---

62. See V. Hunter, "The Prison of Athens: A Comparative Perspective," *Phoenix* 51 (1971) 296–323 for a discussion of the different assumptions affecting prison conditions in antiquity from those after the rise of the penitentiary in the late eighteenth century. See Stark, *Rise of Christianity*, for a sociological interpretation of martyrdom.

63. *Martyrdom of Perpetua and Felicitas* 7.1; *Martyrdom of Pionius* 18.12; cf. 11.7.

64. Lane Fox, *Pagan and Christians*, 471 and Lucian *Peregrinus* 12.

65. *Martyrdom of Marian and James* 5.10. During Clitophon's imprisonment, Achilles

larly shows how those most severely tortured encouraged their prison community: "Some, though tortured so severely that it seemed impossible for them to survive even if they received every kind of care, lived on in prison: deprived of human attention, they were strengthened and given power by the Lord in soul and body, and continued to encourage and exhort the others."[66] The *Acts of Montanus and Lucius* describes the heroics of Lucius who was so worn out by sickness and prison life that he feared he would be crushed to death by the surrounding crowd on his way to martyrdom, so he pushed ahead, lest he miss the opportunity of shedding his blood. All the time, "he would not keep silent, but kept instructing his companions as much as he could."[67]

Felicitas' distress that her pregnancy might keep her from being martyred with the others testifies to her recognition of her group as a major support; she worried that "she might have to shed her holy, innocent blood with common criminals."[68] Fortunately, a premature birth saved her; she died with her companions. The *Acts* show the martyrs steeling themselves for the horror of their deaths by discussing it together. The *Martyrdom of Perpetua and Felicitas* recalls such a discussion: "For whenever they would discuss among themselves their desire for martyrdom, Saturninus indeed insisted that he wanted to be exposed to all the different beasts, that his crown might be all the more glorious.... As for Saturus, he dreaded nothing more than a bear."[69] Thus, in the prisons, martyrs appear in multiple group activities, praying together, reading, encouraging each other, listening to sermons by fellow martyrs, sharing their dreams.[70] Martyrdom was itself a corporate activity and was enmeshed with the larger community.

The letters of Ignatius provide a salient example of the extensive efforts of the wider Christian community to bolster a martyr. Cities along his route sent representatives to honor, encourage, and help him. Perpetua mentioned that many visitors were allowed in their prison "so

---

Tatius also refers to the comfort of prison discussions: "in misfortune man is always inquisitive to hear another's woes; community of suffering is something of a medicine for one's own suffering" (*Leucippe and Clitophon* 7.2.3).

66. *Letter of the Churches of Lyons and Vienne* 1.28
67. *Martyrdom of Montanus and Lucius* 13.4.
68. *Martyrdom of Perpetua and Felicitas* 15.2.
69. *Martyrdom of Perpetua and Felicitas* 19.1
70. See Rapske, *Book of Acts*, 351 (note 44) for references to the dream visions in *Martyr Acts*.

that we might be mutually comforted."[71] The visits were important to the martyrs, as the *Acts of Montanus and Lucius* states: "For a few days we were comforted by the visits of our brethren. The consolation and the joy of the day removed all the agony we endured at night."[72] This same text illumines how far this comfort could extend. The narrator describes his actions supporting Lucius under guard in the prefect's residence: "I was there at his side, clinging closely to him and holding his hand with my hands." Later Lucius is escorted on his way to martyrdom by a group of priests, "all his disciples, whom he had ordained."[73] Christians even brought prisoners the Eucharist.[74] Martyrs clearly remained part of their larger community; their suffering was supported by that community and enacted the community's commitment to the prestige and power of suffering. These examples serve to illustrate that the paradigm of the individual martyr does not do justice to the often corporate character of martyrdom and its representation in the early Church.

Moreover, the *Acts* clearly indicate that both the martyrs themselves and their communities understood martyrdom to have specifically corporate objectives. As I discussed earlier, the language of power inscribed in the public torture and execution of martyrs inculcated the strength and dominance of the Roman state. The state broke the bodies of dissidents to proclaim and graphically symbolize its enduring unity and power. The martyrs, however, usurped this bodily inscribed language of power and recycled and redirected it to bolster Christian corporate existence. In many cases martyrs facing death framed their martyrdom to empower their community's unity and internal concord. Ignatius provides an early example. As William Schoedel notes, the theme of unity "may well represent the central concern of the letters of Ignatius," precisely, the solidarity of the Christian community.[75] Ignatius indicates that his suffering allows him to speak about this unity: "in the bonds which I bear I sing the churches, in which I pray for a union of flesh and spirit of Jesus Christ...and of faith and love."[76] In his strong plea to the Philadelphians, Ignatius equates dissension with a transgression of Christ's passion which his own suffering imitates: "if

---

71. *Martyrdom of Perpetua and Felicitas* 9.1.
72. *Martyrdom of Montanus and Lucius* 4.7.
73. *Martyrdom of Montanus and Lucius* 19.1; 22.1.
74. *Martyrdom of Montanus and Lucius* 9.2.
75. Schoedel, *Ignatius,* 21.
76. *Magnesians* 1.2; cf. Schoedel, *Ignatius,*105.

anyone walks in an alien purpose this person does not conform to the passion."[77] In fact, Ignatius employs his whole journey toward martyrdom as an occasion of community-building as he or his friends rally the churches to support and send embassies to him. He also asks all the churches he writes to send letters to his church in Syria in celebration of their newly forged unity: because they have had restored to them "their own corporate body," τὸ ἴδιον σωματεῖον.[78] Ignatius's focus is as much on Christian unity as it is on his coming suffering.

Like Ignatius, Saturus, the leader of Perpetua's group, wrote from prison to encourage Christian unity and eliminate dissent. The narrator of the *Martyrdom of Perpetua and Felicitas* includes a description of Saturus's dream that "he himself wrote." In this dream Saturus sees Perpetua and himself ascending to heaven. There they meet their bishop and a presbyter who throw themselves at their feet and beg: "Make peace between us. For you have gone away and left us thus." An angel chides these officials and tells them to allow the martyrs to recover (*refrigerent*) and that they should settle their own quarrels. The angel continues with advice for the Bishop: "You must scold your flock. They approach you as though they had come from the games, quarreling about the different teams."[79] Saturus chooses to leave as his last words, authenticated by his suffering, his call for increased authority and unity in his Christian community.

Both sections of the *Acts of Montanus and Lucius* end by linking martyrdom to Christian social unity and harmony. The first section, a group letter to the Carthaginian church, concludes with the martyrs' lengthy exhortation to their community for harmony: "We must cling to the harmony of love and adhere to the bonds of charity."[80] They describe a vision to symbolize the disfiguring effects of disharmony. Two of the martyrs had a falling out over a woman, and one dreamt that he was taken to a very bright spot where his clothes and body began to glow. Indeed, in his words "our flesh became so bright that one's eyes could see the secrets of the heart."[81] What he saw in his own heart

---

77. *Philadelphians* 3.3

78. *Smyrneans* 11.2–3; *Philadelphians* 10; *Polycarp* 8.1; Schoedel, *Ignatius*, 12.

79. *Martyrdom of Perpetua and Felicitas* 13.1–6. Bowersock, *Martyrdom and Rome*, 34, considers Saturus's testimony genuine, but, if it is an addition, it shows the social reading that contemporaries would have given a martyr's actions.

80. *Martyrdom of Montanus and Lucius* 10.4.

81. *Martyrdom of Montanus and Lucius* 11.4.

were stains, and he recognized that these were a result of his not making up at once with his fellow martyr. Immediately after this dream
description, the letter concludes with a call for unity: "Wherefore, dearest brothers, let us all cling to harmony, peace, and unanimity in every
virtue. Let us imitate here what we shall be there."[82] The martyrs take
their last opportunity to communicate and speak in support of their
community's harmony.

The second section of these *Acts*, a continuation commissioned by
Flavian, one of the martyrs, ends with a similar emphasis on unity. His
friend records Flavian's final words: " 'Dearest brothers,' he said, 'you
will keep peace with me, if you acknowledge the peace of the Church
and preserve the bond of love. Do not think that what I have said is in-
significant. Our Lord Jesus Christ himself, when he was close to death,
left us these last words: 'This is my commandment,' he said, 'that you
love one another as I have loved you.' "[83] The commandment for Christian unity may not be Jesus' last words, but it is explicitly a thematic
in the martyrs' last words. They offered their deaths as a mandate to
strengthen the incorporation of their communities.

The letter describing the deaths of the martyrs of Lyons similarly understands the martyrs' actions as promoting stronger corporate
bonds: "Peace they had always loved, and it was peace which they
commended to us for ever. In peace they departed to God, leaving no
pain for their Mother [Church], no strife or conflict for their brothers,
but rather joy, peace, harmony, and love."[84] These martyrs, like many
others, apparently promoted their own deaths as a warrant for Christian
harmony.

My last example of the connection between martyrdom and community harmony comes from the *Acts of Pionius*. This case is a negative
example. Pionius included in his written record of his imprisonment
notes on the sermons he delivered in prison, in one of which he addressed the lapsed who visited the prisoners. He explained that he wept
for them: "It may be that the salt has lost its savor, and cast out, is trod-
den on by men. But let no one imagine, my little children, that the Lord
has failed, but rather we ourselves.... For we have sinned, and indeed,
some of us have been scornful; we have done wrong by backbiting and

82. *Martyrdom of Montanus and Lucius* 11.6.
83. *Martyrdom of Montanus and Lucius* 23.3.
84. *Letter of the Churches of Lyons and Vienne* 2.7.

accusing one another; thus we have been destroyed by one another."[85] The lapsed failed in their martyrdoms, precisely, according to Pionius, because the Christian community failed in its charity toward one another. The lack of harmony, of corporate integrity, resulted in the falling away of members. Just as other martyrs equated martyrdom and Christian unity, Pionius equated the numbers of lapsed with disunity — two sides of the same coin.

Martyr texts and the martyrs themselves insist on the relation between a martyr's death and Christian social unity. Martyrs project their deaths as a warrant for the unity of their community. They face death not as individuals but as members of an incorporation that is strengthened and substantiated by their deaths. In a sense, *contra* Shaw, the martyr's body was never alone but woven into a web of signification that heralded a revised "language of power." Christians rewrote the language that was intended to inscribe their defeat and the reintegration of the Roman social body onto their destroyed bodies. Christians plugged into the power charge, the social energy, that flowed through tortured and destroyed bodies and redirected it to support their corporate existence. Martyrs' bodies had a significant function in the evolving incorporation of the Christian community. Even if this incorporation could not actually subvert "the civic regime of power," it could and did erect an alternate power site.[86]

In the discursive attention afforded the tortured and constrained body in the romance and the *Martyr Acts,* one observes the tactics and strategies of different social entities for social power. The romance affirmed the sheltering strength of the Greek city, displacing danger, torture, and imprisonment outside the city's boundaries. In the figure of the faithful, loving elite couple, the Greek urban elite celebrated their social institutions and harmony.

The *Martyr Acts* opened new social space. Christians often depict a city as the space of a prison or another civic place of punishment. With this representation they resisted the contemporary celebration of civic institutions and revealed the existence of those excluded from its idealized social harmony. This new social space in turn empowered new voices to enter the cultural dialogue of the period.

---

85. *Martyrdom of Pionius* 12.12–15.
86. Shaw, "Body/Power," 83.

# 8

## Facing the Scriptures:
## Mimesis and Intertextuality
## in the *Acts of Philip*

### François Bovon

### INTRODUCTION

The goal of this paper is to describe the relationship that the *Acts of Philip* establishes with other texts, particularly respected and authoritative documents anterior to the *Acts of Philip*.[1] I will examine, of course,

---

1. On the relationship between the apocryphal Acts of the apostles and other texts see Éric Junod and Jean-Daniel Kaestli, *Acta Iohannis*, Corpus Christianorum, Series Apocryphorum 1–2 (2 vols.; Turnhout: Brepols, 1983) 2.694–700; Dennis Ronald MacDonald, ed., *The Apocryphal Acts of Apostles*, Semeia 38 (1986); Richard I. Pervo, *Profit with Delight: The Literary Genre of the Acts of the Apostles* (Philadelphia: Fortress Press, 1987); Christopher R. Matthews, "Philip and Simon, Luke and Peter: A Lukan Sequel and Its Intertextual Success," in Eugene H. Lovering, Jr., ed., *SBL 1992 Seminar Papers* (Atlanta: Scholars Press, 1992) 133–46; Dennis R. MacDonald, "*The Acts of Paul* and *The Acts of Peter:* Which Came First?" ibid., 214–24; Robert F. Stoops, "Peter, Paul, and Priority in the Apocryphal Acts," ibid., 225–33; Richard Valantasis, "Narrative Strategies and Synoptic Quandaries: A Response to Dennis MacDonald's Reading of *Acts of Paul* and *Acts of Peter*," ibid., 234–39; Gonzalo del Cerro, "Los Hechos apócrifos de los Apóstoles su género literario," *Estudios Biblicos* 51 (1993) 207–32; James K. Elliott, "The Apocryphal Acts," *Expository Times* 105 (1993) 71–77; F. Stanley Jones, "Principal Orientations on the Relations between the Apocryphal Acts (*Acts of Paul* and *Acts of John; Acts of Peter* and *Acts of John*)," in Eugene H. Lovering, Jr., ed., *SBL 1993 Seminar Papers* (Atlanta: Scholars Press, 1993) 485–505; MacDonald, *Christianizing Homer*; Enrico Norelli, "Avant le canonique et l'apocryphe. aux origines des récits de la naissance de Jésus," *Revue de théologie et de philosophie* 126 (1994) 305–24; Julian V. Hills, "The Acts of the Apostles in the *Acts of Paul*," in Eugene H. Lovering, Jr., ed., *SBL 1994 Seminar Papers* (Atlanta: Georgia, 1994) 24–54; Richard I. Pervo, "The Ancient Novel Becomes Christian," in Gareth Schmeling, ed., *The Novel in the Ancient World* (Leiden: Brill, 1996) 685–711; Johannes B. Bauer, "Schriftrezeption in den neutestamentlichen Apokryphen," in Gerog Schöllgen and Clemens Scholten, eds., *Stimuli. Exegese und ihre Hermeneutik in Antike und Christentum. Festschrift für Ernst Dassmann*, Jahrbuch für Antike und Christentum, Ergänzungsband 23 (Münster: Aschendorff, 1996) 43–48; and in Robert F. Stoops, Jr., ed., *The Apocryphal Acts of the Apostles in Intertextual Perspectives*, Semeia 80 (1997). Methodologically important is an article by Gary A. Anderson, "Between Biblical Commentaries and Apocryphal Narratives: The Narrativization of Biblical Exegesis in the *Life of Adam and Eve*," *Jewish Studies* 36 (1996) 31*–39*; and a review article of Marc Van Uytfanghe's dissertation by Jacques Fontaine, "Bible et ha-

the explicit biblical quotations, but I will also try to unveil the allusions and imitations, the recasting and reinterpretations of canonical and noncanonical material. Despite some polemics with pagan cults and confrontations with Jewish opponents, the text does not integrate much literary material from these two worlds, which would have been foreign to the author. I do not see in this popular composition any influence of Homer, the tragedies, Plato, nor of any Jewish text independent of a Christian appropriation.

The pioneering scholar Constantin Tischendorf edited in 1851 and 1866 the *Martyrdom of Philip* (in two forms) and APh 2.[2] Years later Maximilien Bonnet discovered the *Vaticanus graecus 824*, then the only manuscript to transmit such long and new sections as APh 1 and 3–9. Bonnet's 1903 edition of vol. 2/2 of the *Acta apostolorum apocrypha* has remained the standard for nearly a century.[3]

In recent years the collation and critical edition of new manuscripts have given me, and my colleagues Bertrand Bouvier and Frédéric Amsler, access to a much longer and more complete text.[4] In these manuscripts the form of the text is less censored than in the *Vaticanus graecus 824* (V).[5] Most important is the manuscript from Mount Athos,

---

giographie dans le royaume franc mérovingien (600–750). Une soutenance remarquée à l'Université de Gand," *Analecta Bollandiana* 97 (1979) 387–96. A general bibliography on the apocryphal Acts can be found in Bovon et al., *Apocryphal Acts*, 355–63. Still important is Eckhard Plümacher, "Apokryphe Apostelakten," *RE Sup* 15. 11–70. A general bibliography on the *Acts of Philip* is available in François Bovon, "Les Actes de Philippe," in Wolgand Haase and Hildegard Temporini, eds., *Aufstieg und Niedergang der römischen Welt* (Berlin: de Gruyter, 1988) 2.25.6: 4523–27; and in Frédéric Amsler, *Acta Philippi. Commentarius*, Corpus Christianorum, Series Apocryphorum 12 (Turnhout: Brepols, 1999) ix–xxxvi.

2. Constantin Tischendorf, *Acta apostolorum apocrypha* (Leipzig: Averianus et Mendelssohn, 1851; reprint, Hildesheim: Olms, 1990) XXXI–XL and 75–104; idem., *Apocalypses apocryphae Mosis, Esdrae, Pauli, Iohannes, item Mariae dormitio, additis evangeliorum et actuum apocryphorum supplementis* (Leipzig: Mendelssohn, 1866; reprint Hildesheim: Olms, 1966) 141–56.

3. Maximilien Bonnet, "Acta Philippi et Acta Thomae, accedunt Acta Barnabae," in Richard Adelbert Lipsius and Maximilien Bonnet, eds., *Acta apostolorum apocrypha*, 2 vols. in 3; (Leipzig: Mendelssohn, 1891–1903; reprint, Darmstadt: Wissenschaftliche Buchgesellschaft, 1959) 2.2: VII–XV, XXXVI–XXXVII, and 1–90; see also Pierre Batiffol, "Actus sancti Philippi apostoli. Nunc primum edidit," *Analecta Bollandiana* 9 (1890) 204–49.

4. See Bovon, "Actes de Philippe," 4431–527; Bertrand Bouvier and François Bovon, "Actes de Philippe, I, d'après un manuscrit inédit,"in Damaskinos Papandreou, Wolfgang A. Bienert, and Knut Schäferdiek, eds., *Oecumenica et Patristica. Festschrift für Wilhelm Schneemelcher* (Stuttgart: Kohlhammer, 1989) 367–94.

5. On this manuscript, see François Bovon, Bertrand Bouvier, and Frédéric Amsler, *Acta Philippi: Textus*, Corpus Christianorum, Series Apocryphorum 11 (Turnhout: Brepols, 1999) XX–XXI.

*Xenophontos 32* (A), which offers several completely new acts (APh 11 [the end], 12, 13, 14, and 15) and a less adulterated version of APh 1–9.[6] The codex *Atheniensis 346* (G) provides an original new text of APh 8, including the commissioning of the apostles and the decisive role played by Mariamne, probably Mary Magdalene, considered here as Philip's sister.[7]

For this paper I am using the Greek text of the *Acts of Philip* according to the new critical edition in the *Series apocryphorum* of the *Corpus Christianorum*. I mention this technicality because it is relevant to our topic. The Orthodox Church in the East and the Catholic Church in the West both condemned the *Acts of Philip* as fraudulent and apocryphal.[8] The only chance for these apocryphal stories to survive was to be hidden in a decent and respected text or to endure a radical cure of orthodoxy, which would have included a rewriting along the lines of biblical phraseology.[9] The *Vaticanus graecus 824* is such a rewriting; it presents a new formulation of APh 3, the calming by Philip of the raging waters, which is here influenced by New Testament narratives (Matt 8:23–27 and parallels) more than is the same story present in the *Xenophontos 32*. No manuscript — not the Nag Hammadi codices nor even the Bodmer papyri — can claim to represent a secured original text.

In my opinion, the *Acts of Philip* belongs to an ascetic marginal movement of the fourth century C.E. probably located in Asia Minor, an encratite community under the criticism of the mainstream Church.[10]

---

6. On this manuscript, see Bovon, *Acta Philippi: Textus*, XIII–XX.

7. On this manuscript, see Bovon, *Acta Philippi: Textus*, XXVI–XXX.

8. See Bovon, "Actes de Philippe," 4466–67. More generally on the condemnation of the apocryphal Acts of the apostles, see Éric Junod, "Actes apocryphes et hérésie: le jugement de Photius," in François Bovon et al., eds., *Les actes apocryphes des apôtres. Christianisme et monde païen*, Publications de la Faculté de théologie de l'Université de Genève 4 (Geneva: Labor et Fides, 1981) 11–24; and Ferdinand Piontek, *Die katholische Kirche und die häretischen Apostelgeschichten bis zum Ausgang des 6. Jahrhunderts. Ein Beitrag zur Literaturgeschichte* (Breslau: Nischkowsky, 1907).

9. See François Bovon, "Byzantine Witnesses for the Apocryphal Acts of the Apostles," Bovon et al., *Apocryphal Acts*, 87–98.

10. One study remains important on the *Acts of Philip*: Richard Adelbert Lipsius, *Die apokryphen Apostelgeschichten und Apostellegenden. Ein Beitrag zur altchristlichen Literaturgeschichte* (2 vols. in 3 and supplement; Braunschweig: Schwetschke, 1893–1900; reprint, Amsterdam: Philo, 1976) 2.2: 1–53, and supplement 64–73; idem., "Zu den Acten des Philippus," *Jahrbücher für protestantische Theologie* 17 (1891) 459–73.

On the religious community behind the *Acts of Philip*, see Erik Peterson, "Die Häretiker der Philippus-Akten," *ZNW* 31 (1932) 172–79; idem., "Zum Messalianismus der Philippus-Akten," *Oriens christianus* 3d ser. 7 (1932) 172; Bovon, "Actes de Phillipe," 1521–23; Frédéric Amsler, "Introduction," in Frédéric Amsler, François Bovon, and Bertrand Bouvier, eds.,

It fits well among those attacked by the Council of Gangra (middle-fourth century C.E.) and by the Cappadocian Fathers, particularly Basil of Caesarea and Amphilochius of Iconium. What is important for our investigation is the way that the author deals with the Christian past. He or she writes from the biblical legacy but does so in a unusual way, finding inspiration in the Bible only through an unorthodox reading of it, a reading enriched by other noncanonical but authoritative texts. Just as it is unwise to read Paul's letter to the Galatians and omit the Jewish exegesis situated between the Hebrew Bible and early Christian interpretation, so it is dangerous to read the *Acts of Philip*, compare it to the Hebrew Scriptures or the New Testament, and neglect earlier Christian apocryphal literature.

What this author produced is an enormous text, longer than the canonical Acts of the Apostles. Put under scrutiny, the work appears to be composite, because its author was not shy to incorporate older material. The first part, APh 1–7, is probably a collection of independent tales by individual authors that have been combined into a patchwork with more or less success by the final author. The second part, APh 8 through the end, forms a literary unit, starting like the *Acts of Thomas* with the sending of the apostle to his mission field.[11]

In this paper I limit my investigation to the second part, APh 8 forward, but it may be helpful to mention some aspects of intertextuality in the first part. APh 1 is an imitation of the resurrection story of Luke 7:10–17 (son of the widow of Nain), itself a rewriting of stories concerning Elijah (1 Kings 17) and Elishah (2 Kings 4). New in the *Xenophontos 32* version, when compared to the *Vaticanus graecus 824* and the Bible, is an impressive tour of Hell undertaken by the young man during his stay in the underworld (APh 1.5–17).[12]

APh 2 is inspired by canonical Acts 17, APh 6, and probably APh Mart: Philip is in Athens and tries to convert the philosophers of the

---

*Actes de l'apôtre Philippe. Introduction, traductions et notes*, Apocryphes 8 (Turnhout: Brepols, 1996) 80–82; Richard N. Slater, "An Inquiry into the Relationship between Community and Text: The Apocryphal *Acts of Philip* 1 and the Encratites of Asia Minor," in Bovon et al., *Apocryphal Acts*, 281–306.

11. On the history of composition of the *Acts of Philip*, see the reconstructions of Amsler, "Introduction," Amsler, *Actes de l'apôtre Philippe*, 25–27, and Amsler, *Acta Philippi: Commentarius*, 429–39 passim, as partly distinct from Bovon, "Actes de Philippe," 4443–56 and 4521–23.

12. On this first act, see Bouvier and Bovon, "Actes de Philippe, I, d'après un manuscrit inédit;" Slater, "Inquiry," and Amsler, *Acta Philippi: Commentarius*, 25–83.

city. Significantly, the apostle does not use philosophical arguments but relies on Jesus' sayings and biblical material. It is therefore logical that in this episode, diverging from canonical Acts 17, the Greek philosophers seek the High Priest from Jerusalem hoping that he will rescue them. Strangely, the controversy between the Jewish leader and the Christian hero does not include (as will be the case in APh 6) a polemic over precise Jewish biblical prophecies but, instead, contains a general theological discussion. Writing the epilogue of this tale, the author imitates a biblical narrative, the revolt of Korah, Dathan, and Abiram (Numbers 16), and mentions the split of the earth as punishment of the high priest.[13]

The influence of canonical Acts, here Acts 8, is also visible in APh 3.1–3. As Philip's new converts in Acts 8:14–17 need the apostolic laying of hands by Peter and John, here Philip himself asks for apostolic support so that he, the evangelist or deacon, may carry on the task of a true apostle.[14]

In APh 5.22–23, during the long description of Ireos's conversion, Philip at one point is transfigured, but when he notices that the brightness of his new appearance becomes a threat to his admirers, he "remembers Jesus" and decides to return to his human condition (APh 5.23). The reference to the New Testament episode is explicit.

In the middle of that same story of Ireos and his family (APh 5–7), there is a controversy between the apostle and a Jewish scholar. The topic of the dispute is the relevance of the prophetic scriptures to the Christian faith (APh 6.13[77]). Following the pattern of a battle of quotations, as found in the canonical Gospels (Matt 4:1–11 and Luke 4:1–13, the dispute during the temptation between Jesus and the Devil) and in the *Acts of Peter* 23–28[15] (the fight between the first apostle and Simon Magus), the two opponents in the Ireos context cast several biblical proofs on each side, and several points deserve attention here. First, the controversy deals explicitly with prophetic oracles of the Bible and doctrinal statements, so the commands of the mosaic law are absent

---

13. See Christopher R. Matthews, "Trajectories through the Philip Tradition" (Th.D. diss., Harvard University, 1993) 248–55; and more recently, "Peter and Philip Upside Down: Perspectives on the Relation of the *Acts of Philip* to the *Acts of Peter*," in Eugene H. Lovering, Jr., ed., *SBL 1996 Seminar Papers* (Atlanta: Scholars Press, 1996) 28–31.

14. On this act see the notes in Bovon, *Acta Philippi: Textus*, 77–83; Amsler, "Introduction, Amsler, et al., *Actes de l'apôtre Philippe*, 37–52.

15. See Matthews, "Peter and Philip Upside Down," 28–31.

from the discussion. Second, the author reaches an anti-Semitic paradox: almost all the biblical quotations are taken from the Septuagint and are spoken by the rabbi with an ostensible lack of accuracy.[16] All are imprecise or truncated. For the Christian author this is an easy and wicked way to scorn his adversary. Third, the Jewish opponent finally admits his defeat and ironically accepts as legitimate and true the Christian interpretation of the Hebrew prophets! Fourth, neither the individual biblical quotations nor their sequence corresponds to any book of *Testimonia* preserved from antiquity. This dissimilarity remains an enigma.

Apart from the controversy just mentioned (APh 6.13–15[77–80]), what I have been concerned with so far is not quotations from the Bible but imitations of biblical episodes. The author had new stories to tell, developments of the Hebrew Bible and the New Testament. It was the author's conviction that God had not achieved the manifestation of a providential love toward humanity. But these new salvific events did not contradict the old wisdom, the old revelation. On the contrary, they were witnesses to the ongoing, divine care for the created world. Furthermore, these testimonies are embedded in a network of harmonious and coherent authoritative texts. This conception, present in the first part of the *Acts of Philip*, will be confirmed in the second.

## THE PRESENCE OF THE HEBREW BIBLE
## IN APh 8 TO APh MARTYRDOM

The presence of the Bible is as irregular and surprising in the second part of the *Acts of Philip* as it was in the first. The Exodus tradition, the Sinai tradition, and the lives of the patriarchs, judges or kings are virtually absent from the text. The God of the author is more the God of the creation than the God of law or covenant. Like a large river, divine providence shares its love toward humanity at each generation. A theological proximity with the Creator of the Hebrew Bible is evident from the following prayer:

> My Lord Jesus Christ, hope and strength of all, King of glory, who created the heavens, locked the depths and condemned the enemy to stay there; you who spread out the firmament and placed in it the lights in order to make blazing your works, who disposed the air for an enjoyable usage and

---

16. See Amsler, *Actes de l'apôtre Philippe*, 163, n. 283 (Frédéric Amsler's note).

for the breathing of all those who need it; you who gave your sweetness to the waters in order that your creatures could live; you who rebuked the sea and provided calm to the waves, you are the Lord of all higher knowledge; the release of those who are in servitude; the Savior of the aeons. (APh 12.7 [A])

The *Acts of Philip* accounts for evil with reference to the first chapters of Genesis, but it emphasizes the role of the snake, not that of Adam, in generating evil. The devil, the dragon, the viper, and the fifty snakes play a considerable role in the narrative. The hostile forces of the enemy constantly confront the apostolic trio — Philip, Mariamne, and Bartholomew — during their missionary journey. In APh 3, during a sea voyage, the apostle Philip has to show his divine power in calming a storm, the symbol of negative forces. In APh 9 there is an initial confrontation and a victory over a dragon. A second episode occurs in APh 11. Then, in APh 13, the apostles have to overcome guardian snakes at the gate of the city, which carries the symbolic name of Ophiorymos, literally the street or promenade, of the snakes. At one point, the dragon explains to the apostolic group not only the origin of evil but also its transmission from generation to generation. In paragraphs that are not always clear, in a prose that tries to be theologically sophisticated, the dragon suggests a direct influence on Eve and, through their coalition, the presence of sin in human history. After Eve, the poison of the snake, like a mortal seed, contaminated Cain and influenced his will to kill Abel. Now it will be Philip's responsibility to oppose the dragon and to overcome the snakes. It will be Mariamne's duty to reverse Eve's fallibility. In his commissioning speech the Savior speaks to the sister of Philip saying:

Concerning you, Mariamne, change your clothing and your appearance: take away everything that outwardly resembles a woman, the summer dress that you wear. Do not let the fringe of your cloth hang on the ground, do not drape it but cut this out; then go on your way in the company of your brother Philip toward the city called Ophiorymos, which means the promenade of the snakes; for the inhabitants of this city worship the mother of the snakes, the viper. As you will enter the city, it is necessary that the snakes of that city see you released from the appearance of Eve, that nothing in your outlook manifests a woman, because the appearance of Eve is the woman, and it is she who embodies the feminine form. Concerning Adam, he embodies the form of the man, and you know that, from the beginning, enmity arose between Eve and Adam. It was the beginning of the rebellion of the snake against this man and of its friendship toward his wife, Eve; consequently Adam has been deceived by his wife Eve; the molting of the snake is its venom; the snake put it on through her, and through this skin the original enemy found a place to stay in Cain, son of Eve, so that he could kill Abel, his brother. Therefore you, Mariamne, escape from Eve's poverty to get rich in yourself. (APh 8.4 [G])

In APh 11.3 one finds a confirmation of this theory on the lips of the dragon itself:

And the dragon who was among them answered: "Here is the place from where I draw my origin: the plot stirred up in Paradise; it was there that the one who now wishes to kill me through you cursed me. For then, after I withdrew from the garden with every kind of plant, I found a place to hide in Cain, because of Abel. After I put up the feminine beauty in the face of the angels, I then hurled them down from heaven. Then, having generated sons of high stature, [+++]. After they had multiplied, they started to devour human beings like grasshoppers. After the flood had killed them off, they generated the race of the demons and snakes, when Moses' rod confounded the nature of the Egyptian wise men and magicians. We are the fifty snakes that Moses' dragon then gobbled down. From now on it is you, Philip, who is victorious over us." (APh 11.3 [A])

An intriguing passage connects the Hebrew Bible and the New Testament. Actually this passage, APh 8.11–12, shows that the biblical traditions of both Testaments were envisaged by the author through the glasses of apocryphal traditions not so different from the ones that can be found behind the *Second Epistle of Clement* (see particularly 2 Clem 4.5 and 5.2–4).[17] In APh 8.11–12 the major concern remains evil, its nature and reality, and how to overcome it. Among the negative forces responsible for the presence of evil on earth, the author often mentions the revolt of the fallen angels and their descent to the so-called Egregores (see APh 8.11 and 11.3).[18] Noah is also mentioned as the agent chosen by God to preserve and save the human race and several species of animals from the flood. Through their number, the seven pairs of pure animals express God's forgiveness. The two pairs of impure animals manifest that God is also a righteous judge who knows how to punish with equity.[19]

---

17. On these passages see the remarks of Klaus Wengst, *Didache (Apostellehre)*, *Barnabasbrief, Zweiter Klemensbrief, Schrift an Diognet*, Schriften des Urchristentums 2 (Darmstadt: Wissenschaftliche Buchgesellschaft, 1984) 222–23.

18. See the note in Bovon, *Acta Philippi: Textus*, 258–59, n. 25.

19. See the note in Bovon, *Acta Philippi: Textus*, 258–59, n. 26.

After that introduction — the Risen Savior here teaches Philip at the moment of his commissioning — one finds an explicit reference to a New Testament episode remembered through an apocryphal tradition:

> Therefore, your brother Peter remembered what Noah had done at the day of the punishment of the sinners, when he told me: "Do you want me to forgive my brother until seven times, in a manner similar to the one Noah forgave?" And I answered him: "I do not want you to be satisfied by following the example of Noah but to forgive seventy times seven!" Now, Philip, do not be tired of practicing the good toward those who do evil to you. (APh 8.12 [G])

For the author of the *Acts of Philip*, the memory of the biblical story of Noah is preserved in the New Testament tradition, and this New Testament tradition is preserved in an apocryphal development that establishes an explicit relation between Jesus' words and Noah's attitude.[20]

Another episode in the *Acts of Philip* is typical of the author's relationship to biblical tradition. The reader of the Bible remembers the episode of Elijah, who destroyed in heavenly fire the messengers of the wicked king Ahaziah (2 Kings 1:9–16). The Gospel of Luke makes a reference to this episode in a critical perspective: Jesus condemns the disciples who suggested the miraculous use of that heavenly fire as a weapon for retaliation against the unwilling Samaritans (Luke 9:54).[21] In the *Acts of Philip*, the apocryphal apostle not only makes the same suggestion as the New Testament disciples but, like the biblical prophet Elijah, does in fact retaliate against his enemies with violence.[22] If his expressed wish is to follow Elijah's steps (APh Mart 21[127] A: "Let us say ourselves that fire from heaven come down and consume them"), then his concrete retaliation recalls Moses' punishment of Korah, Dathan, and Abiram (Num 16). He orders the earth to split and gobble up his opponents (APh Mart 25[131]-28[134]).[23] But what was tolerable in the story of Moses and the rebellious Israelites is contrary, according to our author, to Jesus' teaching on nonretaliation.

---

20. I have not been able to locate that apocryphal tradition.

21. See François Bovon, *Das Evangelium nach Lukas. 2. Teilband Lk 9,51–14,35*, Evangelisch-Katholischer Kommentar zum Neuen Testament 3:2 (Zürich: Benziger, 1996) 27–28.

22. See my article "The Child and the Beast: Fighting Violence in Ancient Christianity," *HTR* 92 (1999) 369–92.

23. The earth swallows not only his opponents but also the inhabitants of the city, worshipers of the Viper.

The whole ending of the Martyrdom story is related to this sin of the apostle, Jesus' verbal rebuke, and future punishment (APh Mart 26[132]–33[139], 34[140], 37[143]). Jesus' teaching not to combat evil with a second evil is the decisive criterion by which Philip's attitude and action are to be judged. Strangely enough, there is no explicit quotation of the Sermon on the Mount in this context but only a general reference to what Jesus taught. We should remember that such a teaching in antiquity was not the appanage of the Christians. The venerable Pythagorean tradition proclaimed the same message on nonviolence and pled the same refusal of violent retaliation.[24]

Similarity and difference also characterize the Savior's protracted sermon at the beginning of the missions of Philip and Mariamne, when compared with the New Testament sayings of Jesus (APh 8.3–7, 9–14). His sermon offers first the advice that Mariamne remain the strong woman, as we have seen. Second, it explains to Philip and his sister that their missionary duty fits into the framework of divine providence. Third, it assures them of his ongoing care and spiritual presence at their sides, even during their confrontation with the enemy. Finally, in dialogue with Philip, the Savior conveys a short catechism on the art of nonretaliation and on the habit of forgiveness. If the literary form is similar to the biblical commissioning stories and farewell speeches, its content has only an occasional kinship with Jesus' teachings in the New Testament.

## NEW TESTAMENT AND APOCRYPHAL TRADITIONS ALIVE IN THE TEXT

The first explicit quotation appears in the martyrdom story (APh Mart 34[140]). Hanging on his cross, Philip succumbs to the temptation to curse his enemies, as we have seen. His Lord, appearing in a heavenly

---

24. According to Diogenes Laertius a book was attributed to Pythagoras, called *The Scopiades*, which had as a beginning an advice not to harm anybody (*De clarorum philosophorum vitis*, 8.8). On the difficulty of Diogenes' text concerning this beginning of Pythagoras' book, see the critical apparatus of Armand Delatte, *La vie de Pythagore de Diogène Laërce. Édition critique avec introduction et commentaire*, Académie royale de Belgique, Classe des lettres et des sciences morales et politiques, deuxième série, 17 (Bruxelles: Lamertin, 1922) 109. Unfortunately, Delatte does not deal with this textual problem in his commentary (165–66). The title *The Scopiades* is not well attested in the textual tradition; see the apparatus of the critical edition by H. S. Long, *Diogenis Laertii vitae philosophorum* (2 vols.; Oxford: Clarendon Press, 1964) 2–396.

vision, corrects the apostle. Finally, ashamed of his vindictive desires, Philip repents, and the reader assists at a collective delivery from the split earth (this part of the martyrdom probably influenced the episode of APh 2 mentioned above). The apostle, deeply moved, then proclaims not curses but praises. Addressing newly baptized converts from the city of Ophiorymos who surround his cross, he explains that he has come to their city not to make any sort of trade but to release them from the power of the Devil. He goes on to say that he is now crucified upside down (a motif taken over from the *Acts of Peter* 37) to fulfill Jesus' command.[25] He then quotes a saying of his Lord, not a canonical but an apocryphal saying, an *agraphon* preserved by ancient Christian writers. Actually, it is quoted by some church fathers and appears in the *Gospel of Thomas* 22 as well as the *Acts of Peter* 38: "I repeat here the command of Christ the Savior: 'If you do not make right the things which are left, if you do not consider as precious the things which are vile, you will not be able to enter into the kingdom of God'" (APh Mart 34[140] A).[26] For the author, as for many ancient Christian writers, the authority of Jesus' words is more important than the canonicity of the books in which they are included. That one saying comes from the Gospel of Matthew and another from an oral source, *Acts of Peter* or *Gospel of Thomas,* does not matter.

Then the apostle communicates his last will to his survivors. To his fellow apostle Bartholomew in particular he commands an ascetic life and reminds him of their Lord's teaching: "'Everyone,' he says, 'who looks at a woman with lust in his heart has already committed adultery in his heart'" (APh 36[142] A; Matt 5:28 is cited).[27] This is one of the few explicit quotations of the New Testament, and is introduced

---

25. On the relation of the *Acts of Peter* to other texts, see MacDonald, "The Acts of Paul and The Acts of Peter," 214–24; Christine M. Thomas, "Word and Deed: The *Acts of Peter* and Orality," *Apocrypha* 3 (1992) 125–64, and idem, "The 'Prehistory' of the *Acts of Peter*," Bovon et al., *Apocryphal Acts,* 39–62; and Dennis R. MacDonald, "Which Came First? Intertextual Relationships Among the Apocryphal Acts of the Apostles," *Semeia* 80 (1997) 11–41.

26. See Jonathan Z. Smith, *Map Is Not Territory: Studies in the History of Religions,* Studies in Judaism in Late Antiquity 23 (Leiden: Brill, 1978) 147–71; and Matthews, "Peter and Philip Upside Down," 31–34.

27. Actually, this is the case only in the recensions (the manuscript A is one of the witnesses of this recension) and of APh Mart; on the recensions of the *Acts of Philip,* see Joseph Flamion, "Les trois recensions grecques du Martyre de l'apôtre Philippe," *Mélanges d'histoire offerts à Charles Moeller,* Université de Louvain, Recueil de travaux publiés par les membres des conférences d'histoire et de philologie 40 (Louvain: Bureaux du Recueil, 1914) 215–25.

by "Teaching us, our Lord said." The quotation, however, is not precise and is followed by a kind of narrative commentary: "Therefore,
our brother Peter fled every place where a woman could have been
present"(APh 36[142]A).[28] The speech goes on to a reminder of the apocryphal episode preserved at the end of the *Papyrus Berolinensis 8502,*
which probably originated in the *Acts of Peter,* or the miraculous and
providential paralysis of Peter's daughter.[29]

Another quotation offers a third type of reference. In APh 9 the
apostolic group faces a horrible dragon. To strengthen his companions'
spirits, Philip refers to words of the Savior promising protection: "Now
we need assistance from the Savior. Remember the word of Christ who
sent us by saying: 'Do not fear anything, neither persecution, nor the
snakes of this country, nor the dark dragon!' Let us therefore remain
firm, like columns strongly established before God, and all the power
of the enemy will be wiped out and his threat will fall down" (APh
9.2 [V]). The saying quoted is not, as one would first expect, from the
New Testament, Luke 10:19 or Mark 16:18. It is neither an *agraphon* nor
a saying of the Lord taken from another apocryphal text. It probably
represents an intratextual, free reference to a saying of the Savior pronounced in an earlier speech, in his commissioning speech, APh 8.7
(G): "Now then, brothers, do not fear the bites of the snakes, nor their
venom; because in front of you their mouth will be shut and their threat
abolished. If they lift up their head, apply to them the sign of the
monad; if the vipers come out and meet you, protect yourselves with
the cross and at once they will bend down their heads."[30] Because the
Lord is a spiritual, divine being, his words may be preserved in the
Gospels but also in oral tradition (*agrapha*), in the stream of apocryphal
literature, or even in the text of the *Acts of Philip* itself.

The most interesting case is to be found on the Savior's lips earlier in
the martyrdom story, while the apostle is still disobedient, sending his
opponents and all the inhabitants of Ophiorymos alive into the abyss.

---

28. On this passage, see Ann Graham Brock, "What's in a Name: The Competition for
Authority in Early Christian Texts," *SBL 1998 Seminar Paper* (Atlanta: Scholars Press, 1999)
1.108 n. 7. Brock refers also to Terence V. Smith, *Petrine Controversies in Early Christianity: Attitudes towards Peter in Christian Writings of the First Two Centuries,* Wissenschaftliche
Untersuchungen zum Neuen Testament 2.15 (Tübingen: Mohr [Siebeck], 1985) 107–8.

29. This episode is analyzed by Michel Tardieu, *Écrits gnostiques. Codex de Berlin,*
Sources gnotiques et manichéennes 1 (Paris: Cerf, 1984) 403–10; see also Matthews, "Peter
and Philip Upside Down," 28.

30. See the notes in Bovon, *Acta Philippi: Textus,* nm. 6 and 253.

At this moment, the Savior appears to his apostle and speaks to him, trying to bring him back to reason, to Christian reason:

> At that moment, the Savior appeared and said to Philip: "Who is the one who puts his hand to the plow, then looks back, and makes his row straight? Or who is the one who gives his lamp to others, then himself remains sitting in the darkness? Or who is the one who lives on a pile of manure and leaves his habitation to foreigners? Or who is the one who undoes his clothes, and goes naked into the hard winter? Or what enemy rejoices in the joy of the one who hates him? Or what soldier goes into the war well-armed and does not put on the vestment of victory? Or what slave, having fulfilled the service of his master, will not be invited by the latter to the meal? Or what athlete runs with ardor in a stadium and does not receive the prize, O Philip? Here, the wedding chamber is ready; blessed is the guest of the spouse, for rich is the harvest of the fields, and blessed is the worker who is able." (APh Mart 29[135] A)

These words are among the last that the Savior tells the apostle. After that, the Lord will leave him, assigning him a final punishment after death, a waiting period of forty days before entering into Paradise.

These sayings represent a strange case of intertextuality.[31] The Savior does not speak here in the usual style of the post-resurrection dialogues frequent in the Nag Hammadi codices but in a collection of sayings similar to the Source Q or the *Gospel of Thomas*. These words, however, are not to be found in the canonical gospels, in any apocryphal collection, nor in any known series of *agrapha*.[32] The closest parallel appears in the *Acts of John* 67, part of the last speech of the apostle John before his death. It is my contention that these sayings of the *Acts of Philip* are not a composition of the author of the *Acts of Philip* but a free quotation

---

31. The notion of intertextuality must be used carefully; see the advice of Matthews, "Peter and Philip Upside Down," 23–26; and Thomas R. Hatina, "Intertextuality and Historical Criticism in New Testament Studies: Is there a Relationship?" *Biblical Interpretation* 7 (1999) 28–43.

32. Although this series was known through the publications of Constantin Tischendorf, *Acta apostolorum apocrypha*, 87, and *Apocalypses Apocryphae*, 147, Alfred Resch mentions only a small part of it, the beatitude about the crown and the bridegroom. Besides this reference, he cites the saying on the prohibition of retaliation (APh Mart 31 [137]), the saying on reversal of left and right (APh Mart 34 [140]), and the passage of the *Acts of Philip* quoted by Pseudo-Athanasius Sinaita, *De tribus quadragesimis*, PG 89 1396–97; see Alfred Resch, *Agrapha: Aussercanonische Evangelienfragmente gesammelt und untersucht*, TU 5.4 (Leipzig: Hinrichs, 1889) 9–10, 79, 129, 131, 245, 254, 416–17, and 480; idem, *Agrapha: Aussercanonische Schriftfragmente gesammelt und untersucht in zweiter völlig neu bearbeiteter durch alttestamentliche Agrapha vermehrter Auflage herausgegeben*, TU n.s. 15:3–4 (Leipzig: Hinrichs, 1906) 279–81. In his second edition Resch does not use Maximilien Bonnet's edition, published in 1903 (Lipsius-Bonnet, *Acta apostolorum apocrypha*, vol. 2.2).

from an unknown gospel. They represent a curious occurrence of inter-textuality (an implicit quotation or adaptation);[33] therefore, they earn a special interest from the historians of early Christianity.[34]

Because all these stories belong to the same salvific plot, to the same ongoing divine fight, the author thought it appropriate to use old mo-tives, past sermons, or ancient episodes to fill a present necessity. The process is understandable and has been followed in later centuries by hagiographers.

The quarrel between Philip and the Jew Aristarchos (APh 6.9–21) borrows without hesitation from the *Acts of Peter* 23–28 (the conflict be-tween Peter and Simon Magus).[35] It is also from the *Acts of Peter* that the author draws the episode of Peter's daughter (APh Mart 36[142]).[36] The celebration of the Eucharist (APh 11.9) rewrites a hymn mentioned in the *Acts of John* 94–96, 109.[37] The commissioning of the apostle Philip (APh 8.1–2) resembles the beginning of the *Acts of Thomas*.[38] The newly discovered beatitudes, pronounced by Philip (APh 5.25), are similar in form to the beatitudes of the canonical gospels (Matt 5:3–12 and Luke 6:20–23) and of the *Acts of Paul* 5–6.[39] The description of the dragons (APh 9.1[102] and 11.2–8) shares common traits with the *Shepherd of Hermas* 22.6–24.1 (Vis. IV 1.6–3.1), the *Acts of Thomas* 31, or the *Questions of Bartholomew* 4.13.[40] Several times (APh 2.9, 17;11.6; APh Mart 25 [re-cension]) Philip, who is here so ready to anger, receives the nickname that the Gospel of Mark attributes to the sons of Zebbedaios, namely "son of thunder" (Mark 3:17).[41]

---

33. The resurrected Christ is quoting the historical Jesus, and that phenomenon occurs also in Luke 24:44–48 and in Acts 1:4–5.

34. On this important passage see my article "The Synoptic Gospels and the Non-canonical Acts of the Apostles," *HTR* 81 (1988) 30–31.

35. On this relationship, see Matthews, "Peter and Philip Upside Down," 28–31.

36. This has been disputed in a still unpublished study by Andrea Molinari, " 'I Never Knew the Man': The Independence of the Coptic *Act of Peter* ( Papyrus Berolinensis 8502.4) from the Apocryphal Acts of Peter, Its Genre and Origins."

37. See Bovon, "Actes de Philippe," 4500–03; and the notes in Bovon, *Acta Philippi: Textus*, 296–99, and Amsler, *Acta Philippi: Commentarius*, 348–54.

38. See Jean-Daniel Kaestli, "Les scènes d'attribution des champs de mission et de départ de l'apôtre dans les Actes apocryphes," *Les actes apocryphes des apôtres*, 249–64.

39. See Bovon, "The Synoptic Gospels and the Non-Canonical Acts," 31.

40. See Erik Peterson, "Die Begegnung mit dem Ungeheuer. Hermas, Visio IV," *Vigiliae christianae* 8 (1954) 52–71; reprint in idem, *Frühkirche, Judentum und Gnosis. Studien und Untersuchungen* (Freiburg: Herder, 1959; reprint, Darmstadt: Wissenschaftliche Buchgesellschaft, 1982) 285–309.

41. See the notes in Bovon, *Acta Philippi: Textus*, 290 n. 29.

This relation to former texts and scriptures can even explain the very composition of the global work by amalgam and appropriation. The final author did not hesitate to bring together several traditions and texts related to Philip, merging together in this huge river the memories of Philip the evangelist, one of the Seven, and Philip the apostle, one of the Twelve.

## CONCLUSION

This author does not consider his reference books or his own composition to be sacred in the sense that only a literal quotation would be admissible and any imitation prohibited. The free use of the Bible, of both Testaments, is confirmed by a similar type of reference to the tales from apostolic times. For the author, there is an ongoing process of revelation and manifestation of divine love through the centuries. The time of Adam and Eve, the time of Cain and Abel, the time of Moses in the wilderness, the construction of the Temple under Solomon, spoken of by a defeated dragon, the time of Jesus understood as the crucified, the teacher and the commissioner, all these periods are marked by the presence of negative forces, dragons, snakes, and the viper, but, at the same time, by powerful divine providence and its successful agents: the prophets, the Savior, the apostles. The creative memory of this group of salvific events can still give direction to readers and believers more than any canonical or noncanonical scriptures.

Salvific events were more important for our author than were the Holy Scriptures. According to him or her, holy periods were not limited to the biblical history of redemption. God has to express love, manifest providence, and overcome the enemy's ferocity in every generation. Therefore, not only biblical quotations but also apostolic memories and apocryphal traditions are welcome and used for shaping the stories of the neglected apostle Philip.

The author and the Christian ascetic community perhaps felt neglected and marginalized.[42] The mainstream Church, the victorious Church of the Councils and bishops, could establish its identity on

---

42. On the social and religious location of the author of the *Acts of Philip* see the hypothesis of Amsler, "Introduction," Amsler, *Actes de l'apôtre Philippe*, 13–86, and idem, "The Apostle Philip, the Viper, the Leopard and the Kid: The Masked Actors of a Religious Conflict in Hierapolis of Phrygia (*Acts of Philip* VIII and *Martyrdom*)," in Eugene H. Lovering, Jr., ed., *SBL 1996 Seminar Papers* (Atlanta: Scholars Press, 1996) 432–37.

Peter, Paul, or John. As Encratites, who preferred vegetables to meat, water to wine for the Eucharist, and accepted as ministers women as well as men,[43] they also wanted to preserve the memory of Philip. Of course, this preservation has little in common with the task of a modern archivist; it is much more the construction of a sacred origin, an initial time which can be actualized or reiterated when faith and obedience cooperate in a polemical struggle against all the possible dragons.

---

43. See APh 1, 12; Bertrand Bouvier and François Bovon, "Actes de Philippe, I, d'après un manuscrit inédit," 393–94; Bovon, *Acta Philippi: Textus*, 29.

# Bibliography
# of Cited Works

Aichele, George, Jr. and Phillips, Gary A. "Exegesis, Eisegesis, Intergesis." *Semeia* 69/70 (1995) 7–18.

Alexander, Loveday. "Ancient Book Production and the Circulation of the Gospels." In Richard Bauckham, ed. *The Gospel for All Christians: Rethinking the Gospel Audiences.* Grand Rapids: Eerdmans, 1998, 71–105.

Alvares, Jean. "Maps." In Gareth Schmeling, ed. *The Novel in the Ancient World.* Leiden: Brill, 1996, 801–14.

Ameling, Walter. "Der Sophist Rufus." *EA* 6 (1985) 27–33.

Amsler, Frédéric. *Acta Philippi. Commentarius.* Corpus Christianorum, Series Apocryphorum 12. Turnhout: Brepols, 1999.

———. "The Apostle Philip, the Viper, the Leopard and the Kid: The Masked Actors of a Religious Conflict in Hierapolis of Phrygia (*Acts of Philip* VIII and *Martyrdom*)." In Eugene H. Lovering, Jr., ed. *SBL 1996 Seminar Papers.* Atlanta: Scholars Press, 1996.

Amsler, Frédéric, François Bovon and Bertrand Bouvier, eds. *Actes de l'apôtre Philippe. Introduction, traductions et notes.* Apocryphes 8. Turnhout: Brepols, 1996.

Anderson, Gary A. "Between Biblical Commentaries and Apocryphal Narratives: The Narrativization of Biblical Exegesis in the *Life of Adam and Eve.*" *Jewish Studies* 36 (1996) 31*-39*.

Barchiesi, Alessandro. *La traccia del modello. Effetti Omerici nella narrazione Virgiliana.* Biblioteca di materiali e discussioni per l'analisi dei testi classici 1. Pisa: Giardini, 1984.

Batiffol, Pierre. "Actus sancti Philippi apostoli. Nunc primum edidit." *Analecta Bollandiana* 9 (1890) 204–49.

Bauckham, Richard. "For Whom Were the Gospels Written." In Richard Bauckham, ed. *The Gospel for All Christians: Rethinking the Gospel Audiences.* Grand Rapids: Eerdmans, 1998, 9–48.

Bauer, Johannes B. "Schriftrezeption in den neutestamentlichen Apokryphen." *Stimuli. Exegese und ihre Hermeneutik in Antike und Christentum. Festschrift für Ernst Dassmann.* Ed. Georg Schöllgen and Clemens Scholten. Jahrbuch für Antike und Christentum, Ergänzungsband 23. Münster: Aschendorff, 1996, 43–48.

Beker, J. Christiaan. "Luke's Paul as the Legacy of Paul." In Eugene H. Lovering, Jr., ed. *SBL 1993 Seminar Papers.* Atlanta: Scholars Press, 1993, 511–19.

Bender, John B. *Imagining the Penitentiary: Fiction and the Architecture of Mind in Eighteenth Century England.* Chicago: University of Chicago Press, 1987.

Binder, Gerhard. "Eine Polemik des Porphyrios gegen die allegorische Auslegung des Alten Testaments durch die Christen." *ZPE* 3 (1968) 81–95.

Blanchard, Alain. "Sur le milieu d'origine du papyrus Bodmer de Ménandre." *CdÉ* 66 (1991) 211–20.

Bloom, Harold. *The Anxiety of Influence.* Oxford: Oxford University Press, 1973.

Boismard, M. E. and Paul Benoit. *Synopse des quatre évangiles en français avec parallels des apocryphes et des Péres.* Paris: Cerf, 1972.

Bonner, Stanley Frederick. *Education in Ancient Rome: From the Elder Cato to the Younger Pliny.* Berkeley: University of California Press, 1977.

Bonz, Marianne Palmer. *The Past as Legacy: Luke-Acts and Ancient Epic.* Minneapolis: Fortress Press, 2000.

Booth, Alan. "Elementary and Secondary Education in the Roman Empire." *Florilegium* 1 (1979) 1–14.

Bouvier, Bertrand, and François Bovon. "Actes de Philippe, I, d'après un manuscrit inédit." In Damaskinos Papandreou, Wolfgang A. Bienert, and Kurt Schäferdiek, eds., *Oecumenica et Patristica: Festschrift für Wilhelm Schneemelcher.* Stuttgart: Kohlhammer, 1989, 367–94.

Bovon, François. "Les Actes de Philippe." In Wolgand Haase and Hildegard Temporini, eds., *Aufstieg und Niedergang der römischen Welt* 2.25.6. Berlin: de Gruyter, 1988, 4523–27.

————. "Byzantine Witnesses for the Apocryphal Acts of the Apostles." In François Bovon, Ann Graham Brock, and Christopher R. Matthews, eds., *The Apocryphal Acts of the Apostles: Harvard Divinity School Studies.* Religions of the World. Cambridge: Harvard University Press, 1999, 87–98.

————. "The Child and the Beast: Fighting Violence in Ancient Christianity." *HTR* 92 (1999) 369–92.

————. *Das Evangelium nach Lukas. 2. Teilband Lk 9,51–14,35.* Evangelisch-Katholischer Kommentar zum Neuen Testament 3. Zürich: Benziger, 1996.

————. "The Synoptic Gospels and the Non-canonical Acts of the Apostles." *HTR* 81 (1988) 19–36.

Bovon, François, Ann Graham Brock and Christopher R. Matthews, eds. *The Apocryphal Acts of the Apostles Harvard Divinity School Studies.* Religions of the World. Cambridge; Harvard University Press. 1999.

Bovon, François, Bertrand Bouvier, and Frédéric Amsler. *Acta Philippi: Textus.* Corpus Christianorum, Series Apocryphorum 11. Turnhout: Brepols, 1999.

Bowersock, Glen Warren. *Martyrdom and Rome.* Cambridge: Cambridge University Press, 1995.

Brock, Ann Graham. "What's in a Name: The Competition for Authority in Early Christian Texts." *SBL 1998 Seminar Papers.* Atlanta: Scholars Press, 1999.

Brodie, Thomas Louis. *The Crucial Bridge: The Elijah-Elisha Narrative as an Interpretive Synthesis of Genesis-Kings and a Literary Model for the Gospels*. Collegeville: Liturgical Press, 2000.

———. "Luke's Redesigning of Paul: Corinthian Division and Reconciliation (1 Corinthians 1–5) as One Component of Jerusalem Unity (Acts 1–5)." *IBS* 17 (1995) 98–128.

———. "Mark 10:1–45 as a Creative Rewriting of 1 Peter 2:18–3:17." *PIBA* 4 (1980) 98.

———. *The Quest for the Origin of John's Gospel: A Source-Oriented Approach*. New York: Oxford University Press, 1993.

———. "Vivid, Positive, Practical: The Systematic Use of Romans in Matthew 1–7." *PIBA* 16 (1993) 36–55.

Carmichael, Calum M. *Women, Law, and the Genesis Traditions*. Edinburgh: Edinburgh University Press, 1979.

Cerro, Gonzalo del. "Los Hechos apócrifos de los Apóstoles su género literario." *Estudios Bíblicos* 51 (1993) 207–32.

Christ, Wilhelm von and Wilhelm Schmid. *Geschichte der griechischen Literatur*. Handbuch der Altertumswissenschaft 7.2.2. Munich. Beck, 1924.

Clarysse, Willy, and Alfons Wouters. "A Schoolboy's Exercise in the Chester Beatty Library." *AncSoc* 1 (1970) 201–35.

Clausen, Wendell. "Callimachus and Latin Poetry." *Greek, Roman and Byzantine Studies* 5 (1964) 181–96.

Cohen, Shaye J. D. "Sosates the Jewish Homer." *HTR* 74 (1981) 391–96.

Coles, R. A. "A New Fragment of a Post-Classical Tragedy from Oxyrhynchus." *Bulletin of the Institute of Classical Studies* 15 (1968) 110–18.

Collart, Paul. "A l'école avec les petits grecs d'Égypte." *CdÉ* 21 (1936) 489–507.

———. *Les papyrus Bouriant*. Paris: Édouard Champion, 1926.

Conte, Gian Biagio. *The Rhetoric of Imitation: Genre and Poetic Memory in Vergil and other Poets*. Charles Segal, ed. Cornell Studies in Classical Philology 44. Ithaca: Cornell University Press, 1986.

Conzelmann, Hans. *The Acts of the Apostles*. Translated by James Linburg et al.; Eldon Jay Epp and Christopher R. Matthews, eds. Hermeneia. Philadelphia: Fortress Press, 1987.

Cribiore, Raffaella. "A Homeric Writing Exercise and Reading Homer in School." *Tyche* 9 (1994) 1–8.

———. "Literary School Exercises." *ZPE* 116 (1997) 53–60.

———. *Writing, Teachers, and Students in Graeco-Roman Egypt*. American Studies in Papyrology 36. Atlanta: Scholars Press, 1996.

Culbertson, Roberta. "Embodied Memory, Transcendence and Telling: Recounting the Trauma, Re-establishing the Self." *New Literary History* 26 (1995) 169–96.

Debut, Janine. "De l'usage des listes de mots comme fondement de la pedagogie dans l'antiquité." *REA* 85 (1983) 261–74.

———. "Les documents scolaires." *ZPE* 63 (1986) 251–78.

Delatte, Armand. *La vie de Pythagore de Diogène Laërce. Édition critique avec introduction et commentaire.* Académie royale de Belgique. Classe des lettres et des sciences morales et politiques, deuxième série 17. Bruxelles: Lamertin, 1922.

Deselaers, Paul. *Das Buch Tobit. Studien zu seiner Entstehung, Komposition und Theologie.* OBO 43. Göttingen: Vandenhoeck & Ruprecht, 1982.

DiLella, Alexander A. "The Deuteronomic Background of the Farewell Discourse in Tobit 14:3–11." *CBQ* 41 (1979) 380–89.

Dilts, Mervin R. and George A. Kennedy, eds. *Two Greek Rhetorical Treatises from the Roman Empire.* Mnemosyne Supplementum 168. Leiden: Brill, 1997.

Dimant, Devorah. "Use and Interpretation of Mikra in the Apocrypha and Pseudepigrapha." In Martin Jan Mulder and Harry Sysling, eds. *Mikra: Text, Translation, Reading and Interpretation of the Hebrew Bible in Ancient Judaism and Early Christianity.* CRINT 2.1. Philadelphia: Fortress Press, 1988, 379–419.

Doran, Robert. "Narrative Literature." In Robert A. Kraft and George W. E. Nickelsburg, eds. *Early Judaism and its Modern Interpreters.* Philadelphia: Fortress Press, 1986, 287–310.

Dupont, Jacques. *The Sources of the Acts: The Present Position.* Translated by Kathleen Pond. New York: Herder, 1964.

Elliott, James K. "The Apocryphal Acts." *Expository Times* 105 (1993) 71–77.

Endres, John C. *Biblical Interpretation in the Book of Jubilees.* CBQMS 18. Washington: Catholic Biblical Association of America, 1987.

Enslin, Morton Scott. "Once Again, Luke and Paul," *ZNW* 61 (1970) 253–71.

Fagles, Robert, trans. *The Iliad.* New York: Viking, 1990.

Farrell, Joseph. *Vergil's Georgics and the Traditions of Ancient Epic: the Art of Allusion in Literary History.* New York: Oxford University Press, 1991.

Felten, J., ed. *Nicolai progymnasmata.* Rhetores graeci 11. Leipzig: Teubner, 1913.

Finkelpearl, Ellen. *Metamorphosis of Language in Apuleius: A Study of Allusion in the Novel.* Ann Arbor: University of Michigan Press, 1998.

Fishbane, Michael A. *Biblical Interpretation in Ancient Israel.* Oxford: Clarendon Press, 1985.

Fitzmyer, Joseph A. *The Gospel According to Luke (I–IX).* AB 28A. Garden City: Doubleday, 1981.

———. "Tobit." In Magen Brochi, et al, eds. *Qumran Cave IV, XIV: Parabiblical Texts. Part II.* DJD 19. Oxford: Clarendon Press, 1995, 1–76.

Flamion, Joseph. "Les trois recensions grecques du Martyre de l'apôtre Philippe." *Mélanges d'histoire offerts à Charles Moeller.* Université de Louvain, Recueil de travaux publiés par les membres des conférences d'histoire et de philologie 40. Louvain: Bureaux du Recueil, 1914, 215–25.

Foerster, Richard, ed. *Libanii opera.* 11 vols. Bibliotheca scriptorum graecorum et romanorum teubneriana. Leipzig: Teubner, 1903–1927. Reprint by Hildesheim: Olms, 1963.

Foerster, Richard, and Karl Münscher. "Libanios." Pauly-Wissowa. *RE* 12.2 (1915) 2485–551.

Fontaine, Jacques. "Bible et hagiographie dans le royaume franc mérovingien (600–750). Une soutenance remarquée à l'Université de Gand." *Analecta Bollandiana* 97 (1979) 387–96.

Foucault, Michel. *Power/Knowledge: Selected Interviews and Other Writings 1992–1997*. Edited and translated by Colin Gordon et al. New York: Pantheon, 1980.

———. "Space, Knowledge, Power." In Paul Rabinow, ed. *The Foucault Reader*. New York: Pantheon, 1984.

Frangoulidis, Stavros A. "Epic Inversion in Apuleius' Tale of Tlepolemus/ Haemus." *Mnemosyne* 45 (1992) 60–74.

Fries, Carl. "Das Buch Tobit und die Telemachie." *ZWTh* 53 (1911) 54–87.

Gerth, K. "Severos von Alexandreia." Pauly-Wissowa. *RE Sup* 8 (1956) 715–18.

Giangrande, Giuseppe. " 'Arte allusiva' and Alexandrian Poetry." *Classical Quarterly* n. s. 17 (1967) 85–97.

Glasson, T. Francis. "The Main Source of Tobit." *ZAW* 71 (1959) 275–77.

Goulder, Michael D. *Luke: A New Paradigm*. JSNTSup 20. Sheffield: Sheffield University Press, 1989.

Grässer, Erich. "Acta-Forschung seit 1960." *ThR* 41 (1976) 141–194, 259–290, and 42 (1977) 1–68.

Greene, Thomas M. *The Light in Troy: Imitation and Discovery in Renaissance Poetry*. New Haven: Yale University Press, 1982.

Greenfield, Jonas C. "Ahikar in the Book of Tobit." In Maurice Carrez, et al. eds. *De la Torah au Messie. Études d'exégèse et d'herméneutique bibliques offertes à Henri Cazelles*. Paris: Desclée, 1981, 329–36.

Gregory, Derek. *Geographical Imaginations*. Oxford: Blackwell, 1994.

Haenchen, Ernst. *The Acts of the Apostles*. Translated by Bernard Noble and Gerald Shinn. Oxford: Blackwell, 1971.

Hanhart, Robert, ed. *Tobit*. Septuaginta. Vetus Testamentum graecum auctoritate Academiae Scientiarum Gottingensis editum 8/5. Göttingen: Vandenhoeck & Ruprecht, 1983.

Harrison, Stephen J. "Some Odyssean Scenes in Apuleius' *Metamorphoses*." *Materiali e discussioni per l'analisi del testi classici* 25 (1990) 193–201.

Hatina, Thomas R. "Intertextuality and Historical Criticism in New Testament Studies: Is There a Relationship?" *Biblical Interpretation* 7 (1999) 28–43.

Hays, Richard B. *Echoes of Scripture in the Letters of Paul*. New Haven: Yale University Press, 1989.

Hesseling, D. C. "On Waxen Tablets with Fables of Babrius." *JHS* 13 (1892–1893) 293–314.

Heubeck, Alfred, Stephanie West, and John Bryand Hainsworth, ed. *A Commentary on Homer's Odyssey*. Vol. 1, Introduction and Books I–VIII. New York: Oxford University Press, 1988.

Hexter, Ralph. *A Guide to the Odyssey: A Commentary on the English Translation of Robert Fitzgerald.* New York: Vintage Books, 1993.

Hilgard, A., ed. *Commentarius Melampodis seu Diomedis in artis Dionysianne 11* (in *Scholia in Dionysii Thracis artem grammaticam*). Grammatici graeci 3.1. Leipzig: Teubner, 1901.

Hills, Julian V. "The Acts of the Apostles in the *Acts of Paul*." In Eugene H. Lovering, Jr., ed. *SBL 1994 Seminar Papers.* Atlanta: Scholars Press, 1994, 24–54.

Hinds, Stephen. *Allusion and Intertext: Dynamics of Appropriation in Roman Poetry.* Roman Literature and Its Contexts. New York: Cambridge University Press, 1998.

Hock, Ronald F. "A Dog in the Manger: The Cynic Cynulcus among Athenaeus' Deipnosophists." In David L. Balch et al., eds. *Greeks, Romans, and Christians: Essays in Honor of Abraham J. Malherbe.* Minneapolis: Fortress Press, 1990.

Hock, Ronald F., and Edward O'Neil, eds. *The Chreia in Ancient Rhetoric. Vol. 1 The Progymnasmata.* SBLTT 27. Atlanta: Scholars Press, 1986.

Hunger, Herbert. *Die hochsprachliche profane Literatur der Byzantiner.* Handbuch der Altertumswissenschaft 12.5. Munich: Beck, 1978.

Hunter, V. "The Prison of Athens: A Comparative Perspective." *Phoenix* 51 (1971) 296–323.

Johnson, Luke Timothy. "The Social Dimensions of *Soteria* in Luke-Acts and Paul." In Eugene H. Lovering, Jr., ed. *SBL 1993 Seminar Papers.* Atlanta: Scholars Press, 1993, 520–36.

Jones, F. Stanley. "Principal Orientations on the Relations between the Apocryphal Acts (*Acts of Paul* and *Acts of John*; *Acts of Peter* and *Acts of John*)." In Eugene H. Lovering, Jr., ed. *SBL 1993 Seminar Papers.* Atlanta: Scholars Press, 1993, 485–505.

Jouguet, Pierre, and Paul Perdrizet. "Le papyrus Bouriant no.1. Un cahier d'écolier grec d'Égypt." *StudPal* 6 (1906) 148–61.

Junod, Éric. "Actes apocryphes et hérésie: le jugement de Photius." In François Bovon et al., eds. *Les actes apocryphes des apôtres. Christianisme et monde païen.* Publications de la Faculté de théologie de l'Université de Genève 4. Geneva: Labor et Fides, 1981, 11–24.

Junod, Éric, and Jean-Daniel Kaestli. *Acta Iohannis.* 2 vols. Corpus Christianorum, Series Apocryphorum 1–2. Turnhout: Brepols, 1983.

Kaestli, Jean-Daniel. "Les scènes d'attribution des champs de mission et de départ de l'apôtre dans les Actes apocryphes." In François Bovon et al., eds. *Les actes apocryphes des apôtres. Christianisme et monde païen.* Publications de la Faculté de theologie de l'Université de Genève 4. Geneva: Labor et Fides, 1981, 249–64.

Kaplan, Caren. *Questions of Travel: Postmodern Discourses of Displacement.* Durham: Duke University Press, 1996.

Karnthaler, Fr. P. "Severus von Alexandreia. Ein verschollener griechischer Schriftsteller des IV. Jahrhunderts n. Chr." *BNGJ* 8 (1929–30) 327–30.

Keith, Michael and Steve Pile. "Introduction Part 2: The Place of Politics." In Michael Keith and Steve Pile, eds. *Place and the Politics of Identity.* London: Routledge, 1993.

Kemp, Alan. "The *Tekhnê Grammatikê* of Dionysius Thrax: English Translation with Introduction and Notes." In Daniel J. Taylor, ed. *The History of Linguistics in the Classical Period.* Philadelphia: John Benjamins, 1987, 169–89.

Kennedy, George Alexander. *Greek Rhetoric under Christian Emperors.* Princeton: Princeton University Press, 1983.

Kenyon, F. G. "Two Greek School-Tablets." *JHS* 29 (1909) 29–40.

Kuch, Heinrich. "A Study on the Margins of the Ancient Novel: Barbarians and Others." In Gareth Schmeling, ed. *The Novel in the Ancient World.* Leiden: Brill, 1996, 209–20.

Lane Fox, Robin. *Pagans and Christians.* New York: Alfred A. Knopf, 1987.

Lefebvre, Henri. *The Production of Space.* Translated by Donald Nicholson-Smith. Oxford: Blackwell, 1991.

Lenaerts, Jean. "Fragment d'Analecta sur Diogène (P. Osl. III, 177)." *CdÉ* 49 (1974) 121–23.

Lipsius, Richard Aldebert. *Die apokryphen Apostelgeschichten und Apostellegenden. Ein Beitrag zur altchristlichen Literaturgeschichte.* 2 vols. in 3 and supplement. Braunschweig: Schwetschke, 1893–1900. Reprint, Amsterdam: Philo, 1976.

———. "Zu den Acten des Philippus." *Jahrbücher für protestantische Theologie* 17 (1891) 459–73.

Lipsius, Richard Aldebert, and Maximilien Bonnet, eds. *Acta apostolorum apocrypha.* 2 vols. in 3. Leipzig: Mendelssohn, 1891–1903. Reprint, Darmstadt: Olms, 1959.

Litwak, Kenneth D. "Echoes of Scripture? A Critical Survey of Recent Works on Paul's Use of the Old Testament." *Currents in Research. Biblical Studies* 6 (1998) 260–88.

Long, H. S. *Diogenis Laertii vitae philosophorum.* 2 vols. Oxford: Clarendon Press, 1964.

Lundon, John. "Leixeis from the Scholia Minora in Homerum." *ZPE* 124 (1999) 25–52.

MacDonald, Dennis Ronald. "The *Acts of Andrew and Matthias* and the *Acts of Andrew.*" *Semeia* 38 (1986) 9–33.

———. "The *Acts of Paul* and *The Acts of Peter:* Which Came First?" In Eugene H. Lovering, Jr., ed. *SBL 1992 Seminar Papers.* Atlanta: Scholars Press, 1992, 214–24.

———. *Christianizing Homer: The "Odyssey," Plato, and the "Acts of Andrew."* New York: Oxford University Press, 1994.

———. *The Homeric Epics and the Gospel of Mark.* New Haven: Yale University Press, 2000.

————. "Which Came First? Intertextual Relationships among the Apocryphal Acts of the Apostles." *Semeia* 80 (1997) 11–41.

Marrou, Henri Irénée. *A History of Education in Antiquity.* Translated George Lamb. New York: Sheed & Ward, 1956. Reprint, Madison: University of Wisconsin Press, 1982.

Matthews, Christopher R. "Peter and Philip Upside Down: Perspectives on the Relation of the *Acts of Philip* to the *Acts of Peter.*" In Eugene H. Lovering, Jr., ed. *SBL 1996 Seminar Papers.* Atlanta: Scholars Press, 1996, 28–31.

————. "Philip and Simon, Luke and Peter: A Lukan Sequel and Its Intertextual Success." In Eugene H. Lovering, Jr., ed. *SBL 1992 Seminar Papers.* Atlanta: Scholars Press, 1992, 133–46.

————. "Trajectories through the Philip Tradition." Th.D. diss., Harvard University, 1993.

Milne, Joseph Grafton. "Relics of Graeco-Roman Schools." *JHS* 28 (1908) 121–32.

Molinari, Andrea. " 'I Never Knew the Man': The Independence of the Coptic Act of Peter (Papyrus Berolinensis 8502.4) from the Apocryphal Acts of Peter, Its Genre and Origins." Unpublished.

Moore, Carey A. *Tobit: A New Translation with Introduction and Commentary.* Anchor Bible 40A. New York: Doubleday, 1996.

Morgan, J. R. "Heliodorus." In Gareth Schmeling, ed. *The Novel in the Ancient World.* Leiden: Brill, 1996, 417–56.

Morgan, Kathleen E. *Ovid's Art of Imitation: Propertius and the Amores.* Mnemosyne Supplementum. Lugduni Batavorum. Leiden: Brill, 1977.

Morgan, Teresa Jean. *Literate Education in the Hellenistic and Roman Worlds.* Cambridge Classical Studies. New York: Cambridge University Press, 1998.

Murphy-O'Connor, Jerome. *1 Corinthians.* New Testament Message 10. Dublin: Veritas, 1979.

Musurillo, Herbert., ed. *The Acts of the Christian Martyrs.* Oxford Early Christian Texts. Oxford: Clarendon Press, 1972.

Nickelsburg, George W. E. "The Bible Rewritten and Expanded." In Michael E. Stone, ed. *Jewish Writings of the Second Temple Period: Apocrypha, Pseudepigrapha, Qumran Sectarian Writings, Philo, Josephus.* CRINT 2. Philadelphia: Fortress Press, 1984, 89–156.

————. "The Search for Tobit's Mixed Ancestry: A Historical and Hermeneutical Odyssey." *RevQ* 17 (1996) 339–49.

————. "Stories of Biblical and Early Post-Biblical Times." In Michael E. Stone, ed. *Jewish Writings of the Second Temple Period: Apocrypha, Pseudepigrapha, Qumran Sectarian Writings, Philo, Josephus.* CRINT 2. Philadelphia: Fortress Press, 1984, 33–87.

————. "Tobit and Enoch: Distant Cousins with a Recognizable Resemblance." In David J. Lull, ed. *SBL 1988 Seminar Papers.* Atlanta: Scholars Press, 1988, 54–68.

Norelli, Enrico. "Avant le canonique et l'apocryphe: aux origines des récits de la naissance de Jésus." *Revue de théologie et de philosophie* 126 (1994) 305–24.

Nowell, Irene. "The Book of Tobit: Narrative Technique and Theology." Ph.D. diss., Catholic University of America, 1983.

Pack, Roger A. *The Greek and Latin Literary Texts from Greco-Roman Egypt.* 2d ed. Ann Arbor: University of Michigan Press, 1965.

Parsons, P. J. "A School-Book from the Sayce Collection." *ZPE* 6 (1970) 133–49.

Perkins, Judith. *The Suffering Self: Pain and Narrative Representation in Early Christian Era.* London: Routledge, 1995.

Pervo, Richard I. "The Ancient Novel Becomes Christian." In Gareth Schmeling, ed. *The Novel in the Ancient World.* Leiden: Brill, 1996, 685–711.

———. *Profit with Delight: The Literary Genre of the Acts of the Apostles.* Philadelphia: Fortress Press, 1987.

Petersen, Norman R. "Tobit." In Bernhard W. Anderson, ed. *The Books of the Bible.* 2 vols. New York: Scribners, 1989, 2.35–42.

Peterson, Erik. "Die Begegnung mit dem Ungeheuer. Hermas, Visio IV." *Vigiliae christianae* 8 (1954) 52–71; Reprint in idem, *Frühkirche, Judentum und Gnosis. Studien und Untersuchungen* Freiburg: Herder, 1959. Reprint, Darmstadt. Wissenschaftliche Buchgesellschaft, 1982.

———. "Die Häretiker der Philippus-Akten." *ZNW* 31 (1932) 97–111.

———. "Zum Messalianismus der Philippus-Akten." Oriens christianus 3d ser. 7 (1932) 172–79.

Petit, Paul. *Les étudiants de Libanius.* Paris: Nouvelles Éditions Latines, 1956.

Pfeiffer, Robert Henry. *History of New Testament Times, with an Introduction to the Apocrypha.* New York: Harper, 1949.

Piontek, Ferdinand. *Die katholische Kirche und die häretischen Apostelgeschichten bis zum Ausgang des 6. Jahrhunderts. Ein Beitrag zur Literaturgeschichte.* Breslau: Nischkowsky, 1907.

Plümacher, Eckhard. "Apokryphe Apostelakten." *RE Sup.* 15.11–70.

Rabe, David. *Hurlyburly: A Play.* New York: Grove Press, 1985.

Rabe, Hugo, ed. *Aphthonii progymnasmata.* Rhetores graeci 10. Leipzig: Teubner, 1926.

———. *Hermogenis opera.* Rhetores graeci 6. Stuttgart: Teubner, 1913.

Rabenau, Merten. *Studien zum Buch Tobit.* BZAW 220. Berlin: Walter de Gruyter, 1994.

Rapske, Brian. *The Book of Acts and Paul in Roman Custody.* The Book of Acts in its First Century Setting 3. Grand Rapids: Eerdmans, 1994.

Reader, William W. *The Severed Hand and the Upright Corpse: The Declamations of Marcus Antonius Polemo.* SBLTT 42. Atlanta: Scholars Press, 1996.

Reardon, Bryan P. "Achilles Tatius and Ego-Narrative." In J. R. Morgan and Richard Stoneman, eds. *Greek Fiction: The Greek Novel in Context.* London: Routledge, 1994, 80–96.

————, ed. *Collected Ancient Greek Novels*. Berkeley: University of California Press, 1989.

Reinhardt, Karl. "Homer und die Telemachie." *Von Werken und Formen. Vortage und Aufsätze*. Godesberg: Kupper, 1948, 37–51.

Renehan, Robert. "Classical Greek Quotations in the New Testament." In David Neiman and Margaret Schatkin, eds. *The Heritage of the Early Church: Essays in Honor of the Very Reverend Georges Florovsky*. Orientalia christiana analecta 195. Rome: Pont. Institutum Studiorum Orientalium, 1973, 17–46.

Renner, Timothy. "Three New Homerica on Papyrus." *HSCP* 83 (1979) 311–37.

Resch, Alfred. *Agrapha: Aussercanonische Evangelienfragmente gesammelt und untersucht*. TU 5.4. Leipzig: Hinrichs, 1889.

————. *Agrapha: Aussercanonische Schriftfragmente gesammelt und untersucht in zweiter völlig neu bearbeiteter durch alttestamentliche Agrapha vermehrter Auflage herausgegeben*. TU n.s. 15.3–4. Leipzig: Hinrichs, 1906.

Riley, Gregory J. *One Jesus, Many Christs*. San Francisco: Harper, 1997.

Robert, L. *Le martyre de Pionios prêtre de Smyrne*. Washington: Dumbarton Oaks Research Library, 1994.

Robins, Robert Henry. *The Byzantine Grammarians: Their Place in History*. Trends in Linguistics, Studies and Monographs 70. New York: Mouton de Gruyter, 1993.

Rolland, Philippe. "Marc, lecteur de Pierre et de Paul." In Frans Van Segbroeck et al., ed. *The Four Gospels*. Festschrift Frans Neirynck. BETL 100. 3 vols. Louvain: Louvain University Press, 1992.

Ross, David O., Jr. *Style and Tradition in Catullus*. Loeb Classical Monographs. Cambridge: Harvard University Press, 1969.

Ruppert, Lothar. "Das Buch Tobias. Ein Modellfall nachgestalteter Erzählung." In Josef Schreiner, ed. *Wort, Lied und Gottesspruch. Festschrift J. Ziegler*, vol. 1: *Beiträge zur Septuaginta*. Forschung zur Bibel 1. Würtzburg: Echter, 1972, 109–19.

Russell, Donald Andrew. *Greek Declamation*. New York: Cambridge University Press, 1983.

Saïd, Suzanne. "The City in the Greek Novel." In James Tatum, ed. *The Search for the Ancient Novel*. Baltimore: Johns Hopkins University Press, 1993.

Scarry, Elaine. *The Body in Pain: The Making and Unmaking of the World*. New York: Oxford University Press, 1985.

Scheid, John and Jesper Svenbro. *The Craft of Zeus. Myths of Weaving and Fabric*. Translated by Carol Volk. Revealing Antiquity 9. Cambridge: Harvard University Press, 1996.

Schenk, Wolfgang. "Sekundäre Jesuanisierungen von primären Paulus-Aussagen bei Markus." In Frans Van Segbroeck et al., eds. *The Four Gospels*. Festschrift Frans Neirynck. BETL 100. 3 vols. Louvain: Louvain University Press, 1992.

Schissel, Otmar. "Die rhetorische Kunstlehre des Rufus von Perinthos." *RhM* 75 (1926) 369–92.

———. "Rhetorische Progymnasmatik der Byzantiner." *BNGJ* 11 (1934–35) 1–11.

———. "Severus von Alexandreia. Ein verschollener griechischer Schriftsteller des IV Jahrhunderts n. Chr." *BNGJ* 8 (1929–1930) 1–13.

Schneider, Gerhard von. *Die Apostelgeschichte.* HTKNT 5. Freiburg: Herder, 1980–1982.

Schoedel, William R. *Ignatius of Antioch.* Helmut Koester, ed. Hermenia. Philadelphia: Fortress Press, 1985.

Schwartz, J. "Un manuel scolaire de l'époque byzantine." *ÉdP* 7 (1948) 93–109.

Shaw, Brent D. "Body/Power/Identity: Passions of the Martyrs." *Journal of Early Christian Studies* 4 (1996) 269–312.

Shumate, Nancy. *Crisis and Conversion in Apuleius' Metamorphoses.* Ann Arbor: University of Michigan Press, 1996.

Sijpesteijn, P. J. "Scholia minora zu Homer *Ilias* 22.184–256." *Mnemosyne* 40 (1987) 158–61.

Slater, Richard N. "An Inquiry into the Relationship Between Community and Text: The Apocryphal *Acts of Philip* 1 and the Encratites of Asia Minor." In François Bovon, Ann Graham Brock, and Christopher R. Matthews, eds. *The Apocryphal Acts of the Apostles: Harvard Divinity School Studies.* Religions of the World. Cambridge: Harvard University Press: 1999, 281–306.

Smith, Jonathan Z. *Map Is not Territory: Studies in the History of Religions.* Studies in Judaism in Late Antiquity 23. Leiden: Brill, 1978.

Smith, Terence V. *Petrine Controversies in Early Christianity: Attitudes towards Peter in Christian Writings of the First Two Centuries.* Wissenschaftliche Untersuchungen zum Neuen Testament 2.15. Tübingen: Mohr (Siebeck), 1985.

Soja, Edward W. *Postmodern Geographies: The Reassertion of Space in Critical Social Theory.* London: Verso, 1989.

Soll, William. "Misfortune and Exile in Tobit: The Juncture of a Fairy Tale Source and Deuteronomic Theology." *CBQ* 51 (1989) 209–31.

———. "Tobit and Folklore Studies with Emphasis on Propp's Methodology." In David J. Lull, ed. *SBL 1988 Seminar Papers.* Atlanta: Scholars Press, 1988, 39–53.

Spengel, Leonardi, and C. Hammer, eds. *Rhetores Graeci.* 3 vols. Leipzig: Teubner, 1884.

Stark, Rodney. *The Rise of Christianity: A Sociologist Reconsiders History.* Princeton: Princeton University Press, 1996.

Stoops, Robert F., Jr., ed. *The Apocryphal Acts of the Apostles in Intertextual Perspectives.* Semeia 80 (1997).

———. "Peter, Paul, and Priority in the Apocryphal Acts." In Eugene H. Lovering, Jr., ed. *SBL 1992 Seminar Papers.* Atlanta: Scholars Press, 1992, 225–33.

Tardieu, Michel. *Écrits gnostiques. Codex de Berlin.* Sources gnostiques et manichéennes 1. Paris: Cerf, 1984.

Thomas, Christine M. "The 'Prehistory' of the *Acts of Peter*." In François Bovon, Ann Graham Brock, and Christopher R. Matthews, eds. *The Apocryphal Acts of the Apostles: Harvard Divinity School Studies*. Religions of the World. Cambridge: Harvard University Press, 1999, 39–62.

———. "Word and Deed: The *Acts of Peter* and Orality." *Apocrypha* 3 (1992) 125–64.

Thomas, Richard F. "Catullus and the Polemics of Poetic Reference." *American Journal of Philology* 103 (1982) 144–64.

Thompson, Michael B. "The Holy Internet: Communications Between Churches in the First Christian Generation." In Richard Bauckham, ed. *The Gospels for all Christians: Rethinking the Gospel Audiences*. Grand Rapids: Eerdmans, 1998, 49–70.

Tischendorf, Constantin. *Acta apostolorum apocrypha*. Leipzig: Averianus et Mendelssohn, 1851. Reprint, Hildesheim: Olms, 1990.

———. *Apocalypses apocryphae Mosis, Esdrae, Pauli, Iohannis, item Mariae dormitio, additis evangeliorum et actuum apocryphorum supplementis*. Leipzig: Mendelssohn, 1866. Reprint, Hildesheim: Olms, 1966.

Tov, Emanuel and Sidnie White. "Reworked Pentateuch." In Harold Attridge, et al., eds. *Qumran Cave 4, VIII: Parabiblical Texts. Part II*. DJD 13. Oxford: Clarendon Press, 1994, 187–351.

Trigg, Joseph W. "Martyrs and Churchmen in Third-Century North Africa." *Studia Patristica* 15 (1984) 242–46.

Uhlig, G., ed. *Dionysii Thracis Ars grammatica*. Grammatici graeci 1.1. Leipzig: Teubner, 1883.

Valantasis, Richard. "Narrative Strategies and Synoptic Quandaries: A Response to Dennis MacDonald's Reading of *Acts of Paul* and *Acts of Peter*." In Eugene H. Lovering, Jr., ed. *SBL 1992 Seminar Papers*. Atlanta: Scholars Press, 1992, 234–39.

VanderKam, James C. *The Book of Jubilees*. CSCO 511. Louvain: Peeters, 1989.

Van Henten, J. W. "The Martyrs as Heroes of the Christian People." In M. Lamberigts and P. Van Deun, eds. *Martyrium in Multidisciplinary Perspective*. Louvain: Louvain University Press, 1995, 303–22.

Vielhauer, Paul. "On the 'Paulism' of Acts." In Leander E. Keck and J. L. Martyn, eds. *Studies in Luke-Acts*. London: SPCK, 1968, 31–50.

Walz, Christian, ed. *Rhetores graeci*. 9 vols. Stuttgart: Cottae, 1832–1836.

Wansink, Craig S. *Chained in Christ: The Experience and Rhetoric of Paul's Imprisonments*. JSNTSup 130. Sheffield: Sheffield Academic Press, 1996.

Wengst, Klaus. *Didache (Apostellehre), Barnabasbrief, Zweiter Klemensbrief, Schrift an Diognet*. Schriften des Urchristentums 2. Darmstadt: Wissenschaftliche Buchgesellschaft, 1984.

Wouters, Alfons. *The Grammatical Papyri from Graeco-Roman Egypt: Contributions to the Study of the 'Ars Grammatica' in Antiquity*. Brussels: Paleis der Academiën, 1979.

Youtie, Herbert Chayyim and John Garrett Winter, eds., *Papyri and Ostraca from Karanis.* 2d series. Michigan Papyri 8. Ann Arbor: University of Michigan Press, 1951.

Zalateo, Giorgio, et al. "Papiri Fiorentini inediti." *Aegyptus* 20 (1940) 3–30.

Ziebarth, Erich Gustav Ludwig. *Aus der antike Schule. Sammlung griechischer Texte auf Papyrus, Holztafeln, Ostraka.* 2d edition. Kleine Texte für Vorlesungen und Übungen 65. Bonn: A. Marcus & E. Weber, 1913.

Zimmerman, Frank. *The Book of Tobit: An English Translation with Introduction and Commentary.* Jewish Apocryphal Literature. New York: Harper, 1958.

# Index